The Usborne First Illustrated English Dictionary and Thesaurus

gleaming

shiny

brave

daring

Jane Bingham, Rachel Ward and Caroline Young

towering

tall

Designed by
Kirsty Tizzard and
Karen Tomlins

swing

sway

Edited by
Felicity Brooks, Phil Clarke,
Sam Smith and Sam Taplin

Cover design: Kirsty Tizzard

Additional design and illustration by
Lizzie Barber, Stephanie Jeffries and
Candice Whatmore

Digital manipulation by Keith Furnival

Proofreading by Hannah Rowley
and Simon Tudhope

Editorial assistant: Olivia Boote

Dictionary advisors: John McIlwain,
Rita D'Apice Gould and Porter Tierney

Copyright ©2017 Usborne Publishing Ltd. The name Usborne and the devices are Trade Marks of Usborne Publishing Ltd. All rights reserved. No part of this publication may be reproduced, stored in a retrieval system, or transmitted in any form or by any means, electronic, mechanical, photocopying, recording or otherwise without the prior permission of the publisher. UKE.

First Illustrated English Dictionary

Illustrated by Villie Karabatzia

Contents

Using your dictionary	2
A-Z dictionary	4
Useful words	253
Spelling quiz	255
Word hunt	256

The Thesaurus section starts on page 257.

USING YOUR DICTIONARY

Finding a word

The words in this dictionary are arranged in alphabetical order from A to Z. This helps you to find them easily.

1 To find a word, such as "beach", think of its first letter, "b".

2 Now look at the alphabet bar down the side of each page. When you see a coloured letter "b" you have found the pages of "b" words.

3 Next, think of the second letter of your word. Look along the top of the page for words that begin "be".

4 Then look down the "be" words until you find your word.

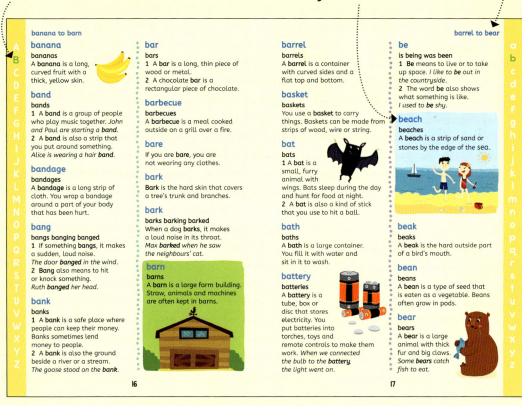

If you can't find a word, you may have spelt it wrongly. For example:

- **Ceiling** and **city** begin with an "s" sound, but are spelt "**ce**" and "**ci**".

- **Knee** and **knife** begin with an "n" sound but are spelt "**kn**".

- **Phone** and **photograph** begin with an "f" sound, but are spelt "**ph**".

Looking at a word
The dictionary tells you lots of things about words and how to use them.

new

newer newest
1 If something is **new**, it has just been made or it has just been bought. *Ruby has a **new** bicycle.*
2 **New** can also mean different. *There is a **new** family next door.*
■ opposite **old**

- You can check how to spell a word.
- You can see other ways of using the word.
- You can find out what the word means.
- You can see how the word is used.
- You can find out if a word has more than one meaning.
- You can see the opposites of some words.

More help with words
Here are some more ways that this dictionary helps you with writing and saying words.

- It gives you ideas for other words to use in your writing.

> Some other words for **big** are **enormous**, **gigantic**, **huge**, **massive** and **vast**.

- It helps you say difficult words.

yolk

yolks
▲ *say yoke*
The **yolk** is the yellow part in the middle of an egg.

Alphabetical order
It's much easier to use a dictionary if you know how to put words into alphabetical order. You compare their first letters, then their second letters, then their third, and so on.

For example, the words bed, ant, bedtime, bear, bad and bedroom are put into alphabetical order like this:

ant	a comes before b
bad	ba comes before be
bear	bea comes before bed
bed	bed comes before bedr
bedroom	bedr comes before bedt
bedtime	

able to action

Aa

able
If you are **able** to do something, you know how to do it. *Zak is **able** to ride a bicycle.*

about
1 **About** means to do with something. *This book is **about** elephants.*
2 **About** also means near to something. *The party ends at **about** six o'clock.*

above
If something is **above** another thing, it is over it or higher than it. *The balloons are **above** the clouds.*
■ opposite **below**

abroad
When you go **abroad**, you go to another country.

absent
If someone is **absent**, they are not here. *Joe is **absent** from school today because he is sick.*

accident
accidents
1 If there is an **accident**, something bad happens that you do not expect. *Rosa had an **accident** and broke her leg.*
2 If something happens **by accident**, nobody has planned or expected it. *I met my friend Peter **by accident**.*

ache
aches aching ached
▲ rhymes with **cake**
If part of your body **aches**, it hurts for a while. *Skating makes my legs **ache**.*

across
Across means from one side to the other. *Owen walked **across** the road.*

act
acts acting acted
1 When you **act**, you do something. *Ranjit **acted** quickly to put out the fire.*
2 If you **act** in a play, you pretend to be one of the people in it.

action
actions
1 An **action** is a movement. *We all copied Simon's **actions**.*
2 An **action** is anything that is done. *My dad was given a medal for his brave **actions**.*

activity to aeroplane

activity
activities
An **activity** is something that you do. *Horse riding is my favourite activity.*

add
adds adding added
1 If you **add** something to another thing, you put it with that thing. *Add butter to the flour.*
2 When you **add** numbers, you put them together. *Jane added five and seven to make twelve.*

■ opposite **subtract**

address
addresses
Your **address** is the name of the place where you live.

admire
admires admiring admired
If you **admire** someone or something, you think that they are very nice or very good. *Jake admired Rachel's painting.*

admit
admits admitting admitted
When you **admit** that you did something, you agree that you did it.

adopt
adopts adopting adopted
When people **adopt** a child, the child comes to live with them and becomes part of their family.

adore
adores adoring adored
If you **adore** something, you love it very much. *Katie adores dogs.*

adult
adults
An **adult** is a grown-up person.

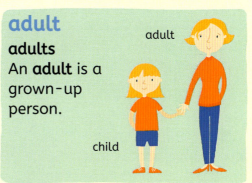

adventure
adventures
An **adventure** is something exciting that people do. Some adventures can be dangerous. *Exploring the castle was a great adventure.*

advice
Advice is information that is meant to help you. *My granny gave me some good advice.*

aeroplane
aeroplanes
An **aeroplane** is a large machine that flies through the air. Aeroplanes have wings and engines. They carry people or things from one place to another.

affect to agree

affect
affects affecting affected
If something **affects** another thing, it does something to it. *Feeling nervous affected June's singing.*

afford
affords affording afforded
If you can **afford** something, you have enough money to buy it.

afraid
If you're **afraid**, you're worried something might go wrong, or something might hurt you. *Jessie is afraid of spiders.*

after
1 When one thing happens **after** another, it happens later than it. *We went for a walk after lunch.*
■ opposite **before**
2 **After** also means following something. *William ran after the ball.*

afternoon
afternoons
The **afternoon** is the part of the day that starts at 12 o'clock and ends at about 6 o'clock.

again
If you do something **again**, you do it one more time. *Beth is singing that song again.*

against
1 If something is **against** another thing, it is next to it and touching it. *Benji leant his bike against the wall.*
2 If you are **against** someone or something, you are on a different side from them. *The teams will play against each other tomorrow.*
3 If you are playing a game and you do something **against the rules**, you do not obey the rules.

age
ages
Your **age** is how old you are. *At the age of five, you have five candles on your birthday cake.*

ago
Ago means before now. *We started school two weeks ago.*

agree
agrees agreeing agreed
1 If you **agree** with someone, you both think the same about something. *Garth and I agreed that the film was dreadful.*
■ opposite **disagree**
2 If you **agree** to do something that someone has asked you to, you say that you will do it. *Jon agreed to tidy his room before he went out.*
■ opposite **refuse**

ahead

If you are **ahead** of someone, you are in front of them. *Skye ran on **ahead** of the others. Grace is **ahead** of Daisy in maths.*

aim

aims aiming aimed

When you **aim** something, you try to make it go in a particular direction. *Robin **aimed** the arrow and fired.*

air

Air is what you breathe. You cannot see air but it is a mixture of gases all around you.

aircraft

aircraft

An **aircraft** is a machine that flies.

airport

airports

An **airport** is a place where aircraft take off and land.

alarm

alarms

An **alarm** is something that makes a loud noise. Alarms wake you up or warn you about something. *An **alarm** clock. A fire **alarm**.*

album

albums

An **album** is a collection of recorded songs.

alien

aliens

In stories, an **alien** is a creature that comes from another planet. *The **alien** had three eyes and four arms.*

alike

If people or things are **alike**, they are the same in some way. *The twins look **alike**.*

alive

If a person, an animal, or a plant is **alive**, they are living.
■ *opposite* **dead**

all

All means everything, everyone, or the whole thing. ***All** the children were excited. Karen ate **all** the chocolate.*

alligator

alligators

An **alligator** is a large reptile that looks similar to a crocodile.

allow to ambulance

allow
allows allowing allowed
If someone **allows** you to do something, they let you do it. *Mum **allowed** us to stay up late.*

almost
Almost means close to, but not quite. *It's **almost** bedtime.*

alone
When you are **alone**, you are not with anyone else.

along
1 **Along** means from one end to the other. *The cat ran **along** the street.*
2 If you bring something **along**, you bring it with you. *George brought his dog **along** to school.*

aloud
When you read **aloud**, you read so that other people can hear you. *Ollie is reading his poem **aloud**.*

alphabet
alphabets
An **alphabet** is a set of all the letters that people use to write words. You can see the order of the letters in the English alphabet at the side of this page.

already
If something has happened **already**, it has happened before now. *I've seen this film **already**.*

alright
1 Something that is **alright** is good enough. *Does this hat look **alright**?*
2 **Alright** also means well and happy. *Are you feeling **alright**?*

also
You use the word **also** to mean something extra. *Hannah ate an apple. She **also** ate my banana.*

always
If you **always** do something, you do it all the time or every time. *I **always** read before I go to sleep.*
■ opposite **never**

amazing
Something that is **amazing** is very surprising or impressive. *Dan scored an **amazing** goal.*

ambulance
ambulances
An **ambulance** is a special van that takes injured or sick people to hospital.

amount

amounts
An **amount** is how much there is of something. *Sarah ate a tiny **amount** of ice cream.*

anchor

anchors
▲ say **an-ker**
An **anchor** is a heavy, metal hook on a long chain that is fixed to a ship. When the anchor is thrown off a ship, it sinks to the bottom of the sea and stops the ship from moving.

angry

angrier angriest
If you are **angry**, you are very annoyed and feel like shouting or fighting. *Kim was **angry** when she saw that her glasses were broken.*

animal

animals
An **animal** is anything that moves and breathes. Horses, lizards, fish, birds and insects are all animals. Plants are not animals.

ankle

ankles
Your **ankle** is the joint between your leg and your foot.

annoy

annoys annoying annoyed
If someone or something **annoys** you, they make you feel angry. *Ed **annoyed** his brother by singing out of tune.*

another

1 You use the word **another** to mean one more. *Please may I have **another** biscuit?*
2 You also use **another** to mean a different one. *Is there **another** way to the station?*

answer

answers
An **answer** is what you say after someone has asked you a question. *Hari gave the right **answer** to the question.*

ant

ants
An **ant** is a small insect. Ants live in large groups in the ground or in trees. *Some **ants** bite leaves off trees and carry them back to their nest.*

any

1 **Any** means some. *Are there any biscuits left?*
2 You also use the word **any** to show that it does not matter which one. *Take any book you like.*

anybody

Anybody means any person. *Has anybody seen my slippers?*

anyone

Anyone means any person. *Anyone is welcome to come to the party.*

anyway

If you do something **anyway**, you do it even though there are reasons not to. *Bella had no umbrella, but went out in the rain anyway.*

anywhere

Anywhere means any place. *I can't find my slippers anywhere!*

apart

1 **Apart** means away from something else. *Stand with your feet apart.*
2 If you take something **apart**, you take it to pieces. *Ben is taking his bicycle apart to see how it works.*
3 **Apart from** means except. *Everyone enjoyed the film, apart from Milo.*

ape

apes

An **ape** is a large animal with long arms and no tail. Chimpanzees and gorillas are apes.

apologize

apologizes apologizing apologized

When you **apologize**, you say sorry for something that you have done or said. *Mark apologized for breaking the chair.*

app

apps

An **app** is a program on a smartphone or tablet. App is short for application.

appear

appears appearing appeared

When something **appears**, it can be seen when it could not be seen before.

■ *opposite* **disappear**

Two birds appeared from inside the hat.

apple to armour

apple
apples
An **apple** is a rounded fruit with a green, red or yellow skin.

apron
aprons
You wear an **apron** to keep your clothes clean when you are cooking or painting.

aquarium
aquariums
An **aquarium** is a glass tank filled with water. You keep fish and other creatures in an aquarium.

area
areas
An **area** is a place or a space.
*A large **area** of grass.*
*A science **area**.*

aren't
Aren't is a short way of saying **are not**. *These strawberries **aren't** ripe yet.*

argue
argues arguing argued
People **argue** because they do not agree about something. When they argue, they say what they think and often get angry.
*We **argued** about which team was the best.*

argument
arguments
An **argument** is when people don't agree with each other. When people have an argument, they say what they think and often get angry.

arm
arms
Your **arm** is the part of your body between your shoulder and your hand.

armchair
armchairs
An **armchair** is a comfortable chair with parts on either side for you to rest your arms on.

armour
Armour is a set of clothes made of metal. Soldiers long ago wore armour to protect themselves when they were fighting.

a b c d e f g h i j k l m n o p q r s t u v w x y z

army to assembly

army
armies
An **army** is a large group of people who fight on the same side in a war.

around
1 **Around** something means in a circle all the way along its outside. *Mo tied a ribbon around her waist.*
2 **Around** also means in every part. *I looked around the house.*
3 **Around** also means near to somewhere. *Kai lives around here.*

arrange
arranges arranging arranged
1 When you **arrange** something, you plan how it will be done. *Mum is arranging a party for next weekend.*
2 If you **arrange** things, you put them together so they look tidy or pretty.

Rana arranged the flowers in a vase.

arrive
arrives arriving arrived
When something or someone **arrives**, they get to where they are going. *The parcel arrived at Lily's house. We arrived at the park.*

arrow
arrows
1 An **arrow** is a thin stick with a point at one end and feathers at the other end. You shoot arrows from a bow.
2 An **arrow** is also a sign that shows you which way to go. *Follow the arrows to get to the sports hall.*

art
Art is something that someone has made to be beautiful, or to show feelings or ideas. Paintings and statues are types of art.

ask
asks asking asked
1 If you **ask** a question, you say that you want to know something. *Jack asked me how old I was.*
2 If you **ask for** something, you say that you want it. *Mia asked for an apple.*

asleep
When you are **asleep**, your eyes are closed and your whole body is resting. *Pickle is asleep on a cushion.*
■ opposite
awake

assembly
assemblies
An **assembly** is a large group of people who are meeting together. *School assembly.*

astonish to autumn

astonish
astonishes astonishing astonished
If you **astonish** someone, you make them feel very surprised.

astronaut
astronauts
An **astronaut** is someone who goes into space. Astronauts travel in spacecraft.

ate
Ate comes from the word **eat**. *Usually we eat at home. Yesterday we ate at a restaurant.*

atlas
atlases
An **atlas** is a book of maps.

attach
attaches attaching attached
When you **attach** one thing to another, you join them together. *Will attached the lead to Fido's collar.*

attack
attacks attacking attacked
If someone **attacks** another person, they try to hurt them.

attention
attention
When you pay **attention**, you watch and listen carefully. *Pay attention to what I'm saying!*

attic
attics
An **attic** is a room at the top of a house, just under the roof.

attic

attract
attracts attracting attracted
When a magnet **attracts** an object, it makes it come nearer.

audience
audiences
An **audience** is a group of people who watch or listen to something, such as a play or a band.

aunt
aunts
Your **aunt** is the sister of your mum or your dad. Another word for aunt is auntie.

autumn
▲ say *aw-tum*
Autumn is one of the four seasons. It comes between summer and winter. In autumn, the weather begins to get cold and leaves fall from the trees.

awake to backwards

awake

Awake means not asleep. Owls stay **awake** at night and sleep in the day.
- opposite **asleep**

away

1 If someone or something goes **away**, they go from where they are to another place.
2 If you put things **away**, you put them where they belong. *Finlay, put your toys **away**.*

awful

Something that is **awful** is very bad. *That programme was **awful**.*

awkward

1 Something that is **awkward** is difficult to use. *My shoelaces are **awkward** to tie because they are too short.*
2 Someone who moves in an **awkward** way is clumsy.
3 Someone who behaves in an **awkward** way is very hard to please.

axe

axes
An **axe** is a tool with a long handle and a large, metal blade. People use axes to chop wood.

Bb

baby

babies
A **baby** is a very young child.

baby-sitter

baby-sitters
A **baby-sitter** is someone who looks after children when their parents are out.

back

backs
1 The **back** of something is the part farthest from the front. *We sat at the **back** of the cinema.*
2 Your **back** is the part of your body between your neck and your bottom.
- opposite **front**

backwards

1 If a word is spelt **backwards**, it is spelt the wrong way round. *"Step" spelt backwards is "pets".*
2 If you move **backwards**, you move the way that your back faces. *Jack is walking **backwards** through the snow.*
- opposite **forwards**

bacon
Bacon is a type of meat that comes from a pig.

bad
worse worst
1 Someone who is **bad** does things that they should not do.
2 Something that is **bad** is not good. *A **bad** cold.*
- opposite **good**

> Some other words for **bad** are **awful**, **terrible**, and **dreadful**.

badge
badges
A **badge** is a small piece of metal, plastic or cloth that you wear on your clothes.

badger
badgers
A **badger** is a black and white animal that lives under the ground.

bag
bags
You use a **bag** to hold or carry things. *A shopping **bag**.*

bake
bakes baking baked
When you **bake** food, you cook it in an oven. *Maggie **baked** a cake.*

balance
balances balancing balanced
If you **balance** something, you keep it steady so it does not fall. *The seal **balanced** a ball on its nose.*

bald
balder baldest
People who are **bald** have little or no hair on the top of their heads.

ball
balls
A **ball** is a round object that you throw, catch or kick.

tennis ball

ballet
▲ say **bal**-*ay*
Ballet is a kind of dance with special steps. Ballet often tells a story.

balloon
balloons
1 A **balloon** is a thin, rubber bag. When you blow into a balloon, it gets bigger.
2 A **balloon** is also a kind of aircraft powered by a very large bag of hot air. Passengers ride in a basket underneath it.

banana to barn

banana
bananas
A **banana** is a long, curved fruit with a thick, yellow skin.

band
bands
1 A **band** is a group of people who play music together. *John and Paul are starting a **band**.*
2 A **band** is also a strip that you put around something. *Alice is wearing a hair **band**.*

bandage
bandages
A **bandage** is a long strip of cloth. You wrap a bandage around a part of your body that has been hurt.

bang
bangs banging banged
1 If something **bangs**, it makes a sudden, loud noise. *The door **banged** in the wind.*
2 **Bang** also means to hit or knock something. *Ruth **banged** her head.*

bank
banks
1 A **bank** is a safe place where people can keep their money. Banks sometimes lend money to people.
2 A **bank** is also the ground beside a river or a stream. *The goose stood on the **bank**.*

bar
bars
1 A **bar** is a long, thin piece of wood or metal.
2 A chocolate **bar** is a rectangular piece of chocolate.

barbecue
barbecues
A **barbecue** is a meal cooked outside on a grill over a fire.

bare
If you are **bare**, you are not wearing any clothes.

bark
Bark is the hard skin that covers a tree's trunk and branches.

bark
barks barking barked
When a dog **barks**, it makes a loud noise in its throat. *Max **barked** when he saw the neighbours' cat.*

barn
barns
A **barn** is a large farm building. Straw, animals and machines are often kept in barns.

barrel

barrels

A **barrel** is a container with curved sides and a flat top and bottom.

basket

baskets

You use a **basket** to carry things. Baskets can be made from strips of wood, wire or string.

bat

bats

1 A **bat** is a small, furry animal with wings. Bats sleep during the day and hunt for food at night.
2 A **bat** is also a kind of stick that you use to hit a ball.

bath

baths

A **bath** is a large container. You fill it with water and sit in it to wash.

battery

batteries

A **battery** is a tube, box or disc that stores electricity. You put batteries into torches, toys and remote controls to make them work. *When we connected the bulb to the battery, the light went on.*

be

is being was been

1 **Be** means to live or to take up space. *I like to be out in the countryside.*
2 The word **be** also shows what something is like. *I used to be shy.*

beach

beaches

A **beach** is a strip of sand or stones by the edge of the sea.

beak

beaks

A **beak** is the hard outside part of a bird's mouth.

bean

beans

A **bean** is a type of seed that is eaten as a vegetable. Beans often grow in pods.

bear

bears

A **bear** is a large animal with thick fur and big claws. *Some bears catch fish to eat.*

beard to beef

beard
beards
A **beard** is the hair that grows on a man's chin and cheeks.

beat
beats beating beat beaten
1 If you **beat** someone in a race or a competition, you do better than they do.
2 If you **beat** something, you keep hitting it.

*Stuart **beat** his drum.*

beautiful
▲ say **byoo**-tih-ful
If something is **beautiful**, it is lovely to look at or listen to.

beaver
beavers
A **beaver** is an animal with very sharp front teeth and a large, flat tail. Beavers build their homes in rivers out of sticks and mud.

became
Became comes from the word **become**. *I thought she might become famous, but she **became** a huge celebrity.*

because
You use the word **because** to explain why something happens. *I was scared **because** it was dark.*

become
becomes becoming became become
If one thing **becomes** something else, it turns into it. *Some caterpillars **become** butterflies.*

bed
beds
A **bed** is something that you lie on when you sleep or rest.

bedroom
bedrooms
Your **bedroom** is the room where you sleep.

bee
bees
A **bee** is an insect with black and yellow stripes. Some bees make honey. Bees can sting, but rarely do.

beef
Beef is meat that comes from a cow.

beetle

beetles
A **beetle** is a common insect. There are thousands of different beetles.

before

If something happens **before** something else, it happens earlier than it.
■ opposite **after**

begin

begins beginning began begun
When you **begin** to do something, you start to do it. *Jo began to cry.*

behave

behaves behaving behaved
1 The way you **behave** is the way that you do things. *Annie is behaving very strangely today.*
2 If you **behave yourself**, you do what you are supposed to.

behind

1 If you are **behind** something, you are further back than it. *Mike was behind Sam in the race.*
2 **Behind** also means round the back of. *Ramel hid behind the shed.*

believe

believes believing believed
If you **believe** something, you think that it is true. *Patrick believed Buster's story.*

bell

bells
A **bell** is a metal object shaped like a cup. Bells make a ringing noise when you hit them or shake them.

belong

belongs belonging belonged
1 If something **belongs** to you, it is yours. *This hat belongs to me.*
2 If you **belong** to a club, you are a member of it.
3 If something **belongs** in a place, that is where it should be. *The spade belongs in the shed.*

below

If something is **below** another thing, it is under it. *Katy sank below the surface of the water.*
■ opposite **above**

belt

belts
A **belt** is a thin band of leather, cloth or plastic that you wear around your waist. *Henry's new belt is red with a silver buckle.*

bench

benches
A **bench** is a long, hard seat for several people.

bend

bends bending bent
If something **bends**, it changes its shape so that it is not straight. *These straws **bend** in the middle. Janie **bent** over and touched her toes.*

beneath

If something is **beneath** another thing, it is below it. *Spot is hiding **beneath** the table.*

bent

If something is **bent**, it is not straight. *The fork was **bent** out of shape.*

berry

berries
A **berry** is a small, soft fruit. Some berries are poisonous.

beside

If you are **beside** someone or something, you are next to them. *I sit **beside** Sam at school.*

best

Something that is the **best** is better than all the others. *Jan won a prize for doing the **best** painting.*
■ opposite **worst**

better

1 You use the word **better** to mean very good compared with something else. *My bike is **better** than yours.*
2 If you feel **better**, you do not feel ill any more.
■ opposite **worse**

between

If you are **between** two things, you are in the middle of them. *Kate sat **between** Mike and Sarah.*

beware

The word **beware** tells you to be careful because something is dangerous. ***Beware** of the bull.*

bicycle

bicycles
A **bicycle** is a vehicle with two wheels. You push the pedals to turn the wheels.

big

bigger biggest
A **big** person or thing is large.
■ opposite **small**

Some other words for big are **enormous, gigantic, huge, massive** and **vast**.

bike

bikes
Bike is short for **bicycle**.

bin

bins
You put rubbish in a **bin**.

bird

birds
A **bird** is an animal with two wings. Birds have beaks and are covered with feathers. Most birds can fly.

*Toucans are **birds** with very big beaks.*

birthday

birthdays
Your **birthday** is the date that you were born. People give you gifts every year on your birthday.

biscuit

biscuits
A **biscuit** is a small snack. Biscuits are baked in the oven until they are hard.

bit

bits
A **bit** is a part of something, often a small part.

bite

bites biting
bit bitten
When you **bite** something, you cut into it with your teeth.

*Tamsin **bit** into a pear.*

bitter

If something is **bitter**, it has a sharp taste that many people don't like. Orange peel and coffee taste bitter.

black

Black is a colour. The letters in this sentence are black.

blade

blades
A **blade** is the flat, sharp part of a knife that is used for cutting. Scissors have two blades.

blame

blames blaming blamed
If you **blame** someone, you think or say that they have made something bad happen. *Alexander **blamed** his brother for breaking his model aeroplane.*

blank

A **blank** piece of paper has nothing on it.

blanket

blankets
A **blanket** is a thick cover. You put blankets on your bed to keep you warm.

bleed

bleeds bleeding bled
If you **bleed**, blood comes out of your body. *Jared's nose bled when he bumped into the door.*

blew

Blew comes from the word **blow**. *Amy can blow very hard. She blew out all the candles on her cake.*

blind

Blind people cannot see.

blink

blinks blinking blinked
When you **blink**, you close and then open your eyes very quickly.

block

blocks
A **block** is a thick piece of something, such as wood or stone. Blocks usually have straight sides. *Building blocks*.

blog

blogs
A **blog** is someone's website or web page where they often add new comments, stories or pictures. Blog is short for web log.

blood

▲ *rhymes with* **mud**
Blood is the red liquid inside your body. Your heart pushes blood round your body.

blow

blows blowing blew blown
1 When the wind **blows**, it moves the air. *The wind has blown away dad's newspaper*.
2 When you **blow**, you push air out of your mouth.

Amy is blowing out all the candles.

blue

Blue is a colour. The sky on a sunny day is blue.

blunt

blunter bluntest
Something that is **blunt** is not sharp. *A blunt knife.*
■ *opposite* **sharp**

board

boards
A **board** is a flat piece of wood or card. *A dartboard.*

boast

boasts boasting boasted

Someone who **boasts** enjoys telling other people about what they have done, or about the things that they own. *Annie is boasting about her new bicycle.*

boat

boats

A **boat** is a vehicle that carries people or things across rivers, lakes or seas. Some boats have engines and some have sails.

body

bodies

The **body** of a person or an animal is every part of them. Your legs, shoulders and head are all parts of your body.

head
hand
arm
chest
stomach
knee
leg
foot

boil

boils boiling boiled

1 When water **boils**, it becomes very hot. There are bubbles in the water and steam rises from it.
2 When you **boil** food, you cook it in boiling water.

bone

bones

Your **bones** are the hard, white parts inside your body. Skeletons are made of bones.

bonfire

bonfires

A **bonfire** is a large fire that is lit outdoors.

book

books

A **book** is a group of pages fixed inside a cover. The pages can have writing or pictures on them.

boot

boots

1 A **boot** is a kind of shoe that covers your foot and part of your leg.
2 The **boot** of a car is the space at the back for carrying things.

bored

If you are **bored**, you are annoyed because you have nothing to do or because you have to do something you don't want to.

born

When a baby is **born**, it comes out of its mother.

borrow

borrows borrowing borrowed
If you **borrow** something, someone lets you have it for a short time. *I borrowed Jo's hat.*

both

Both means two together. *Keep both hands on the handlebars.*

bother

bothers bothering bothered
If something or someone **bothers** you, they worry you or annoy you.

bottle

bottles
Bottles are containers that hold liquid. They are made from glass or plastic.

bottom

bottoms
1 The **bottom** is the lowest part of something. *The ship sank to the bottom of the sea.*
■ *opposite* **top**
2 Your **bottom** is the part of your body that you sit on.

bought

Bought comes from the word **buy**. *We always buy Mum a birthday present. Last year, we bought her some flowers.*

bounce

bounces
bouncing
bounced
When something **bounces**, it springs back after hitting another thing. *Hannah bounced on her big ball.*

bow

bows
▲ *rhymes with* **low**
1 A **bow** is a knot with two loops. You tie your shoelaces in a bow.
2 A **bow** is also a curved piece of wood with a string stretched from one end to the other. You use a bow to shoot arrows.
3 You also use a **bow** to play the violin or cello. A bow is made from a long piece of wood with hair stretched from one end to the other.

bow

bowl

bowls
▲ rhymes with **goal**
You use a **bowl** to hold food or drink. Bowls are usually round and deeper than plates.

box

boxes
Boxes are containers that usually have straight sides.

boy

boys
A **boy** is a male child.

bracelet

bracelets
A **bracelet** is a chain or a band that you wear around your wrist.

brake

brakes
You use the **brakes** on a car or a bike to make it slow down or stop.

branch

branches
A **branch** is part of a tree. Branches grow from the trunk of a tree.

brave

braver bravest
If you are **brave**, you are willing to do something frightening. *Ellie was **brave** about staying in hospital.*

bread

Bread is a food that is made with flour and baked in an oven.

break

breaks breaking broke broken
1 When something **breaks**, it splits into pieces. *The mug **broke** when Anna dropped it.*
2 When a machine **breaks**, it stops working. *Toby has **broken** my radio.*

breakfast

breakfasts
▲ say **brek**-fust
Breakfast is the first meal of the day.

breathe

breathes breathing breathed
When you **breathe**, you suck air into your body and then let it out again. You can breathe through your nose or your mouth.

breeze

breezes
A **breeze** is a light wind.

brick

bricks
A **brick** is a block of baked clay. Bricks are used for building.

bridge

bridges
A **bridge** is something that is built over a river, a road or a railway so that people can get across.

bright

brighter brightest
1 Something that is **bright** gives out a lot of light. *The Sun is very bright.*
2 A **bright** colour is strong and easy to see. *Jemima wore a bright pink jumper.*

brilliant

Something that is **brilliant** is very good. *A brilliant idea.*

bring

brings bringing brought
If you **bring** something, you take it with you. *Please bring a packed lunch tomorrow.*

broad

broader broadest
Something that is **broad** is wide. *The boat drifted down the broad, brown river.*

broken

Broken comes from the word **break**. *Toby breaks everything. He's even broken Dad's camera.*

brother

brothers
Your **brother** is a boy who has the same mum and dad as you.

brought

Brought comes from the word **bring**. *Lucy often brings something interesting to school. Last week, she brought her pet snake.*

brown

Brown is a colour. Wood and chocolate are brown.

bruise

bruises
A **bruise** is a purple mark on your skin. You get a bruise when part of your body is hit by something. *Marc has a bruise on his knee where he knocked it.*

brush
brushes
A **brush** has lots of hairs or wires fixed to a handle. Toothbrushes, paintbrushes and hairbrushes are types of brush.

bubble
bubbles
A **bubble** is a ball of gas inside a liquid. There are bubbles in boiling water and fizzy drinks. Soap bubbles can float through the air.

bucket
buckets
A **bucket** is a container with a flat bottom and a handle.

build
builds building built
If you **build** something, you make it by fixing things together. *Harry is building a castle.*

building
buildings
A **building** is a place with walls and a roof. Houses, shops, schools and offices are buildings.

built
Built comes from the word **build**. *Hannah won our competition to build the tallest tower. She built one that was three metres high.*

bulb
bulbs
1 A **light bulb** shines when you turn on a light. Light bulbs are made of glass.
2 A **bulb** is the part of some plants that is under the ground. Flowers such as daffodils and crocuses grow from bulbs.

bull
bulls
A **bull** is a male cow. Bulls are bigger and stronger than female cows.

bulldozer
bulldozers
A **bulldozer** is a large machine that moves rocks and soil.

bully to bus

bully
bullies bullying bullied
Bullying is trying to hurt or frighten other people.

bump
bumps
A **bump** is something round that sticks out. *Osman has a **bump** on his head.*

bump
bumps bumping bumped
If you **bump** into something, you hit it without meaning to. *Osman **bumped** into a shelf.*

bunch
bunches
A **bunch** is a group of things. *A **bunch** of flowers. **Bunches** of grapes.*

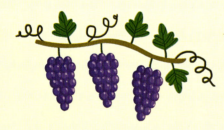

bungalow
bungalows
A **bungalow** is a house that only has one level.

burglar
burglars
A **burglar** is someone who gets into a building and steals things.

burn
burns burning burned burnt
1 If you **burn** something, you set it on fire. *We **burn** logs in our fireplace.*
2 **Burn** also means to damage something with fire or heat. *Alfie has **burnt** the toast again.*
3 If you **burn** yourself, you touch something hot and get hurt.

burst
bursts bursting burst
When something **bursts**, it breaks apart suddenly. *The bag **burst** and scattered apples all over the floor.*

bury
buries burying buried
▲ rhymes with **very**
If you **bury** something, you put it in the ground and cover it with earth. *The pirates **buried** the treasure under a tree.*

bus
buses
A **bus** is a large vehicle that carries lots of people. Buses usually carry people on short journeys between towns or around cities.

bush
bushes
A **bush** is a plant with lots of branches, but no trunk. Bushes are usually smaller than trees.

busy
busier busiest
▲ rhymes with **dizzy**
1 **Busy** people have lots of things to do.
2 If a place is **busy**, there is a lot going on, or a lot of people there.

butcher
butchers
A **butcher** is someone who sells meat.

butter
Butter is a yellow food made from milk. You can spread butter on bread or use it for cooking.

butterfly
butterflies
A **butterfly** is an insect with four large wings.

button
buttons
1 A **button** is something that you press to make something work. *Jacob pressed the **button** to turn on the TV.*
2 A **button** is a small object that is sewn onto clothes. Buttons fit into buttonholes to fasten clothes together.

buy
buys buying bought
When you **buy** something, you pay money so that you can have it. *Chloe is **buying** a new dress.*
▪ opposite **sell**

Cc

cabbage
cabbages
A **cabbage** is a vegetable with lots of leaves. Cabbages can be green, white or purple.

café
cafés
▲ say **kaf-ay**
A **café** is a place that sells food and drink, with tables and chairs where you can sit.

cage
cages
A **cage** is a box or a room with bars. Some pets and zoo animals are kept in cages.

cake to can

cake
cakes
A **cake** is a sweet food that is baked in an oven. Cakes are made with eggs, flour, sugar and butter.

calculator
calculators
A **calculator** is a machine that gives you answers to sums.

calendar
calendars
A **calendar** is a list of all the days, weeks and months in a year. *Olivia marked her birthday on the **calendar**.*

calf
calves
A **calf** is a baby cow. Baby elephants, giraffes and whales are also called calves.

call
calls calling called
1 If you **call** someone, you shout to them so that they come to you. *Dad **called** us to come inside for dinner.*
2 When you **call** someone something, you give them a name. *Tom **called** his kitten Pepper.*
3 **Call** also means to telephone. *David **calls** his uncle every week.*

calm
calmer calmest
If you are **calm**, you are quiet and not worried.

came
Came is from the word **come**. *Henry comes to stay with us every summer. Last year, he **came** in August.*

camel
camels
A **camel** is a large animal with one or two humps on its back. Camels carry people and things across deserts.

camera
cameras
A **camera** is a machine that you use to take photographs.

camp
camps camping camped
When you **camp**, you live in a tent for a short time.

can
cans
A **can** is a metal container with curved sides.

can to caravan

can
could
If you **can** do something, you are able to do it. *Oscar can juggle.*
■ opposite **cannot**

canal
canals
A **canal** is a man-made river.

candle
candles
A **candle** is a stick of wax with a string through the middle, called a wick. When a candle burns, it shines.

> Some words that begin with a "c" sound, such as **kangaroo**, are spelt with a "k".

cannot
If you **cannot** do something, you are not able to do it. *Rebecca cannot come.*
■ opposite **can**

canoe
canoes
▲ *say kan-oo*
A **canoe** is a narrow, light boat that you move with paddles.

can't
Can't is a short way of saying **cannot**. *Rebecca can't come.*

cap
caps
A **cap** is a soft hat with a peak at the front.

capital
capitals
1 A **capital** is the main city of a country. The leaders of a country work in the capital. *The capital of Japan is Tokyo.*
2 A **capital** is also a big letter of the alphabet, such as R or Z. You use a capital when you begin a sentence or write a name. You can see all the capital letters in the strip down the side of the opposite page.

car
cars
A **car** is a vehicle with an engine and four wheels. People drive from place to place in cars.

caravan
caravans
A **caravan** is a small home on wheels. Some caravans can be pulled along by a car.

card

cards
1 **Card** is stiff paper.
2 A greetings **card** is a folded piece of stiff paper. It has a picture on the front and a message inside. You send cards to people at special times, such as birthdays.

3 **Playing cards** are pieces of stiff paper with numbers or pictures on them, used to play games.

cardboard

Cardboard is thick, strong paper. It is used to make boxes.

cardigan

cardigans
A **cardigan** is a knitted jacket. Cardigans fasten at the front.

care

cares caring cared
1 If you **care for** a person or an animal, you look after them. *Harry has two rabbits and he cares for them himself.*
2 If you **care about** something, you think that it is important.

careful

If you are **careful**, you think about what you are doing and try not to make mistakes.
■ *opposite* **careless**

*Ben was **careful** not to spill the drinks.*

careless

Someone who is **careless** does not think about what they are doing. *It was **careless** of Fergus to forget his coat.*
■ *opposite* **careful**

carpet

carpets
A **carpet** is a thick, soft covering for a floor.

carriage

carriages
Carriages are the parts of a train that contain the passengers.

carrot

carrots
A **carrot** is a long, orange vegetable that grows under the ground. You can eat carrots raw or cooked.

carry

carries carrying carried
If you **carry** something, you take it somewhere with you. *James carried his bag to the station.*

carton

cartons
Cartons are containers used to hold food or drink. They are made from card or plastic.

cartoon

cartoons
1 A **cartoon** is a film that uses drawings rather than actors.
2 A **cartoon** is also a funny drawing.

case

cases
You use a **case** to store or carry things. *Ginny keeps her glasses in a case.*

cash

Cash is money in coins or notes.

castle

castles
A **castle** is a big building with high walls to keep enemies out. Most castles were built a long time ago.

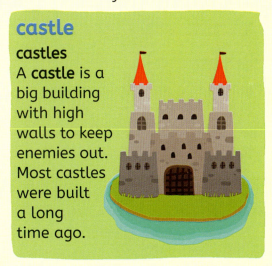

cat

cats
A **cat** is a furry animal with a long tail. Cats are often kept as pets. Large, wild cats, such as lions and tigers, are known as big cats.

catch

catches catching caught
1 When you **catch** something, you take hold of it while it is moving or in the air. *Joseph ran to catch the ball.*
2 If you **catch** a bus or a train, you get on it. *David caught the last bus home.*

caterpillar

caterpillars
A **caterpillar** is a small animal that looks like a worm with lots of short legs. Caterpillars turn into butterflies or moths.

cattle

Cattle is a word for cows and bulls. *We saw some cattle in the field.*

caught

Caught comes from the word **catch**. *Joseph ran to catch the ball. He caught it easily.*

cauliflower to centre

cauliflower

cauliflowers

A **cauliflower** is a round vegetable. Cauliflowers have green leaves and a white centre.

cause

causes causing caused

If something **causes** something else, it makes it happen. *Running with scissors can cause accidents.*

cave

caves

A **cave** is a large hole in the side of a cliff or a mountain, or under the ground.

CD

CDs

A **CD** is a round piece of plastic with music or information stored on it. CD is short for compact disc.

> Some words that begin with a "c" sound, such as **keep**, **kennel**, **kettle** and **key**, are spelt with a "k".

ceiling

ceilings
▲ say **see**-ling

The **ceiling** is the part of a room that is above your head. Lights hang from ceilings.

celebrate

celebrates celebrating celebrated

When people **celebrate**, they have fun together to mark a special occasion. *We celebrated Auntie's birthday with a big party.*

celebrity

celebrities

A **celebrity** is a famous person, such as a singer or footballer.

cellar

cellars

A **cellar** is a room under a house, often used to store things.

cello

cellos
▲ say **chel**-lo

A **cello** is a musical instrument like a large violin.

Rosalind loves to play the cello.

cement

Cement is a grey powder that is mixed with water and goes very hard when it dries. People use cement to stick bricks together.

centre

centres

The **centre** of something is the middle of it.

century

centuries
A **century** is a period of one hundred years.

cereal

cereals
1 **Cereal** is a food that you eat for breakfast. Most people eat cereal with milk.
2 **Cereals** are also farm plants such as wheat or rice. Their seeds are used for food.

certain

If you are **certain** about something, you are sure about it. *Robert is **certain** that his team will win.*

certificate

certificates
A **certificate** is a piece of paper that says you have done something. *A cycling **certificate**.*

chain

chains
A **chain** is a row of metal loops that are joined together.

chair

chairs
A **chair** is a seat with four legs and a back. Chairs are made for one person to sit on.

chalk

chalks
A **chalk** is a stick of powdered rock used for drawing. Chalks can be white or coloured.

champion

champions
A **champion** is the winner of a race or a competition.

chance

chances
1 When you have the **chance** to do something, it is possible for you to do it. *Petra has the **chance** to go skiing.*
2 If there is a **chance** that something will happen, it might happen, or it might not. *There's a **chance** it will snow later.*
3 If something happens **by chance**, it has not been planned.

change

Change is the money given back to you when you hand over more money than something costs.

change

changes changing changed
1 When something **changes**, it is different from how it was before. *If the weather **changes**, we'll go back inside.*
2 When you **change**, you put on different clothes. *Molly **changed** before she went out.*

channel to check

channel
channels
A **channel** is what you choose on a television or radio to see or hear programmes shown by a certain station.

chapter
chapters
A **chapter** is a part of a book.
*The book has 12 **chapters**.*

character
characters
▲ *say **karrak**-ter*
1 A **character** is a person in a story, a film or a play.
2 Your **character** is the sort of person you are.

charge
If someone is **in charge** of something, they look after it.
*Mrs Parsnip is **in charge** of our class.*

charge
charges charging charged
1 When you **charge** a battery or a phone, you fill up the electricity stored inside it.
2 If someone **charges** you for something, they ask you to pay money for it.

chart
charts
A **chart** is a picture, a map or a list that shows information clearly.

chase
chases chasing chased
If you **chase** a person or an animal, you run after them and try to catch them.
*Finn **chased** Flora.*

chat
chats chatting chatted
When you **chat** to someone you talk to them in a relaxed, friendly way.

cheap
cheaper cheapest
Something that is **cheap** does not cost much.
■ *opposite* **expensive**

cheat
cheats cheating cheated
If you **cheat**, you break the rules so that you can win or get something that you want.

check
checks checking checked
If you **check** something, you make sure that it is right.
*Lola **checked** a spelling in her dictionary.*

cheek

cheeks
Your **cheeks** are the soft sides of your face.

cheer

cheers cheering cheered
1 When you **cheer**, you shout happily to show that you like something.
2 When you **cheer** someone **up**, you do or say something to make them feel better.

cheerful

Someone who is **cheerful** feels and looks happy.

cheese

cheeses
Cheese is a food that is made from milk. Cheese can be hard or soft.

cheetah

cheetahs
A **cheetah** is a large wild cat. Cheetahs can run very fast.

cherry

cherries
A **cherry** is a small, round fruit with a hard seed called a stone in the middle. Cherries can be red, black or yellow.

chess

Chess is a game for two people. You play chess by moving special pieces, such as a queen or a knight, across a board of black and white squares.

chest

chests
1 Your **chest** is the front part of your body between your neck and your stomach.
2 A **chest** is a large, strong box that you keep things in. Chests are usually made of wood.

chew

chews chewing chewed
When you **chew** food, you bite it many times before you swallow it.

chick

chicks
A **chick** is a very young bird.

chicken

chickens
1 A **chicken** is a bird that is kept on a farm.
2 **Chicken** is also the meat that comes from chickens.

chickenpox to chunk

chickenpox
Chickenpox is a disease. When you have chickenpox, lots of itchy red spots appear on your skin.

child
children
A **child** is a young boy or girl.

chimney
chimneys
A **chimney** is a wide pipe above a fire that carries smoke out of a building. *Our chimney is made of red brick.*

chimpanzee
chimpanzees
A **chimpanzee** is an ape with dark fur. The short name for chimpanzee is chimp.

chin
chins
Your **chin** is the part of your face below your mouth.

chip
chips
A **chip** is a long, thin piece of potato that is either fried in oil or baked.

choir
choirs
▲ *say kwire*
A **choir** is a group of people who sing together.

choose
chooses choosing chose chosen
If you **choose** something, you pick the thing that you want. *Dave is choosing a shirt.*

chop
chops chopping chopped
If you **chop** something, you cut it into pieces.

Roberto chopped a carrot.

chosen
Chosen comes from the word **choose**. *Robbie is allowed to choose what we will do. He has chosen a trip to the fair.*

chunk
chunks
A **chunk** is a thick piece of something. *Milo ate a chunk of cheese.*

> Some words that begin with a "**c**" sound, such as **kick, king, kiss** and **kitchen**, are spelt with a "**k**".

cinema
cinemas
A **cinema** is a place where people go to watch films.

circle
circles
A **circle** is a perfectly round shape.

circus
circuses
A **circus** is a show that is held in a big tent.

city
cities
A **city** is a very big place where many people live and work. Cities are usually larger than towns.

clap
claps clapping clapped
When you **clap**, you make a loud noise by slapping your hands together. People clap to show they have enjoyed something, such as a play or a concert.

class
classes
A **class** is a group of people who are taught together. *We are in Mrs Parsnip's class at school.*

classroom
classrooms
A **classroom** is a room in a school where children have lessons.

claw
claws
A **claw** is one of the sharp, curved nails on the feet of some animals. Bears, cats, crocodiles and eagles have claws.

claw

clay
Clay is a kind of earth. When clay is wet, it can be made into different shapes. When it dries or is baked, it becomes hard. *Kate made a pot out of clay.*

clean
cleans cleaning cleaned
When you **clean** something, you take the dirt off it. *Pete needs to clean his boots.*

clean
cleaner cleanest
Something that is **clean** does not have any dirt or food on it. *Raj wore a clean shirt to go to the party. Fetch some clean plates.*
■ opposite **dirty**

clear to clothes

clear
clears clearing cleared
When you **clear** something, you remove things from it to make space.

clear
clearer clearest
1 If a thing is **clear**, you can see through it. *A **clear** plastic ruler.*
2 Something that is **clear** is easy to understand. *The instructions were **clear** and easy to follow.*

clever
cleverer cleverest
Someone who is **clever** finds it easy to learn and to understand things. *Chen is the **cleverest** girl in our class.*

cliff
cliffs
A **cliff** is the very steep side of a hill, mountain or coast.

cliff

climb
climbs climbing climbed
▲ *rhymes with* **time**
When you **climb** something, you move up it. People sometimes use their hands and feet to climb.

cloak
cloaks
A **cloak** is a loose coat without sleeves.

clock
clocks
A **clock** is a machine that shows you what time it is.

*The **clock** says 11.45.*

close
closes closing closed
▲ *say* **kloze**
If you **close** something, you shut it. ***Close** the door behind you.*
■ opposite **open**

close
closer closest
▲ *say* **klose**
If something is **close**, it is near. *Stay **close** to me.*

cloth
cloths
1 **Cloth** is material that is used to make clothes and curtains.
2 A **cloth** is a piece of material that you use to wipe up a mess.

clothes
Clothes are things that you wear, such as shirts, socks and trousers.

cloud to cobweb

cloud
clouds
Clouds are white or grey shapes that you see in the sky. They are made of tiny drops of water. Rain, snow and hail come from clouds.

clown
clowns
A **clown** is someone who makes people laugh. Clowns wear make-up and funny clothes and do tricks.

club
clubs
A **club** is a group of people who meet together because they enjoy doing the same thing. *Ali has joined a computer club.*

clue
clues
A **clue** is something that helps you to find the answer to a question. *The police need some clues to help them find the burglar.*

clumsy
clumsier clumsiest
Clumsy people are not very careful about the way they move and often knock things over.

coach
coaches
1 A **coach** is a large vehicle that carries lots of people. Coaches are mostly used for longer journeys than buses.
2 A **coach** is also someone who teaches you to play a sport.

coal
Coal is a black rock found under the ground. It burns well, making lots of heat.

coast
coasts
The **coast** is the land next to the sea.

coat
coats
1 A **coat** is a piece of clothing that you wear over your other clothes. Coats have long sleeves and are usually made from thick material.
2 An animal's **coat** is the fur or hair that covers its body. *Fido has a long, thick coat.*

cobweb
cobwebs
A **cobweb** is an old spider's web, usually found in a dusty corner.

41

cockerel to colour

cockerel
cockerels
A **cockerel** is a male chicken. The short name for cockerel is cock.

coffee
coffees
Coffee is a drink made by pouring hot water onto the roasted seeds of the coffee tree.

coin
coins
A **coin** is a small, flat piece of metal. Coins are used as money.

cold
colds
When you have a **cold**, you have a sore throat and you cough and sneeze a lot.

cold
colder coldest
1 If something is **cold**, it is not hot or warm. *A **cold** drink.*
2 If the weather is **cold**, the temperature is low. *It was so **cold** that Isla shivered.*
■ opposite **hot**

collar
collars
1 The **collar** of a shirt or a jacket is the part of it that fits round your neck.
2 A **collar** is also a band that goes round the neck of a dog or a cat.

collect
collects collecting collected
1 If you **collect** things, you keep them as a hobby. *Sam **collects** stamps.*
2 When you **collect** things, you put them together. *Tilly **collected** the empty cups.*
3 If you **collect** someone, you take them from a place. *Dad **collected** me from school.*

college
colleges
A **college** is a place where people can learn after they have left school.

colour
colours
Red, yellow and blue are the main **colours**. You can make other colours by mixing the main ones.

red   *yellow*   *blue*

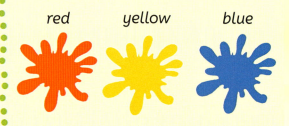

comb

combs
▲ rhymes with **home**
A **comb** is a flat piece of plastic or metal with thin teeth. You use a comb to tidy your hair.

come

comes coming came come
When you **come** to a person or a place, you move towards them. *Come here so that I can hear you.*
■ opposite **go**

comfortable

If something is **comfortable**, it feels good. *A comfortable chair.*

comic

comics
A **comic** is a magazine with stories told in pictures.

common

commoner commonest
Things that are **common** are often seen. *Computers are common in schools.*
■ opposite **rare**

compare

compares comparing compared
When you **compare** two things, you look at them carefully to see if they are the same or different. *Maisie compared the two dresses to decide which she liked best.*

compass

compasses
1 A **compass** is something that shows you which way you are facing. A compass has a needle that always points north.
2 A **compass** is also a tool that you use to draw a circle.

competition

competitions
When you take part in a **competition**, you try to do better than other people. *I came first in the swimming competition.*

complete

completes completing completed
When you **complete** something, you finish it. *Alice completed her homework and went out to play.*

complete

Something that is **complete** does not have anything missing. *Amy checked to make sure that the jigsaw puzzle was complete.*

computer

computers
A **computer** is a machine that stores words, pictures and numbers, and is often used to go on the internet. *Jake loves playing games on his computer.*

concentrate

concentrates concentrating concentrated
When you **concentrate** on something, you think hard about it. *Akil is **concentrating** on his history project.*

concert

concerts
When people give a **concert**, they play music or sing to an audience.

concrete

Concrete is a mixture of cement, small stones, sand and water. It becomes very hard when it dries. Concrete is used for building.

confuse

confuses confusing confused
If someone **confuses** you, they make it difficult for you to understand something. *Hermione **confused** me with her long words.*

connect

connects connecting connected
If you **connect** two things, you join them together. *Ed **connected** the computer to the printer.*

consonant

consonants
A **consonant** is any letter of the alphabet except the vowels a, e, i, o and u. B and f are consonants.

contact lens

contact lenses
Contact lenses are small circles of soft, clear plastic that you put in your eyes to help you see better.

contain

contains containing contained
If a box **contains** something, it has that thing inside it.

container

containers
A **container** is something you use to hold things or keep things in. Boxes, bottles and baskets are all containers.

continue

continues continuing continued
If you **continue** to do something, you don't stop doing it.

control

controls controlling controlled
When you **control** something, you make it do what you want.

*Arthur can **control** his toy car.*

conversation

conversations
When people have a **conversation**, they talk to each other.

cook

cooks
cooking cooked
When you **cook** food, you heat it until it is ready to eat.

cool

cooler coolest
Something that is **cool** feels quite cold. *We enjoyed our **cool** drinks.*

copy

copies
A **copy** is a thing that looks the same as something else. *Jamila liked the painting so much that she made a **copy** of it.*

copy

copies copying copied
If you **copy** someone, you do the same as they do. *Fergus is **copying** the way his dad walks.*

cord

cords
Cord is a type of string. Some bags have a cord around the top that you pull to close them.

corner

corners
A **corner** is a place where two sides join together. *We met at the **corner** of the field.*

correct

corrects correcting corrected
If you **correct** something, you make it right where it was wrong.

correct

If something is **correct**, it does not have any mistakes in it.

corridor

corridors
A **corridor** is a long, indoor passage. *The **corridor** was full of passengers.*

cost

costs costing cost
If something **costs** an amount of money, that's how much you need to buy it. *How much does that hat **cost**?*

costume

costumes
A **costume** is a set of clothes that you wear to make yourself look different. *Freddie wore a bear **costume** for the school play.*

cot

cots
A **cot** is a bed for a baby. Cots have high sides so the baby cannot fall out.

cottage

cottages
A **cottage** is a small house. You often see cottages in the country.

cotton

1 **Cotton** is a material that is used to make clothes. Cotton comes from the cotton plant.
2 **Cotton** is thread that you use for sewing.

cough

coughs coughing coughed
▲ *rhymes with* **off**
When you **cough**, you force air out of your throat with a sudden, loud noise. You often cough when you have a cold.

could

Could comes from the word **can**. *Oscar can juggle with four balls. Last month, he could only juggle with three.*

couldn't

Couldn't is a short way of saying **could not**. *Sebastian couldn't swim before he had lessons.*

count

counts counting counted
1 When you **count**, you say numbers one after the other in order.
2 When you **count** a number of things, you add them up to find out how many there are. *I have counted all the jigsaw pieces and there are 30.*

counter

counters
1 A **counter** is a long table in a shop. Someone stands behind the counter and serves you.
2 A **counter** is also a small piece of plastic that you use in some games.

country

countries
1 A **country** is a part of the world with its own people and laws.
2 The **country**, or countryside, is the land outside towns and cities. There are fields, woods and farms in the country.

courage

▲ *say* **cur-idge**
Someone who has **courage** is brave.

court

courts
1 A **court** is an area where you play sports. *A tennis court.*
2 A **court** is a place where a judge and a group of people decide if someone has broken a law or not.

cousin

cousins
▲ say **kuz**-un
Your **cousin** is the son or daughter of your aunt or uncle.

cover

covers covering covered
If you **cover** something, you put something else over it, or all around it. *Monica covered the cake with icing.*

cow

cows or **cattle**
A **cow** is a large farm animal kept for its milk and its meat.

crab

crabs
A **crab** is a sea creature with a hard shell. Crabs have ten legs and walk sideways.

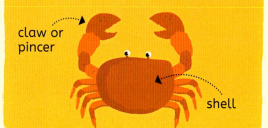
claw or pincer
shell

crack

cracks
A **crack** is a line that shows where something is starting to break. *This mug has a crack in it.*

cracker

crackers
1 A **cracker** is a thin biscuit. People often eat crackers with cheese.
2 A **cracker** is a paper tube that bangs when two people pull it apart. Crackers often have something in them, and are pulled at Christmas meals.

crane

cranes
A **crane** is a tall machine that lifts heavy loads.

crash

crashes
1 A **crash** is a sudden, loud noise. *The plates fell to the ground with a crash.*
2 A **crash** is also a traffic accident.

crash

crashes crashing crashed
When something **crashes**, it hits something else very hard and makes a sudden, loud noise. *The car crashed into a tree.*

crawl to crop

crawl
crawls crawling crawled
When you **crawl**, you move around on your hands and knees. *Jemima **crawled** under the table to hide.*

crayon
crayons
A **crayon** is a coloured pencil. Some crayons are made from wax.

cream
Cream is the thick part of milk. You can use cream in cooking or pour it over puddings and fruit.

creature
creatures
A **creature** is anything that moves and breathes. Horses, lizards, fish, birds and insects are all creatures.

creep
creeps creeping crept
If you **creep** somewhere, you move very slowly and quietly. *Christopher **crept** past his sleeping brother.*

crew
crews
A **crew** is a group of people who work together on a boat or a plane.

cricket
Cricket is a game with a bat and a ball played by two teams. The players have to hit the ball and run up and down the pitch.

cried
Cried comes from the word **cry**. *Poppy began to cry. She **cried** for half an hour.*

crime
crimes
A **crime** is something someone does that is against the law of a country.

crisp
crisps
Crisps are very thin slices of potato that are cooked and eaten cold as a snack.

crocodile
crocodiles
A **crocodile** is a large reptile that lives in rivers in hot countries. Crocodiles have sharp teeth, short legs and a long tail.

crop
crops
Crops are plants grown in fields and used for food. Wheat, potatoes and corn are crops.

corn

cross to cruel

cross
crosses
A **cross** is a sign. It looks like **+** or **X**.

cross
crosses crossing crossed
When you **cross** something, you go from one side of it to the other. *Why did the chicken cross the road?*

cross
crosser crossest
If you are **cross**, you are not pleased about something and you feel angry.

> Some other words for **cross** are **angry, annoyed, irritated** and **furious**.

crowd
crowds
A **crowd** is a large group of people. *A football crowd.*

crown
crowns
A **crown** is a special kind of hat made from gold, silver and jewels. Kings and queens wear crowns.

cruel
crueller cruellest
Cruel people are unkind and often hurt other people or animals.
■ opposite **kind**

crossword
crosswords
A **crossword** is a word puzzle with clues. You work out the answer to a clue, then write the word in squares on the puzzle.

ACROSS
1 Coloured pencil
5 Sound of a cow
6 Cuddly toy bear
8 Sound of a pig
9 Loud noise
12 Pastime
14 What you breathe
15 Very dry place

DOWN
1 Queen's hat
2 Small insects
3 Not young
4 Not rough
7 A thick food made out of milk
10 Not together
11 Write using a keyboard
13 Insect that makes honey

a completed crossword

a b c d e f g h i j k l m n o p q r s t u v w x y z

crumb to curtain

crumb
crumbs
A **crumb** is a very small piece of dry food. *Cake* **crumbs**.

crust
crusts
The **crust** is the hard part on the outside of a pie or a loaf of bread. *Nathan never eats his* **crusts**.

cry
cries crying cried
When you **cry**, tears come from your eyes. People cry when they are sad or hurt.

cube
cubes
A **cube** is a solid shape with six square sides. Most dice are cubes.

cucumber
cucumbers
A **cucumber** is a long, green vegetable that you eat in salads.

cuddle
cuddles cuddling cuddled
When you **cuddle** someone, you hold them closely in your arms.

cup
cups
You drink from a **cup**. Cups are usually round and often have a handle on one side.

cupboard
cupboards
▲ say **cub**-erd
A **cupboard** is a piece of furniture which you keep things in. *Biff put his toys in the* **cupboard**.

curious
If you are **curious** about something, you want to find out about it. *Edward was* **curious** *about the parcel*.

curl
curls
A **curl** is a piece of hair that is curved. *Caroline has beautiful* **curls**.

curtain
curtains
A **curtain** is a piece of material that you pull across a window to cover it.

curve
curves
A **curve** is a line that bends.

cushion
cushions
A **cushion** is a soft pad that you use to make sofas and chairs more comfortable.

customer
customers
Anyone who buys something from a shop is a **customer** of that shop.

cut
cuts cutting cut
1 If you **cut** something, you use a knife or a pair of scissors to divide it into pieces. *Mum cut the potatoes into chips.*
2 When you **cut** yourself, something sharp pushes through your skin and makes you bleed.

cyberbully
cyberbullies
A **cyberbully** is someone who uses the internet or a mobile phone to bully people.

cycle
cycles cycling cycled
To **cycle** is to ride a bicycle. *My dad cycles to work every day.*

Dd

dad
dads
Dad is a name for your father.

daily
If something happens **daily**, it happens every day.

daisy
daisies
Daisies are common flowers with white petals and a yellow centre.

damage
damages damaging damaged
If you **damage** something, you spoil it or break it.

damp
damper dampest
Something **damp** is a little bit wet. *The dew has made our lawn damp.*

dance
dances dancing danced
When you **dance**, you move your body to music.

danger

You are in **danger** when something could very easily happen to hurt you.

dangerous

If something is **dangerous**, it can hurt or kill you.

dare

dares daring dared
1 If you **dare** to do something, you are brave enough to do it. *Peter **dared** to jump off the top diving board.*
2 If you **dare** someone to do something, you test them by asking them to do it. *Fiona **dared** James to climb the tree.*

dark

darker darkest
1 When it is **dark**, there is no light or very little light.
2 **Dark** colours are not pale. *Dark blue.*
■ opposite **light**

date

dates
When someone asks you what the **date** is, you tell them the day and the month.

*The **date** today is 20th June.*

daughter

daughters
A **daughter** is somebody's female child.

day

days
1 **Day** is the time when it is light outside. *We've been out all **day**.*
■ opposite **night**
2 A **day** is a period of 24 hours, starting and ending at midnight. There are seven days in a week. Tuesday and Saturday are days.

dead

If people, animals or plants are **dead**, they are no longer living.
■ opposite **alive**

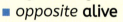

deaf

Deaf people cannot hear at all or cannot hear very well.

dear

dearer dearest
1 If someone is **dear** to you, you love them. *Rachel is a **dear** friend.*
2 You use the word **dear** when you begin a letter. *Dear Mrs Bott.*

decide

decides deciding decided
When you **decide** something, you work out what you're going to do. *Poppy **decided** to wear her purple shorts.*

deck to desert

deck
decks
A **deck** is a floor on a boat or a ship.

decorate
decorates decorating decorated
1 When you **decorate** something, you add things to it to make it look prettier. *Billy decorated the hall for his party.*
2 If you **decorate** a room, you paint it or put wallpaper on its walls.

deep
deeper deepest
Something that is **deep** goes down a long way. *A deep well.*
■ opposite **shallow**

deer
deer
A **deer** is an animal with four legs and brown fur. Deer live in forests and can run very fast. Male deer have big horns called antlers.

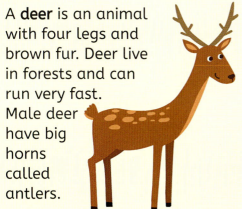

delicious
Food or drink that is **delicious** tastes or smells very good.

deliver
delivers delivering delivered
If you **deliver** something, you take it to somebody. *The postman delivered a parcel.*

dentist
dentists
A **dentist** is someone who takes care of your teeth.

depth
depths
The **depth** of a thing is how far it goes down. *We measured the depth of the pool.*

describe
describes describing described
When you **describe** something, you say what it is like. *Alfie described his new house to me.*

desert
deserts
A **desert** is a large piece of land where very few plants grow. Deserts are very dry and are often covered with sand.

deserve to different

deserve
deserves deserving deserved
If you **deserve** a thing, you earn it by doing something. *Eleanor **deserves** a rest after all her hard work.*

desk
desks
A **desk** is a kind of table that you sit at to write or to do work.

dessert
desserts
A **dessert** is a sweet food that you eat at the end of a meal. *Evie chose ice cream for **dessert**.*

destroy
destroys destroying destroyed
Destroy means to damage something so badly that it cannot be mended. *The storm **destroyed** our garden shed.*

diagram
diagrams
A **diagram** is a drawing that shows something in a clear and simple way.

diamond
diamonds
1 A **diamond** is a jewel. Diamonds are clear and bright.
2 A **diamond** is also a shape with four sides.

diary
diaries
A **diary** is a book in which you write down things that happen to you each day.

dice
dice
A **dice** is a cube with a different number of spots on each side. You use dice in some games.

dictionary
dictionaries
A **dictionary** is a book of words. Dictionaries tell you what words mean and how to spell them.

didn't
Didn't is a short way of saying **did not**. *Harry **didn't** like the new wallpaper.*

die
dies dying died
When a person, an animal or a plant **dies**, they stop living.

different
If a thing is **different**, it is not the same as something else.
■ *opposite* **same**

difficult

If something is **difficult**, you need to try hard to do it.
■ opposite **easy**

dig

digs digging dug
When you **dig**, you make a hole in the ground. You usually dig with a spade.

dinner

dinners
Dinner is a name for the biggest meal of the day.

dinosaur

dinosaurs
Dinosaurs were reptiles that lived millions of years ago. Some dinosaurs were bigger than any land animals alive today.

direction

directions
1 A **direction** is the way that you go to get to a place. *The station is in this direction.*
2 **Directions** are pictures and words that show you how to do something. *These directions show you how to make a kite.*

dirty

dirtier dirtiest
If something is **dirty**, it has mud, food, or other marks on it.
Dirty boots.
■ opposite **clean**

disagree

disagrees disagreeing disagreed
If you **disagree** with someone, you do not think the same as they do about something. *We disagreed about the album. Jack thought it was good, but I thought it was awful.*
■ opposite **agree**

disappear

disappears disappearing disappeared
If something **disappears**, you cannot see it any more. *The Sun disappeared behind a cloud.*
■ opposite **appear**

disappointed

If you are **disappointed**, you are sad because something has not gone the way you wanted it to. *Jo was disappointed that her friend couldn't come.*

disaster to display

disaster
disasters
A **disaster** is something terrible that happens.

disco
discos
A **disco** is a party with music for dancing. There are often flashing lights at discos.

discover
discovers discovering discovered
When you **discover** something, you find out about it for the first time. *Megan **discovered** that her friend had been lying.*

discuss
discusses discussing discussed
When you **discuss** something, you talk about it with someone else. *We **discussed** which way we would go home.*

disease
diseases
A **disease** is something that makes you ill. Chickenpox is a disease.

disguise
disguises
A **disguise** is something you wear so that people won't recognize you.

dish
dishes
You put food in a **dish**. Dishes are deeper than plates.

dishonest
▲ *say diss-**on**-ist*
Someone who is **dishonest** does not tell the truth.
■ *opposite* **honest**

dishwasher
dishwashers
A **dishwasher** is a machine that washes and dries plates and dishes.

dislike
dislikes disliking disliked
When you **dislike** something, you do not like it.
■ *opposite* **like**

disobey
disobeys disobeying disobeyed
If you **disobey** someone, you do not do what they tell you to do.
■ *opposite* **obey**

display
displays
A **display** is a group of things that have been arranged for people to look at. *Luca thought the art **display** was brilliant.*

distance

distances
The **distance** between two things is the space between them. *We measured the **distance** between the tables.*

disturb

disturbs disturbing disturbed
If you **disturb** someone, you stop them doing something for a short time. *Jayden keeps **disturbing** me when I am trying to read.*

dive

dives diving dived
When you **dive** into water, you jump in head first, with your arms stretched out in front of you.

divide

divides dividing divided
1 When you **divide** numbers, you find out how many times one number goes into another. *Hans **divided** 12 by 2.*

$$12 \div 2 = 6$$

■ *opposite* **multiply**

2 When you **divide** something, you make it into smaller pieces. *Ed **divided** the cake into six pieces.*

doctor

doctors
A **doctor** is someone who helps sick people to get better.

doesn't

Doesn't is a short way of saying **does not**. *Elsa **doesn't** mind cold weather.*

dog

dogs
A **dog** is an animal with four legs and a tail, that is often kept as a pet. Dogs come in many shapes and sizes. Some are trained to do work.

doll

dolls
A **doll** is a toy that looks like a person.

dolphin

dolphins
A **dolphin** is a sea animal. Dolphins are clever and playful.

donkey to drain

donkey
donkeys
A **donkey** is an animal that looks like a small horse. Donkeys have long ears and a furry coat.

don't
Don't is a short way of saying **do not**. *I don't like strawberries.*

door
doors
You use a **door** to get into a building, a room or a cupboard.

double
Double means twice as much, or twice as many. *Your lolly is double the size of mine.*

doubt
doubts doubting doubted
▲ say **dowt**
If you **doubt** something, you are not sure about it. *I doubted Simon's story.*

doughnut
doughnuts
▲ say **doe**-nut
A **doughnut** is a small cake covered in sugar or icing.

down
When something moves **down**, it goes from a higher place to a lower place. *We rode our bikes down the hill.*
■ opposite **up**

download
downloads downloading downloaded
When you **download** information, music or a program, you copy it from the internet onto your computer.

drag
drags dragging dragged
If you **drag** something, you pull it along the ground. *Davina dragged her sledge up the hill.*

dragon
dragons
A **dragon** is a fire-breathing monster that you read about in stories. Dragons often have wings and a long tail.

drain
drains
A **drain** is a pipe or tunnel that carries away liquids.

drama
When you do **drama**, you act or make up plays.

drank
Drank comes from the word **drink**. *Leo likes to drink milk. He drank three glasses this morning.*

draughts
▲ rhymes with **rafts**
Draughts is a game for two people. You play draughts by moving counters across a board of black and white squares.

draw
draws drawing drew drawn
1 When you **draw**, you use pencils or crayons to make a picture.
2 If you **draw** a game with someone, neither of you wins or loses.
3 When you **draw** curtains, you close them.

drawer
drawers
A **drawer** is a box that slides in and out of a piece of furniture. You use drawers to keep things in.

drawing
drawings
A **drawing** is a picture made with pens, pencils or crayons.

drawn
Drawn comes from the word **draw**. *Laura likes to draw. She has drawn a picture of a house.*

dream
dreams
A **dream** is a story that you see and hear while you are sleeping.

dress
dresses
A **dress** looks like a skirt and a top joined together. Women and girls wear dresses. *Erin wore her new dress.*

dress
dresses dressing dressed
When you **dress**, you put on your clothes. *Billy dressed quickly.*

drew
Drew comes from the word **draw**. *We all had to draw our favourite food. I drew a bowl of ice cream.*

dried
Dried comes from the word **dry**. *We hung the clothes outside to dry. They had dried by lunch time.*

drill to dry

drill
drills
A **drill** is a tool that makes holes in hard surfaces.

drink
drinks drinking drank drunk
When you **drink**, you swallow liquid.

drip
drips dripping dripped
When something **drips** it falls in drops, or drops fall from it. *The tap is **dripping**.*

drive
drives driving drove driven
When someone **drives** a vehicle, they make it go somewhere.

drop
drops
A **drop** is a tiny amount of liquid. *Drops of rain.*

drop
drops dropping dropped
If you **drop** something, you let it fall, usually by accident. *Daisy dropped her dinner on the floor.*

drove
Drove comes from the word **drive**. *Joseph drives a truck. He drove thousands of miles last month.*

drown
drowns drowning drowned
If someone **drowns**, they die because they are under water and cannot breathe.

drum
drums
A **drum** is a hollow musical instrument with a thin skin stretched over the end. You hit the skin with sticks or with your hands.

drunk
Drunk comes from the word **drink**. *Fiona drinks tea all the time. She has drunk six cups already today.*

dry
dries drying dried
When you **dry** something, you take liquid out of it or off it. *Matilda is **drying** the dishes.*

dry
drier driest
Something that is **dry** does not have any liquid in it or on it.
■ opposite **wet**

duck to eager

duck
ducks
A **duck** is a bird that can swim. Ducks have short legs and can dive underwater.

dug
Dug comes from the word **dig**. *The pirates began to dig. They dug a hole to hide their treasure.*

dull
duller dullest
1 A **dull** colour is not very bright.
2 Something that is **dull** is not very interesting. *Ellis thought the story was very dull.*

dungeon
dungeons
A **dungeon** is a prison under the ground. Dungeons are usually found in castles.

dust
Dust looks like powder and is made up of tiny, dry pieces of dirt. *The furniture was covered in dust.*

dustbin
dustbins
A **dustbin** is a large container with a lid. You put your rubbish in a dustbin.

duvet
duvets
▲ *say **doo**-vay*
A **duvet** is a thick cover for a bed. Duvets are filled with feathers or other soft material.

DVD
DVDs
A **DVD** is a round piece of plastic with a film or information stored on it. *Millie is watching her new DVD.*

dying
Dying comes from the word **die**. *Plants die if you do not give them water. Our plants were dying when we returned from holiday.*

Ee

each
Each means every one. *Joel gave each puppy a name. The roses cost £1 each.*

eager
If you are **eager** to do something, you really want to do it. *Zach is eager to learn the guitar.*

eagle to edge

eagle

eagles
An **eagle** is a large bird with a curved beak and sharp claws. Eagles hunt small animals.

ear

ears
Your **ears** are the parts of your body on the sides of your head that you use to hear.

early

earlier earliest
1 If you arrive **early**, you arrive before the time that you were expected. *Sally was **early** because her watch was wrong.*
2 **Early** also means near the beginning of something. *We set off **early** in the morning.*
■ *opposite* **late**

earn

earns earning earned
If you **earn** money, you work to get it. *Clare **earned** some money by working in her uncle's garden.*

earth

1 **Earth** is another word for soil. Plants grow in the earth.
2 The **Earth** is the planet that we live on.

earthquake

earthquakes
When there is an **earthquake**, the ground shakes and buildings sometimes fall down.

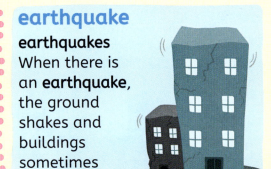

east

East is a direction. The Sun rises in the east.
■ *opposite* **west**

easy

easier easiest
If something is **easy**, you do not have to try hard to do it.
■ *opposite* **difficult**

eat

eats eating ate eaten
When you **eat**, you chew and swallow food. *Simon is **eating** his lunch.*

echo

echoes
▲ *say **ek**-oh*
An **echo** is a sound that you hear again and again. *Our voices made **echoes** in the cave.*

edge

edges
An **edge** is the outside part of something, where it begins or ends. *We walked along the **edge** of the lake.*

effect

effects
An **effect** is a thing that happens because of something else. *Meeting his hero had a powerful **effect** on Ali.*

effort

If you put **effort** into something, you try hard at it. *Misha has put a lot of **effort** into her project.*

egg

eggs
Eggs contain young birds, reptiles or insects, which break out when they are ready to be born. People often eat hens' eggs.

either

Either means one or the other of two. *You can have **either** an apple or an orange.*

elbow

elbows
Your **elbow** is the joint in the middle of your arm, where it bends.

electricity

Electricity is a kind of energy that is used to make light and heat. Electricity is also used to make machines work.

elephant

elephants
An **elephant** is a large, grey animal with a long trunk and two tusks.

else

1 **Else** means other, or different. *Jamelia decided to try something **else**.*
2 **Else** also means more. *I can't see anybody **else** here.*

email

emails
An **email** is a typed message sent across the internet from one email address to another. It is short for electronic mail.

emergency

emergencies
An **emergency** is a serious problem that happens suddenly. You need to act quickly in an emergency.

empty

emptier emptiest
If something is **empty**, there is nothing inside it.
■ opposite **full**

encyclopedia to envelope

encyclopedia
encyclopedias
An **encyclopedia** is a book that contains information about many different subjects.

end
ends
The **end** of something is its last part. *The **end** of the story. The **end** of the train.*

end
ends ending ended
If you **end** something, you finish it. *Leah **ended** the argument by walking out.*

enemy
enemies
Your **enemy** is someone who hates you and wants to hurt you.

energy
1 **Energy** is the power that makes machines work and produces heat and light.
2 When you have **energy**, you have the strength to do things.

Mo is full of energy.

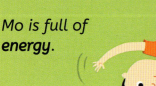

engine
engines
1 An **engine** is a machine that makes things move or work. Cars, planes and ships have engines.
2 An **engine** is also the front part of a train that pulls it along.

enjoy
enjoys enjoying enjoyed
If you **enjoy** something, you like doing it. *Akiko **enjoys** skating.*

enormous
Something that is **enormous** is very big. *Whales are **enormous**.*

enough
If you have **enough** of something, you have as much as you need. *Have you had **enough** lunch?*

enter
enters entering entered
When you **enter** a place, you go into it.

entrance
entrances
An **entrance** is a way into a place. *We searched for the **entrance** to the secret passage.*
■ opposite **exit**

envelope
envelopes
An **envelope** is a paper cover for a letter or a card.

environment

Your **environment** is the land, water and air around you.

equal

Things that are **equal** are the same. *Mix **equal** amounts of red and blue paint. We both had an **equal** number of sweets.*

equipment

Equipment is a name for the things that you need to do something. *Bowls and saucepans are types of kitchen equipment.*

escape

escapes escaping escaped
When people or animals **escape**, they get away from somewhere. *The budgie **escaped** from its cage.*

especially

1 **Especially** means more than the others. *I **especially** liked the purple hat.*
2 If something is **especially for** you, it is meant just for you.

even

1 An **even** number is a number that you reach when you count in twos. *2, 4, 6 and 8 are even numbers.*
■ opposite **odd**
2 Something that is **even** is flat or smooth. *An **even** road.*
■ opposite **uneven**

evening

evenings
The **evening** is the part of the day between the afternoon and the night.

ever

Ever means at any time. *Have you **ever** been skating?*

every

Every means all the people or things in a group. *Matt tried **every** chocolate in the box.*

evil

Someone who is **evil** is very bad and likes to hurt other people.

example

examples
An **example** is a thing that you use to show what similar things are like. *Vikram showed us an **example** of his drawings.*

except

Except means leaving out someone or something. *Everyone except Oliver enjoyed the play.*

excited

If you are **excited**, you feel very happy about something and you keep thinking about it. *The night before his birthday, Sam was too excited to sleep.*

excuse

excuses

An **excuse** is a reason that you give for doing or for not doing something. *Hannah is often late for school, but she always has an excuse.*

exercise

exercises

1 You do **exercise** to keep you fit and strong. Running and swimming are kinds of exercise.

2 An **exercise** is a short piece of work that helps you to practise something you have learnt. *A maths exercise.*

exit

exits

An **exit** is a way out of a place.
■ opposite **entrance**

expect

expects expecting expected

If you **expect** something, you think that it will happen.

expensive

Something that is **expensive** costs a lot of money.
■ opposite **cheap**

experience

experiences

An **experience** is something that you have done or been through. *Going to the zoo was a great experience.*

experiment

experiments

An **experiment** is a test that you do to find out something. *We did an experiment to see which things would float.*

explain

explains explaining explained

When you **explain** something, you talk about it clearly so that other people will understand it. *Madhur explained to her brother how the engine worked.*

explode

explodes exploding exploded
When something **explodes**, it bursts apart with a very loud noise.

explore

explores exploring explored
If you **explore** a place, you look around it for the first time. *The girls explored the old house.*

extinct

If a plant or an animal is **extinct**, there are no more of them alive. *Dodos became extinct about 300 years ago.*

dodo

extra

Extra means more than the usual amount. *Ellen had an extra cake.*

extraordinary

Something that is **extraordinary** is very unusual.

eye

eyes
Your **eyes** are the parts of your body that you use to see.

face

faces
Your **face** is the front of your head.

forehead
nose
chin
eye
cheek
mouth

face

faces facing faced
If you **face** something, you look towards it. *Turn to face the wall.*

fact

facts
A **fact** is something that is true.

factory

factories
A **factory** is a place where things are made by machines or people. *Cars are made in factories.*

fade

fades fading faded
When a colour **fades**, it gets paler. *My red shirt has faded to pink.*

fail to fan

fail
fails failing failed
If you **fail** at something, you are not successful at it. *James searched for his watch, but **failed** to find it.*

faint
faints fainting fainted
When someone **faints**, they feel weak and dizzy, and often fall over.

faint
fainter faintest
If a noise or a colour is **faint**, it is not very loud or strong. *The baby bird made a **faint** sound.*

fair
fairs
A **fair** is a place with rides and games where people go to have fun.

fair
fairer fairest
If you are **fair**, you treat everybody by the same rules. If something is fair, it follows the rules. *If I have a sweet, it is **fair** that you should have one too.*

fairy
fairies
In stories, **fairies** are a kind of tiny people with wings and magical powers.

fall
falls falling fell fallen
When someone **falls**, they suddenly drop to the ground. *Leo **fell** off the ladder.*

false
Something that is **false** is not real or not true.

family
families
A **family** is a group of people who live together. Families are usually made up of parents and their children.

famous
Someone who is **famous** is very well known.

fan
fans
1 A **fan** pushes air onto you to keep you cool. Some fans you wave with your hand, others are electric.
2 A **fan** is someone who admires something or someone. *Alex is a football **fan**.*

fang to favour

fang
fangs
A **fang** is a long, pointed tooth.

far
farther farthest
Far means a long way. *My friend has moved **far** away.*
■ opposite **near**

fare
fares
A **fare** is the money that you pay to travel on a bus or a train.

farm
farms
A **farm** is an area of land where farmers grow crops and keep animals.

farmer
farmers
A **farmer** is someone who owns or runs a farm.

fashion
fashions
Clothes that are **in fashion** are popular.

fast
faster fastest
Something that is **fast** can move quickly.
■ opposite
slow

*A **fast** car.*

Some other words for **fast** are **quick, swift, rapid** and **speedy**.

fasten
fastens fastening fastened
When you **fasten** something, you close it up. *Jamal **fastened** his seat belt.*

fat
fatter fattest
A person or an animal that is **fat** has a big, round body.
■ opposite **thin**

father
fathers
A **father** is a man who has a child.

fault
If something bad is your **fault**, you made it happen. *It's Ben's **fault** that we are late.*

favour
favours
If you do someone a **favour**, you do something helpful for them.

favourite

Your **favourite** thing is the one you like most of all. *Polly is wearing her **favourite** cap.*

fear

Fear is the feeling you have when you think that something bad might happen. *Jon shook with **fear** as he entered the cave.*

feather

feathers
Feathers cover a bird's body and keep it warm. They are very soft and light.

feed

feeds feeding fed
When you **feed** a person or an animal, you give them food. *Vicky never forgets to **feed** her cat.*

feel

feels feeling felt
1 When you **feel** something, you touch it to find out more about it. ***Feel** how cold my hands are!*
2 If you **feel** happy or sad, warm or cold, that is how you are at the time. *Megan **felt** upset when Alfie left.*

feeling

feelings
A **feeling** tells you how you are or what mood you are in. *A warm, happy sort of **feeling** came over Theo.*

fell

Fell comes from the word **fall**. *Joe often falls when he climbs trees. He **fell** last year and broke his leg.*

felt

Felt comes from the word **feel**. *I feel alright today, but yesterday I **felt** terrible.*

felt-tip

felt-tips
Felt-tips are pens with soft tips. They come in many colours.

female

A **female** person or animal belongs to the sex that can have babies.

fence

fences
A **fence** is an outdoor wall made from wood or wire. *A garden **fence**.*

ferry

ferries

A **ferry** is a boat that takes people and cars across water.

festival

festivals

A **festival** is a special day or a special time of the year.

fetch

fetches fetching fetched

When you **fetch** something, you go to it and then bring it back. *Katie fetched her book from upstairs.*

fever

If you have a **fever**, you have a high temperature because you are ill.

few

If you only have a **few** things, you don't have many of them. *Don't eat my sweets, I've only got a few.*

field

fields

A **field** is a piece of land covered in grass, or used to grow crops. Farmers keep animals in fields.

fierce

fiercer fiercest

Something **fierce** is wild and could hurt you. *A fierce tiger.*

fight

fights fighting fought

When people **fight**, they try to hurt each other. *The knights fought with swords.*

fill

fills filling filled

When you **fill** something, you put so much into it that you cannot add any more.

film

films

When you watch a **film**, you see moving pictures with sounds on a screen. Films are shown in cinemas or on television.

filthy

filthier filthiest

Something that is **filthy** is very dirty. *Sam's boots are filthy.*

fin

fins

A **fin** is a thin, flat part that sticks out of a fish's body. Fins help fish to swim.

find to first aid

find
finds finding found
When you **find** something that you have lost, you see where it is. *Daisy **found** her hamster under the bed.*
■ opposite **lose**

fine
1 When the weather is **fine**, it is dry and often sunny.
2 If you feel **fine**, you feel well and happy.

finger
fingers
Your **fingers** are the long, thin parts at the end of your hand. You have five fingers on each hand. One of these fingers is called a thumb.

finish
finishes finishing finished
When you **finish** something, you come to the end of it. *Lexi quickly **finished** her lunch.*

fire
fires
A **fire** is very hot and bright and is made by burning something. *The firefighters tried to put out the **fire**.*

fire engine
fire engines
A **fire engine** is a kind of truck that carries firefighters and equipment to put out fires.

firefighter
firefighters
A **firefighter** is someone whose job is to put out fires.

firework
fireworks
When a **firework** is lit, it makes loud noises and flashes of coloured light. Some fireworks shoot up high into the sky.

firm
firmer firmest
Something that is **firm** does not move or change shape easily. *A **firm** mattress is best to sleep on.*

first
If something is **first**, it comes before everything else. *Henry came **first** in the race.*
■ opposite **last**

first aid
First aid is the help that you give people who are hurt or ill before a doctor sees them.

fish

fish or **fishes**
A **fish** is a creature that lives in water. Fish use slits in their sides called gills to breathe under water. *Many different fishes live around coral reefs.*

fist

fists
When you make a **fist**, you close your hand tightly.

fit

fits fitting fitted
If something **fits**, it is just the right size. *These jeans fit me perfectly.*

fit

fitter fittest
Someone who is **fit** is healthy. *Jessie runs every day to keep fit.*

fix

fixes fixing fixed
1 If you **fix** something that is broken, you mend it. *Lucas is fixing our radio.*
2 When you **fix** something to another thing, you join them together. *Dad has fixed the shelf to the wall.*

fizzy

fizzier fizziest
A **fizzy** drink has lots of bubbles in it.

flag

flags
A **flag** is a special piece of cloth with coloured shapes on it. Flags are usually attached to the ends of long poles. Each country of the world has its own flag.

Swedish flag

flame

flames
A **flame** is the hot, bright light that comes from something that is burning. *A candle flame.*

flash

flashes
A **flash** is a bright light that starts and stops quickly and suddenly. *A flash of lightning.*

flask

flasks
You use a **flask** to carry drinks. Some flasks keep drinks hot or cold. *Lauren took some orange juice in a flask for her lunch.*

flat

flats
A **flat** is a home on one floor of a building.

flat to flower

flat
flatter flattest
Something that is **flat** does not curve or have any bumps. *A **flat** roof. A **flat** lawn.*

flavour
flavours
The **flavour** of something is what it tastes like. *What flavour is your ice cream?*

flew
Flew comes from the word **fly**. *I am going out to fly my new kite. Yesterday, I flew it all afternoon.*

float
floats floating floated
1 When something **floats** in water, it stays on the surface.
2 When something **floats** through the air, it moves slowly above the ground.

The balloon floated over the trees.

flock
flocks
A **flock** is the name for a group of sheep or birds. *A **flock** of starlings.*

flood
floods
▲ rhymes with **mud**
A **flood** is a large amount of water that covers ground which is usually dry. *There was a **flood** in our town.*

floor
floors
1 A **floor** is the part of a room that you walk on.
2 A **floor** is also all the rooms on one level of a building. *Jonah lives in a flat on the second **floor**.*

flour
Flour is a powder made from wheat. You use flour to make bread and cakes.

flow
flows flowing flowed
When a liquid **flows**, it moves from one place to another. *The river **flows** through the valley to the sea.*

flower
flowers
A **flower** is part of a plant. Flowers are often brightly coloured and some flowers smell nice.

petal
leaf
stem

flown

Flown comes from the word **fly**. *The baby birds are learning to fly. Some of them have **flown** away already.*

flu

If you have **flu**, your body aches and you have a high temperature.

fly

flies
A **fly** is an insect with very thin, clear wings.

fly

flies flying flew flown
When something **flies**, it moves through the air.

foal

foals
A **foal** is a baby horse. *The foal is six months old.*

fog

Fog is thick cloud that is close to the ground. When there is fog, you cannot see very far.

fold

folds folding folded
When you **fold** something, you bend one part of it over another part. *Samantha folded the paper in half.*

folder

folders
1 A **folder** is something you keep pieces of paper in. *A homework folder.*
2 A **folder** is also something you use to store a group of files on a computer.

follow

follows following followed
1 If you **follow** someone, you go behind them.
2 If something **follows** another thing, it happens after it. *Summer follows spring.*

fond

fonder fondest
If you are **fond** of someone, you like them very much.

> Some words that begin with an "f" sound, like **phone** and **photograph**, are spelt "ph".

food

Food is what people eat to help them stay healthy and grow.

foot

feet
Your **foot** is the part of your body at the end of your leg.

ankle
heel
big toe
toe
toenail

football to fortnight

football
footballs
1 **Football** is a game played by two teams on a pitch. Each team tries to score goals by kicking a ball into a net.
2 A **football** is the ball used in football games.

footprint
footprints
A **footprint** is the mark made by a foot or a shoe.

forehead
foreheads
Your **forehead** is the part of your face above your eyebrows.

foreign
Something that is **foreign** comes from another country. *Katy collects foreign coins.*

forest
forests
A **forest** is a place where many trees grow close together. Forests are bigger than woods.

forever
If something goes on **forever**, it never ends. *The talk seemed to go on forever.*

forgave
Forgave comes from the word **forgive**. *Ellie found it hard to forgive her sister, but she forgave her in the end.*

forget
forgets forgetting forgot forgotten
If you **forget** something, you do not remember it.

forgive
forgives forgiving forgave forgiven
When you **forgive** someone, you stop being angry with them for something they did.

forgotten
Forgotten comes from the word **forget**. *Archie may forget to bring his book. He's forgotten it before.*

fork
forks
You use a **fork** to eat. Forks have three or four sharp points called prongs.

fortnight
fortnights
A **fortnight** is two weeks. There are 14 days in a fortnight.

forwards

If you move **forwards**, you move ahead or towards the front. *Gary ran **forwards** to catch the ball.*
■ opposite **backwards**

fossil

fossils
A **fossil** is what is left of an animal or a plant that lived millions of years ago. Fossils are found in rocks.

foster

fosters fostering fostered
When people **foster** a child, the child comes to live with them and becomes part of their family for a short time.

fought

Fought comes from the word **fight**. *My brothers often fight. Yesterday, they **fought** over who would have the last biscuit.*

found

Found comes from the word **find**. *Mum asked me to find my book. I **found** it under the bed.*

fountain

fountains
A **fountain** is a spray of water that is pushed up into the air.

fox

foxes
A **fox** is a wild animal that looks like a dog with reddish fur. Foxes have pointed ears and very thick tails.

fraction

fractions
A **fraction** is a part of a whole thing. Halves and quarters are fractions.

frame

frames
A **frame** fits around the edge of something, like a picture or a window.

freckles to frog

freckles
Freckles are light brown spots on your skin. *Ginger's nose is covered with **freckles**.*

free
1 If something is **free**, you do not have to pay any money for it.
2 If a person or an animal is **free**, they can go where they like or do what they like.

freeze
freezes freezing froze frozen
When water **freezes**, it becomes so cold that it turns into ice.

freezer
freezers
A **freezer** is a machine that keeps food very cold so that it does not go bad.

fresh
fresher freshest
If food is **fresh**, it has just been made or picked. *Scarlett loves **fresh** strawberries.*

fridge
fridges
A **fridge** is a machine that keeps food and drinks cool. Fridge is short for refrigerator.

fried
Fried comes from the word **fry**. Fried food has been cooked in hot oil or butter.

friend
friends
▲ rhymes with **bend**
A **friend** is someone you like and who likes you. *Archie and his **friend** enjoy relaxing together.*

friendly
friendlier friendliest
A **friendly** person likes to meet other people and is kind to them.

frightening
If something is **frightening**, it makes you feel afraid. *The story was so **frightening** that Maisie couldn't sleep.*

> Some other words for **frightening** are **scary**, **spooky**, **terrifying** and **petrifying**.

fringe
fringes
Your **fringe** is the hair that hangs down over your forehead.

frog
frogs
A **frog** is a small creature with smooth skin, large eyes and strong back legs that it uses for jumping and swimming.

front

fronts
The **front** of something is the part that faces forwards or comes first. *Karen sat at the front of the bus.*
- opposite **back**

frost

Frost is a thin layer of ice that covers things outside when it is very cold. *Jack scraped the frost off the windscreen.*

frown

frowns frowning frowned
When you **frown**, you push your eyebrows together and wrinkle your forehead. You frown because you are cross or because you are thinking about something.

frozen

Frozen comes from the word **freeze**.
1 If a pond is **frozen**, the surface of the water has turned into ice.

2 **Frozen** food is kept very cold so that it does not go off.

fruit

fruits
A **fruit** is the part of a plant that holds the seeds.

apple
watermelon
kiwi fruit

fry

fries frying fried
When you **fry** food, you cook it in hot oil or butter. *Dad fried an egg for his lunch.*

fudge

Fudge is a soft sweet that is made from butter, cream and sugar.

full

fuller fullest
If something is **full**, it cannot hold any more. *The jar is full of biscuits.*
- opposite **empty**

fumes

Fumes are gases that smell bad and make you cough. Cars make fumes.

fun

When you have **fun**, you have a good time and you are happy.

funny

funnier funniest
1 If something is **funny**, it makes you laugh. *A funny joke.*
2 **Funny** also means strange or peculiar. *We heard a funny noise coming from the attic.*

fur

Fur is the soft hair that covers some animals' bodies. *Polar bears have thick, white fur.*

furious

If you are **furious**, you are very angry. *Sophie was furious that her watch had been stolen.*

furniture

Furniture is the name for all the big things, like tables, chairs and beds, that people have in their houses. *When we moved house, we bought some new furniture.*

fuss

fusses fussing fussed
When you **fuss**, you worry about something more than you need to. *Mum is always fussing about my clothes.*

fussy

If someone is **fussy**, they are hard to please.

future

The **future** is the time that has not happened yet. *In the future, we might have robots to look after us.*

gallop

gallops galloping galloped
When a horse **gallops**, it runs very fast.

Fury galloped away.

game

games
A **game** is something that you play. Games have rules. Football and draughts are games.

gang

gangs
A **gang** is a group of people who do things together.

gap

gaps

A **gap** is a space between two things. *Marcus has a gap between his two front teeth.*

garage

garages

1 A **garage** is a building where a car is kept.
2 **Garages** are also places where people get their cars mended.

garden

gardens

A **garden** is a piece of land near a house where people grow grass, flowers and other plants.

gas

gases

A **gas** is very light and usually cannot be seen. The air is made of gases. Some gases burn easily and are used in ovens and fires.

gate

gates

A **gate** is a kind of door in a fence, wall or hedge.

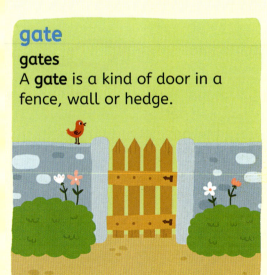

gave

Gave comes from the word **give**. *I want to give my dad a present. Last year I only gave him a card.*

generous

A **generous** person likes to help people and give them things. *It was very generous of Uncle Bill to buy me a bicycle.*

gentle

gentler gentlest

When you are **gentle**, you are careful and kind. *Rosa is gentle with her baby sister.*

gerbil

gerbils

A **gerbil** is a small, furry animal with long back legs. People often keep gerbils as pets.

germ

germs

A **germ** is a tiny living thing that can make you ill. You need a microscope to see germs. *Cover your mouth when you cough, so that you don't spread your germs.*

ghost

ghosts

A **ghost** is a person who has died who some people think they can see.

giant to glove

giant
giants
A **giant** is a very big person that you read about in stories. *The **giant** bent down and picked up the man.*

gift
gifts
A **gift** is something special you give to someone. *We wrapped Yasmin's **gift** carefully.*

giggle
giggles giggling giggled
When you **giggle**, you laugh in a silly way. *Alice kept **giggling** at her dad's new shorts.*

giraffe
giraffes
A **giraffe** is an animal with a very long neck and long legs. Giraffes live in herds and are the tallest animals in the world.

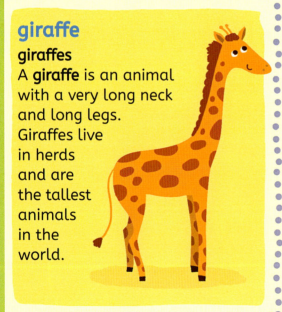

girl
girls
A **girl** is a female child or a young woman.

give
gives giving gave given
1 If you **give** something to someone, you hand it to them. *Anna **gave** the dice to Reuben.*
2 When you **give** something to someone, you let them have it to keep. *Phoebe loves **giving** presents to her friends.*

glad
When you are **glad**, you are pleased and happy about something. *I'm **glad** you are feeling better.*

glass
glasses
1 **Glass** is a hard material that you can see through. Windows and bottles are made of glass. It is quite easy to break glass.
2 A **glass** is a container that you drink from. Glasses are made from glass. *Dan poured some juice into his **glass**.*

glasses
People wear **glasses** to help them see better. Glasses have a frame that holds two special lenses in front of your eyes.

glove
gloves
Gloves are clothes that you wear on your hands to keep them warm or to protect them.

glue to goose

glue
Glue is something you use to stick things together. You use glue to make things or to mend things that are broken.

go
goes
If you have a **go** at something, you try doing it, or take a turn at doing it. *Noah wanted to have a **go** at sailing.*
*It's your **go** next.*

go
goes going went gone
1 When you **go**, you move from one place to another, or you leave. *We're **going** to the park. Let's **go**!*
■ opposite **come**
2 You use **going to** for something that will happen. *Ben is **going to** be eight next week.*

goal
goals
You score a **goal** by kicking, hitting or throwing a ball into a net.

goat
goats
A **goat** is an animal with horns and a short tail. Most goats have beards.

gold
Gold is a yellow metal that is very valuable. *A **gold** ring.*

goldfish
goldfish
A **goldfish** is a small, orange fish. People often keep goldfish as pets.

gone
Gone comes from the word **go**. *Let's go to the park. The others have **gone** there already.*

good
better best
1 If something is **good**, you like it. *A **good** book.*
2 **Good** people do what is right.
3 **Good** work is work that has been done well.
■ opposite **bad**

Some other words for **good** are **marvellous, fantastic, great** and **terrific**.

goodbye
You say **goodbye** when someone goes away.

goose
geese
A **goose** is a large bird with a long neck. Geese can swim and fly.

grab to graze

grab
grabs grabbing grabbed
If you **grab** something, you pick it up in a quick, rough way. *Jacob grabbed his bag and ran.*

gradual
If something is **gradual**, it happens slowly.
A gradual change.

grain
grains
1 A **grain** of something, such as sand or salt, is a tiny piece of it.
2 A **grain** is also a seed, such as a grain of rice, or a grain of wheat.

grandfather
grandfathers
Your **grandfather** is the father of your mother or your father. Children often call their grandfather grandpa or grandad.

grandmother
grandmothers
Your **grandmother** is the mother of your mother or your father. Children often call their grandmother granny or grandma.

grape
grapes
A **grape** is a small, round fruit that grows in bunches. Grapes are green or purple.

grapefruit
grapefruits
A **grapefruit** is a large, round fruit with a thick skin. It is yellow or pink and has a sour taste.

grass
grasses
Grass is a plant with thin, green leaves. Grass grows in fields and gardens.

grateful
If you are **grateful**, you want to thank someone for something they have done.

gravy
Gravy is a hot, brown sauce that you eat with meat.

graze
grazes grazing grazed
1 If you **graze** your skin, you scrape it against something. *I grazed my elbow on the wall and made it bleed.*
2 When animals **graze**, they eat grass that is growing in a field.

great to grow

great
greater greatest
▲ say *grate*
1 **Great** means large. *The trees grew to a **great** height.*
2 **Great** also means very important. *Nelson Mandela was a **great** man.*
3 **Great** also means very good. *We had a **great** holiday.*

greedy
greedier greediest
Greedy people want more of something than they need. *Augustus was so **greedy** that he ate five bowls of ice cream.*

green
Green is the colour that you make when you mix blue and yellow. Grass is green.

greenhouse
greenhouses
A **greenhouse** is a building with a glass roof and walls. People grow plants in greenhouses.

grew
Grew comes from the word **grow**. *Sunflowers grow very fast. Last week, ours **grew** five centimetres.*

grey
Grey is the colour that you make when you mix black and white. Rain clouds are grey.

grin
grins
A **grin** is a big smile.

grip
grips gripping gripped
If you **grip** something, you hold onto it tightly. *I **gripped** the bat.*

ground
The **ground** is the surface that you walk on outside.

group
groups
A **group** is a number of people or things that are together or are the same in some way.

grow
grows growing grew grown
When something **grows**, it gets bigger. *John's sunflower has **grown** bigger than May's.*

growl to gum

growl
growls growling growled
When a dog **growls**, it makes a long, low sound in its throat. *Fido **growled** every time the cat came near.*

grown
Grown comes from the word **grow**. *My auntie is amazed at the way I grow. She says I have **grown** five centimetres since the summer.*

grown-up
grown-ups
A **grown-up** is someone who is no longer a child.

grumble
grumbles grumbling grumbled
If you **grumble**, you keep on saying that you are not happy or that you do not like something.

guard
guards guarding guarded
If you **guard** something, you watch it carefully to keep it safe.

guess
guesses guessing guessed
If you **guess**, you give an answer to something without being sure it is right. *Sam tried to **guess** how many sweets were in the jar.*

guest
guests
A **guest** is someone who comes to visit you. *We have **guests** coming to dinner tonight.*

guilty
guiltier guiltiest
If you are **guilty** of something bad, you made it happen.

guinea pig
guinea pigs
A **guinea pig** is a small, furry animal with no tail. People often keep guinea pigs as pets.

guitar
guitars
A **guitar** is a musical instrument with strings. You play a guitar by pressing the strings with the fingers of one hand and plucking them with the other.

gum
gums
1 Your **gums** are the firm, pink skin around your teeth.
2 **Gum** is a kind of sweet that you chew, but do not swallow.

gun

guns
A **gun** is a weapon that is used to shoot something.

gymnastics
Gymnastics are exercises that you do to make you fit and strong. *James is practising **gymnastics**.*

Hh

habit
habits
A **habit** is something that you do often, usually without thinking about it. *Hayley's worst **habit** is biting her nails.*

had
Had comes from the word **have**. *We often have fish for dinner. We **had** it twice last week.*

hadn't
Hadn't is a short way of saying **had not**. *Natasha **hadn't** slept very well.*

hail
hails hailing hailed
When it **hails**, small pieces of frozen rain fall from the sky. *It is **hailing** on my umbrella.*

hair
hairs
Hair is what grows on your head and on many animals' bodies. *Rachel has very long **hair**.*

half
halves
A **half** is one of two parts of equal size that together make the whole of something. *Amelie cut her apple into **halves**.*

hall
halls
1 A **hall** is a room with other rooms coming off it.
2 A **hall** is also a large room that is used for meetings or plays.

ham
Ham is a type of meat that comes from pigs.

hammer
hammers
A **hammer** is a tool that you use for hitting nails. It has a handle and a heavy metal end.

hamster to happy

hamster
hamsters
A **hamster** is a small, furry animal that looks like a mouse. Hamsters have short tails and store food in their cheeks. They are often kept as pets.

hand
hands
Your **hand** is the part of your body at the end of your arm. You use your hand to hold things.

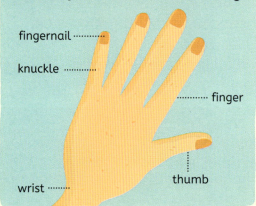

fingernail
knuckle
finger
thumb
wrist

hand
hands handing handed
If you **hand** something to someone, you place it in their hands. *Please **hand** me a brush.*

handbag
handbags
A **handbag** is a bag used to carry money and other small things.

handle
handles
You use a **handle** to hold something or to move something. *The **handle** on my suitcase is broken. Sophie turned the door **handle** slowly.*

handsome
Men and boys who are **handsome** are good-looking.

handwriting
Your **handwriting** is the way that you write letters and words. *Harley has beautiful **handwriting**.*

hang
hangs hanging hung
If you **hang** something, you fix it somewhere above the ground. *Granny **hung** the washing on the line.*

happen
happens happening happened
When something **happens**, it takes place. *What **happens** at the end of the book?*

happy
happier happiest
When you are **happy**, you feel pleased about things.
■ opposite **sad**

Some other words for **happy** are **glad**, **cheerful**, **pleased** and **delighted**.

harbour to have

harbour
harbours
A **harbour** is a safe place where boats can be tied up.

hard
harder hardest
1 Something that is **hard** is firm and solid. *A **hard** bed.*
■ opposite **soft**
2 If something is **hard**, it is difficult to do or to understand. *This homework is too **hard**!*

hard
harder hardest
If you do something **hard**, you do it with a lot of energy. *Biff hit him really **hard**. The teacher says you must try **harder**.*

harmful
If something is **harmful**, it could hurt you or make you ill.

harvest
harvests
Harvest is the time when crops are cut or picked.

has
Has comes from the word **have**. *Adam will have a party for his birthday. He **has** one every year.*

hasn't
Hasn't is a short way of saying **has not**. *Oscar **hasn't** arrived yet.*

hat
hats
A **hat** is something that you wear on your head.

hatch
hatches hatching hatched
When an egg **hatches**, a baby bird or animal breaks out of it.

hate
hates hating hated
If you **hate** something, you really do not like it at all. *Mark **hates** cabbage.*

haunted
If a place is **haunted**, people think that there are ghosts in it.

have
has having had
1 If you **have** something, it is yours. *I **have** a new bicycle. Sarah **has** a cold.*
2 If you **have to** do something, you need to do it. *I **have to** do my homework.*

haven't

Haven't is a short way of saying **have not**. *We haven't got any money.*

head

heads
1 Your **head** is the part of your body where your hair, ears, eyes, mouth and nose are. Your brain is inside your head.
2 The **head** of something is the person in charge. *The head of a school.*

heal

heals healing healed
When a cut **heals**, it gets better.

healthy

healthier healthiest
1 A **healthy** person is well and strong.
2 Something that is **healthy** is good for you. *I try to eat healthy food, such as fruit and vegetables.*

heap

heaps
A **heap** is an untidy pile of things. *Samir left his clothes in a heap on the floor.*

hear

hears hearing heard
When you **hear**, you notice sounds with your ears.

heart

hearts
▲ rhymes with **part**
1 Your **heart** is the part of your body that pushes blood around your body.
2 A **heart** is also this shape: It stands for love.

heat

heats heating heated
When you **heat** something, you make it warmer. *Anna heated the soup in a saucepan.*

heavy

heavier heaviest
Something that is **heavy** weighs a lot. *Kenton tried to lift the heavy suitcase.*
■ opposite
light

he'd

1 **He'd** is a short way of saying **he had**. *He'd always wanted to ride an elephant.*
2 **He'd** is also a short way of saying **he would**. *Tyler says he'd love to go.*

hedge

hedges
A **hedge** is a row of bushes that make a kind of wall. You often see hedges around fields.

hedgehog

hedgehogs
A **hedgehog** is a small animal with lots of spikes on its back. When hedgehogs are frightened, they curl into a ball.

heel

heels
Your **heel** is the back part of your foot.

height

heights
▲ rhymes with **light**
Your **height** is how tall you are. *Kate checked Leo's **height** to see how much he'd grown.*

held

Held comes from the word **hold**. *Henry offered to hold the ladder for his dad. He **held** it until his arms ached.*

helicopter

helicopters
A **helicopter** is an aircraft without wings. It has blades on top that spin around to make it fly or hover.

he'll

He'll is a short way of saying **he will**. *James is finishing his lunch. **He'll** be here soon.*

hello

You say **hello** when you meet someone.

helmet

helmets
A **helmet** is a hard hat that you wear to protect your head.
*Nadia is wearing her bicycle **helmet**.*

help

helps helping helped
If you **help** someone, you do something for them, or you do it with them to make it easier. *Lauren **helped** her dad to put up the tent.*

helpful

A **helpful** person often helps other people.

hen

hens
A **hen** is a female chicken. Hens are kept on farms for their eggs.

herd

herds
A **herd** is a large group of animals such as cattle, deer or elephants.

here

Here means the place where you are. *I've lived **here** for six years.*
■ opposite **there**

here's

Here's is a short way of saying **here is**. *Here's today's newspaper.*

hero

heroes
A **hero** is someone who is very brave. Stories are often about heroes.

hers

If something belongs to a girl or a woman, then it is **hers**. *The doll is **hers**.*

herself

Herself means her and nobody else. *Emily has hurt **herself**.*

he's

1 **He's** is a short way of saying **he is**. *I'm waiting for Kai to arrive. **He's** coming at two o'clock.*
2 **He's** is also short for **he has**. *He's actually done it.*

hibernate

hibernates hibernating hibernated
When animals **hibernate**, they sleep through the winter. They hibernate to stay alive when it is cold and there is not much food.

hiccup

hiccups
When you have **hiccups**, you keep making a sudden sound in your throat.

hide

hides hiding hid hidden
1 When you **hide** something, you put it where no one can see it. *Zak **hid** the present under the bed.*
2 If you **hide** your feelings, you keep them secret. *Lola **hid** her disappointment.*

high

higher highest
1 Something that is **high** is a long way from the ground. *A **high** tower.*
2 **High** also means bigger than usual. ***High** prices.*
3 A **high** voice goes up a long way. Girls and young boys have high voices when they sing.
■ opposite **low**

hill

hills
A **hill** is a high piece of land. Hills are not as tall as mountains.

himself

Himself means him and nobody else. *Max has hurt **himself**.*

hippopotamus
hippopotamuses

A **hippopotamus** is a large animal with short legs and thick skin. Hippopotamuses live in and around rivers.

his

If something belongs to a boy or a man, then it is **his**. *The ball is **his**.*

history

History is the story of what has happened in the past.

hit
hits hitting hit

When two things **hit** each other, they come together very hard. *The car **hit** a wall. Peter **hit** his head.*

hobby
hobbies

A **hobby** is something you enjoy doing in your spare time. *Jon's **hobby** is collecting badges.*

hold
holds holding held

1 If you **hold** something, you have it in your hands or your arms. *Liz **held** the kitten gently.*
2 **Hold** also means to have room for something. *This jug **holds** two litres. The hall **holds** about two hundred people.*

> Some words that begin with an "**h**" sound, such as **whole**, are spelt "**wh**".

hole
holes

A **hole** is a gap or a hollow place. *I see a **hole** in your shirt. The workers dug a **hole** in the road.*

holiday
holidays

A **holiday** is a time when you do not have to work or go to school. People often spend their holidays away from home.

hollow

Something that is **hollow** has an empty space inside it. *We crawled through the **hollow** log.*

home to horrible

home
homes
Your **home** is the place where you live. *We are going to stay at home today.*

homework
Homework is work that a teacher gives you to do at home.

honest
Someone who is **honest** tells the truth and can be trusted.
■ *opposite* **dishonest**

honey
Honey is a sweet, sticky food that is made by bees. You can eat honey on bread.

hood
hoods
The **hood** of a coat is the part that covers your head.

As soon as it started to rain, Ruth put up her hood.

hoof
hooves
An animal's **hoof** is the hard part of its foot. Horses, deer and cows have hooves.

hook
hooks
A **hook** is a curved piece of metal or plastic. Some hooks are used for hanging things up. Other hooks are used for catching things, like fish.

hop
hops hopping hopped
1 When you **hop**, you jump on one foot.
2 When birds and rabbits **hop**, they jump forwards with their feet close together.

hope
hopes hoping hoped
If you **hope** something, you want it to happen and think that it might. *I hope we'll go to the seaside tomorrow.*

horn
horns
1 A **horn** is one of the hard, pointed bones that grow out of some animals' heads. Goats and bulls have horns.
2 A **horn** is also a musical instrument that you blow. *Gabe enjoyed playing his French horn.*

horrible
Something that is **horrible** is awful or frightening. *That soup was horrible. In my dream, I was chased by a horrible monster.*

horse

horses
A **horse** is a large animal with four legs and a long tail. People ride horses.

bridle
mane
saddle
reins
stirrup
hoof

hose

hoses
A **hose** is a long, narrow tube made of rubber or plastic. People use hoses to put water on gardens.

hospital

hospitals
A **hospital** is a building where people who are ill or hurt are looked after. Doctors and nurses work in hospitals.

hot

hotter hottest
Something that is **hot** has a high temperature. *Be careful, the drink is **hot**.*
■ opposite **cold**

hotel

hotels
A **hotel** is a big building with many bedrooms and a restaurant. People pay to stay in hotels when they are away from home.

hour

hours
An **hour** is an amount of time. There are 60 minutes in an hour, and 24 hours in a day.

house

houses
A **house** is a building that people live in. *Where is your **house**?*

hover

hovers hovering hovered
When something **hovers**, it stays in one place in the air.

*The hummingbird **hovered** in front of the flower.*

how

1 **How** means in what way. *How do I turn off the computer?*
2 You also use **how** when you ask about an amount. *How much money do you have? How many people are coming to the play?*

how's

1 **How's** is a short way of saying **how is**. *How's your brother feeling today?*
2 **How's** is also short for **how has**. *How's he managed that?*

hug

hugs hugging hugged
When you **hug** someone, you hold them tightly in your arms. *Gary hugged Mario when he scored the final goal.*

huge

Something **huge** is very big. *Whales are huge.*

human being

human beings
A **human being** is a person. Men, women and children are all human beings.

hump

humps
A **hump** is a big, rounded lump. Camels have humps on their backs.

hung

Hung comes from the word **hang**. *Christopher decided to hang up the picture. He hung it in his room.*

hungry

hungrier hungriest
If you are **hungry**, you want to eat something.

hunt

hunts hunting hunted
1 When animals **hunt**, they chase another animal, then kill it and eat it.
2 If you **hunt for** something, you look for it carefully. *Tony hunted everywhere for his other sock.*

hurry

hurries hurrying hurried
When you **hurry**, you do something quickly. *Hannah hurried to catch the bus.*

hurt

hurts hurting hurt
If something **hurts** you, you feel pain. *Keira's elbow hurt where she had hit it.*

husband

husbands
Someone's **husband** is the man they are married to.

hut

huts
A **hut** is a small building. Huts can be made from wood, metal, mud or grass.

hutch

hutches
A **hutch** is a kind of cage made from wood and wire. People keep rabbits and other small pets in hutches.

ice

Ice is frozen water. It is very cold, and hard. *The pond was covered in **ice**.*

iceberg

icebergs
An **iceberg** is a very large piece of ice that floats in the sea.

ice cream

Ice cream is a sweet, frozen food made from milk or cream. There are many different flavours of ice cream.

icicle

icicles
An **icicle** is a long, thin stick of ice. Icicles are made from dripping water which has frozen.

icing

Icing is used to cover cakes. It is made from sugar mixed with water or butter. *Wayne covered the cake with **icing**.*

icon

icons
An **icon** is a small picture that you click on to start a computer program or open an app.

I'd

1 **I'd** is a short way of saying **I had**. ***I'd** already eaten supper by the time William came.*
2 **I'd** is also a short way of saying **I would**. ***I'd** love to come to your birthday party.*

idea

ideas
1 An **idea** is a thought, or a picture in your mind.
2 If you have an **idea**, you think of something to do, or a way of doing it. *Dylan had lots of **ideas** for a story.*

identical

If two things are **identical**, they are exactly the same. *Holly and Vashti have **identical** umbrellas.*

I'll

I'll is a short way of saying **I will**. *I'll be home before it gets dark.*

ill

When you are **ill**, you are not well. *Nathan was **ill**, so he had to stay in bed.*

I'm

I'm is a short way of saying **I am**. *I'm feeling happy today.*

imagine

imagines imagining imagined
If you **imagine** something, you have a picture of it in your mind. *Esme **imagined** what it would be like to meet a dragon.*

immediately

If you do something **immediately**, you do it now. *Go to your room **immediately**!*

impatient

If somebody is **impatient**, they get annoyed if they have to wait.
■ opposite **patient**

important

If something is **important**, it matters a lot. *It is **important** to clean your teeth every day.*

impossible

If something is **impossible**, it cannot be done. *It is **impossible** to control the weather.*
■ opposite **possible**

impress

impress impressing impressed
If something or someone **impresses** you, you think they are very good. *Isaac was very **impressed** by Ben's magic trick.*

improve

improves improving improved
If something **improves**, it gets better. *My cooking has **improved** a lot this year.*

in

1 **In** means not outside.
■ opposite **out**
2 **In** also shows when something is going to happen. *I'll be back **in** an hour.*

indoors

If you are **indoors**, you are inside a building.
■ opposite **outdoors**

infant to instead

infant
infants
An **infant** is a baby or a very young child.

infectious
If a disease is **infectious**, you can catch it from another person.

inflate
inflates inflating inflated
If you **inflate** something, you fill it with air, or another gas. *Dad inflated the air mattress.*

information
If you ask for **information** about something, you want to find out about it. *I'm looking for information about judo classes.*

ingredient
ingredients
An **ingredient** is one of the things that goes into food. *Katie bought the ingredients for her cake.*

cake ingredients

initial
initials
An **initial** is the first letter of a word or a name. *Edward Thompson's initials are E.T.*

injure
injures injuring injured
If something **injures** you, it harms you. *Libby injured her back when she fell off a stool.*

ink
inks
Ink is a coloured liquid that is used for writing or printing.

insect
insects
An **insect** is a small creature with six legs. Most insects have wings.

dragonfly

inside
1 If something is **inside** a thing, it is in it. *A plum has a stone inside it.*
2 **Inside** also means indoors. *We went inside when it began to rain.*

instead
Instead means in place of something else. *Leon caught the bus instead of walking home.*

instructions to invisible

instructions

Instructions are words or pictures that show you how to do something. *Read the **instructions** before you make the model.*

instrument

instruments
1 An **instrument** is something that helps you to do a job. *Doctors and dentists use **instruments**.*
2 An **instrument** is also something that you use to make music. *Pianos, guitars and horns are all **instruments**.*

horn

intelligent

An **intelligent** person finds it easy to learn and understand things.

interesting

If you find something **interesting**, you want to know more about it.

internet

The **internet** is a way for computers all around the world to share words, pictures, videos and music.

interrupt

interrupts interrupting interrupted
If you **interrupt** someone, you stop them in the middle of what they are doing. *Stephen's sister **interrupted** him while he was listening to music.*

into

1 If you go **into** a building, you go inside it.
2 If something turns **into** something else, it becomes that thing. *Caterpillars turn **into** butterflies.*

invent

invents inventing invented
If you **invent** something, you make something that nobody has made before.

invention

inventions
An **invention** is something that nobody has made or thought of before. *My uncle's latest **invention** is a machine that makes his bed.*

invisible

If something is **invisible**, no one can see it.

invitation

invitations
When you give someone an **invitation**, you ask them to do something with you.

iron

irons
▲ rhymes with **lion**
1 **Iron** is a strong, hard metal. Gates are often made of iron.
2 People use an **iron** to make their clothes smooth. An iron has a handle and a flat metal bottom that gets hot.

irritable

If someone feels **irritable**, they are cross and easily annoyed. *Sam gets **irritable** when he hasn't had enough sleep.*

island

islands
▲ say **eye**-lund
An **island** is a piece of land with water all around it.

isn't

Isn't is a short way of saying **is not**. *Todd **isn't** coming today.*

itch

itches itching itched
If your skin **itches**, you want to scratch it.

it's

1 **It's** is a short way of saying **it is**. ***It's** very cold today.*
2 **It's** is also a short way of saying **it has**. ***It's** been a long day.*

its

Its means belonging to it. *The cat is playing with **its** ball.*

itself

Itself means it and nothing else. *This machine works by **itself**.*

I've

I've is a short way of saying **I have**. ***I've** got an idea for a story.*

Jj

jacket

jackets
A **jacket** is a short, light coat.

jam to jigsaw

jam
jams
Jam is a sweet food that is made by boiling fruit and sugar together. *Strawberry **jam** on toast.*

jar
jars
Jars are containers with lids, usually made of glass. People buy jam and honey in jars.

jaw
jaws
Your **jaw** is the bone at the bottom of your face. It moves when you speak or eat.

jealous
If you are **jealous**, you are upset because somebody else has something that you do not. *Tom was **jealous** when Charlie got his new computer.*

jeans
Jeans are trousers that are made from a strong cotton material called denim.

jelly
jellies
Jelly is a sweet, clear food that wobbles when you move it.

> Some words that begin with a "j" sound, such as **generous**, **gentle**, **gerbil** and **giant**, are spelt with a "g".

jet
jets
A **jet** is an aircraft that travels very fast. Jets have special engines.

jewel
jewels
A **jewel** is a very valuable stone. Diamonds are jewels.

jewellery
Jewellery is the name for pretty things, such as necklaces, rings and earrings, that you wear on your body or on your clothes.

jigsaw
jigsaws
A **jigsaw** is a type of puzzle in which you put lots of pieces back together to make a picture. *Josiah played with his **jigsaw**.*

job
jobs
1 A **job** is the work that someone does to earn money. *Mum has a job in an office.*
2 A **job** is also something that needs to be done. *There are lots of jobs to do in the garden.*

join
joins joining joined
1 If you **join** things, you put them together. *Louise joined the pieces of wood to make a table.*
2 If you **join** a club, you become a member of it. *Heidi has joined a gymnastics club.*

joint
joints
A **joint** is a part of your body where bones meet. Elbows and knees are joints.

joke
jokes
A **joke** is something that you say to make people laugh.

journey
journeys
When you go on a **journey**, you travel from one place to another. *Annabel has a long journey to school.*

jug
jugs
A **jug** is a container with a handle used to hold and pour liquid.

juggle
juggles juggling juggled
When you **juggle**, you keep things in the air by throwing and catching them, one after the other. *Leo can juggle with balls and clubs.*

juice
juices
Juice is the liquid that comes from fruit or vegetables. *Zoe loves mango juice.*

jump
jumps jumping jumped
When you **jump**, you bend your knees and push yourself into the air.

Leah jumped over the puddle.

Some other words for **jump** are **leap**, **spring** and **bound**.

jumper
jumpers
A **jumper** is a piece of clothing that covers the top part of your body. Jumpers are often made of wool, and are worn over other clothes.

jungle to keep

jungle
jungles
A **jungle** is a place in a hot country where lots of trees and plants grow closely together.

junk
Junk is a name for things people do not want.

jury
juries
A **jury** is a group of people in a court who decide whether someone has broken a law or not.

just
1 If something has **just** happened, it happened a very short time ago. *Hamish just left.*
2 **Just** also means in every way. *That's just what I mean.*
3 **Just** also means only. *Don't worry about the noise. It's just the wind in the trees.*

kangaroo
kangaroos
A **kangaroo** is a large animal that moves by jumping. Female kangaroos carry their babies in a bag on their stomach called a pouch.

keen
keener keenest
If you are **keen** to do something, you really want to do it.

keep
keeps keeping kept
1 When you **keep** something, you have it and do not give it away. *Alex keeps all his old comics.*
2 If you **keep** doing something, you do it again and again. *Maya kept laughing at me.*
3 If you **keep** doing something, you don't stop doing it. *Keep going, everyone.*
4 **Keep** also means to make something stay the same. *Please keep the door closed.*

kennel

kennels

A **kennel** is a small hut that is made for a dog to sleep in.

kept

Kept comes from the word **keep**. *Connor keeps his diary under his bed. He has always kept it there.*

kettle

kettles

You use a **kettle** to boil water. A kettle has a handle and a spout.

The kettle is boiling.

key

keys

1 A **key** is a piece of metal that has been cut into a special shape. You use a key to open a lock or to start a car.
2 A **key** is also one of the parts of a piano or a computer that you press to make it work.

keyboard

keyboards

1 A **keyboard** is the part of a computer with lots of buttons that you use to type letters and numbers.
2 A **keyboard** is also a musical instrument like a piano.

kick

kicks kicking kicked

When you **kick** something, you hit it with your foot. *Rhys kicked the football into the air.*

kid

kids

1 A **kid** is a child.
2 A **kid** is also a young goat.

kill

kills killing killed

To **kill** means to make something die. *The frost has killed most of the plants.*

kind

kinds

Things of the same **kind** are alike or belong to the same group. *A butterfly is a kind of insect.*

kind

kinder kindest

A **kind** person cares about how people feel, and tries to help them. *It was kind of Dot to give us tea.*
■ opposite **cruel**

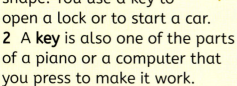

king to knight

king
kings
A **king** is a man who rules a country. Kings come from royal families and are not chosen by the people.

kiss
kisses kissing kissed
When you **kiss** someone, you touch them with your lips.

kitchen
kitchens
A **kitchen** is a room where you cook meals.

kite
kites
A **kite** is a frame covered with paper or cloth with a very long string attached to it. You can fly a kite in the wind.

kitten
kittens
A **kitten** is a very young cat.

> Words that start with **"kn"** are said with an **"n"** sound.

knee
knees
Your **knee** is the joint in the middle of your leg, where it bends.

kneel
kneels kneeling knelt
When you **kneel**, you get down on your knees.

knew
Knew comes from the word **know**. *Chloe didn't know about the party, but she **knew** that we were planning something.*

knife
knives
A **knife** is a tool that you use to cut things. Knives have a handle and a metal blade.

knight
knights
A **knight** was a type of soldier who lived hundreds of years ago. Knights wore armour and fought for their king.

knit

knits knitting knitted
When you **knit**, you make clothes from wool using two long needles. *Meg is knitting a scarf.*

knob

knobs
A **knob** is a round handle on a door or a drawer.

knock

knocks knocking knocked
1 If you **knock** something, you hit it. *I knocked on the door until someone heard me.*
2 If you **knock** something **over**, you make it fall. *Charlie has knocked over a glass of milk.*

knot

knots
A **knot** is a place where something, such as string, is tied. *Tie a knot to fasten your laces.*

know

knows knowing knew known
1 If you **know** something, you have it in your mind. *Eva knows the answers to all the teacher's questions.*
2 If you **know** someone, you have met them before. *I have known Henry for years.*

Ll

label

labels
A **label** is a piece of paper or cloth that is attached to something. Clothes often have labels that tell you how to wash them.

lace

laces
Laces are like long pieces of string. You use laces to tie your shoes or boots.

ladder

ladders
A **ladder** is a set of steps that can be moved around. *Dad used a ladder to climb up to the roof.*

lady

ladies
Lady is a polite word for a woman.

ladybird

ladybirds
A **ladybird** is a small, spotted beetle.

laid

Laid comes from the word **lay**. *I asked Mason to lay the clothes on the chair, but he laid them on the bed.*

lake to lap

lake
lakes
A **lake** is a large area of water with land all around it.

lamb
lambs
1 A **lamb** is a young sheep.
2 **Lamb** is also the meat that comes from lambs.

lamp
lamps
A **lamp** makes light. Most lamps work by electricity. *Jenny has a **lamp** by her bed.*

land
Land is the name for the parts of the Earth that are not covered by water.

land
lands landing landed
When a plane **lands**, it comes down from the air to the ground.

landing
landings
A **landing** is the area of a house at the top of the stairs. A landing has other rooms coming off it.

lane
lanes
1 A **lane** is a narrow road, usually in the country.
2 A **lane** is also one of the strips that a wide road is divided into.

language
languages
Language is a name for the set of words people use to speak and write to each other. *Fritz can speak three **languages**.*

lantern
lanterns
A **lantern** is a lamp that you carry. Lanterns sometimes have a candle inside them.

lap
laps
Your **lap** is the top part of your legs when you are sitting down. *The kitten sat on Daisy's **lap**.*

lap
laps lapping lapped
When an animal **laps up** a drink, it uses its tongue to drink it.

laptop

laptops
A **laptop** is a small computer that you can carry around with you.

large

larger largest
If something is **large**, it takes up a lot of space. *A **large** room. A **large** bag of sweets.*

last

lasts lasting lasted
If something **lasts**, it carries on happening. *The party **lasted** for three hours.*

last

1 Something that is **last** comes at the end. *Z is the **last** letter of the alphabet.*
▪ opposite **first**
2 **Last** also means the one before this. *I saw Liam **last** week.*
▪ opposite **next**

late

later latest
1 If you are **late**, you arrive after the right time. *Tom was **late** because his watch was wrong.*
2 **Late** also means near the end of something. *We arrived home **late** in the evening.*
▪ opposite **early**
3 **Latest** also means most recent. *Have you heard his **latest** song?*

laugh

laughs laughing laughed
▲ rhymes with **staff**
When you **laugh**, you make sounds that show that you think that something is funny. *Laura always **laughs** at Mike's jokes.*

law

laws
A **law** is a rule that everyone in a country must obey.

lawn

lawns
A **lawn** is an area of grass that is kept short. Parks and gardens have lawns.

lay

lays laying laid
1 If you **lay** something somewhere, you put it down carefully.
2 If you **lay a table**, you get it ready for a meal. *Tony **laid the table** for dinner.*
3 When a bird **lays** an egg, the egg comes out of its body. *Our hen has **laid** an egg.*

lay

Lay comes from the word **lie**. *Sienna decided to lie on the sofa. She **lay** there for hours.*

layer to leather

layer
layers
A **layer** is something flat that lies on top of, or beneath, something else.

My birthday cake has three layers.

lazy
lazier laziest
Someone who is **lazy** does not want to do any work. *Jack is too lazy to do his homework.*

lead
leads
1 A **lead** is a long strip of leather or a chain that you fix to a dog's collar. You hold the end of the lead and use it to control the dog.
▲ *rhymes with* **seed**
2 The **lead** in a pencil is the black part that makes a mark.
▲ *rhymes with* **head**

lead
leads leading led
▲ *rhymes with* **seed**
1 If you **lead** someone to a place, you go in front of them to show them where it is.
2 If you **lead** a group of people, you are in charge of them.

leaf
leaves
A **leaf** is one of the thin, flat parts of a plant or a tree. Leaves are usually green but many change colour in autumn.

leak
leaks leaking leaked
If a container **leaks**, the liquid inside it comes out slowly through a small hole when you don't want it to.

lean
leans leaning leant
If something **leans**, it bends to one side. *The tower leant to one side.*

learn
learns learning learnt
When you **learn** something, you get to know it or understand it. *Emma is learning to play tennis.*

least
Least means the smallest amount. *Nobody ate much, but Amelia ate least.*
■ *opposite* **most**

leather
Leather is made from animal skin. It is used to make shoes and bags.

leather bag

leave

leaves leaving left
1 If you **leave** a place, you go away from it. *I **left** home early this morning.*
2 When you **leave** something in a place, you let it stay where it is. *I **left** my jacket at home.*

led

Led comes from the word **lead**. *Chris will lead us up the mountain. He has **led** us before.*

leek

leeks
A **leek** is a long, white vegetable with green leaves at one end.

left

You have a **left** hand and a right hand. Most people write with their right hand, but some people use their left hand.
- opposite **right**

left

Left comes from the word **leave**. *We promised to leave before it got dark, so we **left** at about five o'clock.*

leg

legs
1 Your **legs** are the parts of your body that you use for standing and walking.
2 The **legs** on a table or a chair are the parts that hold it up.

lemon

lemons
A **lemon** is a yellow fruit with a thick skin. Lemons are juicy and have a sharp taste.

lend

lends lending lent
If you **lend** something to someone, you let them have it for a short time. *I **lent** Craig my pen.*

length

lengths
The **length** of something is how long it is. *Dad measured the **length** of the wood.*

lens

lenses
A **lens** is a special, curved piece of glass or plastic. Lenses are used in glasses and telescopes to make things look clearer or bigger.

lent

Lent comes from the word **lend**. *Robby often lends me his bicycle. He **lent** it to me yesterday.*

leopard to lettuce

leopard
leopards
▲ say **lep**-erd
A **leopard** is a large wild cat. Leopards have dark yellow fur with black spots.

leotard
leotards
▲ say **lee**-oh-tard
A **leotard** is a piece of clothing that fits tightly. You may wear a leotard when you dance or do exercise. *Laura wears a **leotard** for her ballet class.*

less
Less means not as much. *I had **less** to eat than my brother.*
■ opposite **more**

lesson
lessons
A **lesson** is a period of time when you are taught something. *A swimming **lesson**.*

let
lets letting let
If someone **lets** you do something, they say that you can do it. *Dad **let** us stay up late.*

let's
Let's is a short way of saying **let us**. ***Let's** go to the cinema.*

letter
letters
1 A **letter** is a sign that you use to write words. A, m and z are letters.
2 A **letter** is also a message that you write on paper. You usually put letters in envelopes to post them.

23 Duck St
Puddletown
Dorset
DT2 3SH
20th March

Dear Gran,
 Thank you so much for the art set you sent for my birthday. I've painted a picture of you. I hope you like it!

Lots of love,
 Meg xXx

lettuce
lettuces
▲ say **let**-iss
A **lettuce** is a vegetable with large leaves that are usually green. You use lettuce to make salads.

level

levels
In computer games, **levels** measure your progress, and usually get more difficult as you go on. *I've got to level four already.*

level

Something that is **level** is flat and not sloping. *Football pitches should be level.*

library

libraries
A **library** is a place where a lot of books are kept. You can borrow books from a library to read at home.

lick

licks licking licked
If you **lick** something, you move your tongue along it.

Leila licked her lolly.

lid

lids
A **lid** is the top of a box or other container. To open the container, you lift up the lid or take it off.

lie

lies lying lied
If you **lie**, you say something that is not true.

lie

lies lying lay lain
When you **lie** down, you rest with your body flat on a bed or another surface.

life

lives
Life is the time that someone is alive. *My grandfather had a long and interesting life.*

lift

lifts
A **lift** is a little room that goes up and down. Lifts carry people between the floors of a building.

lift

lifts lifting lifted
If you **lift** something, you pick it up. *Jonathan lifted the kitten out of the basket.*

light

lights
1 When there is **light**, you can see things. The Sun, lamps and torches make light.
2 A **light** is something that gives out light, such as a lamp.

light

lights lighting lit
When you **light** a fire, you make it burn. *Mum lit the bonfire.*

light

lighter lightest
1 If it is **light**, you can see things.
■ opposite **dark**
2 **Light** colours are pale.
■ opposite **dark**
3 Something that is **light** does not weigh very much.
■ opposite **heavy**

lighthouse

lighthouses
A **lighthouse** is a tower with a flashing light on top. Lighthouses warn ships of dangers, such as hidden rocks.

lightning

Lightning is a sudden flash of light in the sky. You sometimes see lightning when there is a storm.

like

likes liking liked
When you **like** something, it pleases you.
■ opposite **dislike**

like

1 If two people are **like** each other, they are the same in some way.
2 **Like** also means such as. *Will enjoys hobbies like dancing and cycling.*

line

lines
1 A **line** is a long, thin mark. *My writing paper has lines printed on it.*
2 A **line** is also a number of people or things in a row. *We stood in a line for the team photograph.*

link

links
A **link** is a word or a picture on a web page that you can click on to go to another web page or website.

lion

lions
A **lion** is a large wild cat with light brown fur. Lions live in Africa and India.

lip

lips
Your **lips** are the edges of your mouth.

liquid

liquids
A **liquid** is something that can be poured. Water, oil and fruit juice are all liquids.

list

lists
A **list** is a group of things that are written down one after the other. *A shopping list.*

listen

listens listening listened
When you **listen**, you pay attention to what you are hearing. *Mrs Parsnip asked everybody to listen carefully.*

lit

Lit comes from the word **light**. *Dad decided to light a fire. He lit it a long way from the house.*

litter

1 **Litter** is rubbish that has been dropped outside. *The streets were dirty and full of litter.*
2 A **litter** is a group of baby animals born at the same time to the same mother. *A litter of puppies.*

little

1 If something is **little**, it is small.
2 **Little** also means not much. *Martin eats very little.*

live

lives living lived
▲ rhymes with **give**
1 Something that **lives** is alive.
2 If you **live** somewhere, your home is there. *Mohammed lives in London.*

live

▲ rhymes with **hive**
Live means happening at the same time as you watch it. *This show comes to you live from New York City.*

lively

livelier liveliest
Someone who is **lively** has a lot of energy. *Laura is a lively dancer.*

lizard

lizards
A **lizard** is a reptile with a long body and a tail. Lizards lay eggs.

load to look

load
loads
A **load** is something heavy that has to be moved. *The truck took a **load** of sand to the house.*

loaf
loaves
A **loaf** is bread that has been baked in a shape.

lobster
lobsters
A **lobster** is a sea creature with a shell and ten legs. You can eat lobsters. Lobsters turn pink when you cook them.

claw or pincer

feeler

lock
locks
A **lock** keeps things such as doors and cupboards shut. You need a key to open a lock. *My diary has a **lock** on it.*

log
logs
A **log** is a thick piece of wood that has been cut from a tree.

lolly
lollies
A **lolly** is a sweet or ice cream on a stick.

lonely
lonelier loneliest
If you are **lonely**, you feel unhappy because you are alone.

long
longer longest
1 If something is **long**, its ends are far away from each other. *Kamala has very **long** hair.*
2 If something takes a **long** time, it takes a lot of time.
■ *opposite* **short**

look
looks looking looked
1 When you **look** at something, you use your eyes to see it. *Jemima is **looking** at the view.*
2 How something **looks** is how it seems. *That new game **looks** amazing.*
3 If you **look for** something, you try to find it.

loop

loops

A **loop** is a circle made with a rope, a string or a ribbon.

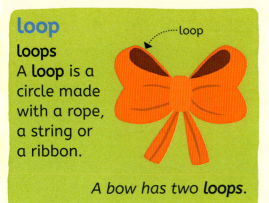

*A bow has two **loops**.*

loose

looser loosest

▲ *rhymes with* **goose**

1 Clothes that are **loose** do not fit closely. ***Loose** trousers.*
2 Something that is **loose** is not fixed firmly. *A **loose** handle.*

■ opposite **tight**

lorry

lorries

A **lorry** is a large vehicle used for carrying things.

lose

loses losing lost

▲ *rhymes with* **shoes**

1 If you **lose** a game or a race, you do not win it.

■ opposite **win**

2 If you **lose** something, you do not know where it is. *Justin has **lost** his watch.*

■ opposite **find**

lost

If you are **lost**, you do not know where you are, or which way to go.

lot

lots

A **lot** is a large amount. *I had a **lot** of birthday cards. **Lots** of people came to my party.*

loud

louder loudest

Something that is **loud** makes a lot of noise. *Mum hates **loud** music.*

■ opposite **quiet**

lounge

lounges

A **lounge** is a room where you can sit and relax.

love

loves loving loved

If you **love** someone, you like them very much.

lovely

lovelier loveliest

If you think something is **lovely**, it really pleases you. *A **lovely** view. A **lovely** song.*

low

lower lowest

1 Something that is **low** is not far from the ground.
2 **Low** also means smaller than usual. ***Low** prices. A **low** temperature.*
3 A **low** voice goes down a long way. Most men have low voices.

■ opposite **high**

*A **low** chair.*

lucky to magic

lucky
luckier luckiest
If you are **lucky**, good things happen to you that you have not planned.

luggage
Luggage is the name for the cases and bags that you take with you when you travel.

lump
lumps
1 A **lump** is a piece of something. *A **lump** of pastry. A **lump** of coal.*
2 A **lump** is something round that sticks out. *My sauce has **lumps** in it. Look at this **lump** on my head!*

lunch
lunches
Lunch is the meal that you eat in the middle of the day. *Florence always takes a packed **lunch** to school.*

lung
lungs
Your **lungs** are inside your chest. When you breathe, air goes in and out of your lungs.

lying
Lying comes from the word **lie**. *Mum told me never to lie. She was very angry when she heard me **lying** to Jack.*

machine
machines
A **machine** is something that does a job. Machines have many moving parts. Cars, computers and cranes are all machines.

made
Made comes from the word **make**. *Freya makes excellent cakes. Yesterday, she **made** a fruitcake.*

magic
1 In stories, **magic** is the power to make impossible things happen.
2 **Magic** is also a name for clever tricks that look impossible.

*He worked his **magic** and a rabbit came out of the hat!*

magician

magicians
A **magician** is someone who does surprising tricks. *Dan had a magician at his party.*

magnet

magnets
A **magnet** is a special piece of metal that makes other metals stick to it. Things that are made of iron and steel stick to magnets.

magnifying glass

magnifying glasses
A **magnifying glass** is a glass lens that makes things look bigger.

mail

Mail is a name for the letters and parcels that people post.

main

Main means the biggest or the most important. *The main entrance to the station. The main meal of the day.*

make

makes making made
1 If you **make** something, you put it together. *Evan loves making model planes.*
2 If you **make** something happen, it happens because of what you do. *Sophia teased her sister and made her cry.*
3 If you **make** something **up**, you invent it. *Alice is always making up stories.*
4 If you **make up** with someone, you become friends again after a quarrel.

make-up

Make-up is something such as lipstick that people put on their face or body to change how they look.

male

A **male** person or animal belongs to the sex that cannot have babies.

mammal

mammals
A **mammal** is an animal that has babies and can feed them with its own milk. Human beings, dogs and whales are all mammals.

man

men
A **man** is an adult, male human being.

manage

manages managing managed
If you **manage** to do something, you do it even though it is difficult. *Poppy **managed** to swim 20 lengths of the pool.*

manners

Your **manners** are the way that you behave. *Gregory has very good **manners**. He is always polite and helpful.*

many

Many means a large number. *There are **many** flowers in our garden.*

map

maps
A **map** is a drawing that shows you where places are. Maps can show roads, rivers and buildings.

marble

marbles
1 A **marble** is a small, glass ball that is used to play a game called marbles.
2 **Marble** is a hard rock. Statues and buildings can be made from marble.

march

marches marching marched
When soldiers **march**, they all walk together with steps of the same size.

margarine

▲ *say marj-er-**een***
Margarine is a soft, yellow food like butter. You can spread margarine on bread or use it for cooking.

margin

margins
A **margin** is a long, blank space along the edge of a page.

mark

marks
1 A **mark** is a dirty spot or a stain on something.
2 Teachers give you a **mark** to show how good or bad your work is.

market

markets
A **market** is a place where you can buy things. Markets are often held outdoors.

marmalade

Marmalade is a sweet, sticky food made from oranges or lemons. People eat marmalade on toast for breakfast.

marry

marries marrying married
When two people **marry**, they promise to spend their lives together.

marsh

marshes
A **marsh** is an area of wet and muddy land. Many birds and animals live in marshes.

mask

masks
A **mask** is something you wear to cover your face.

mat

mats
1 A **mat** is a small piece of carpet or other material that is used to cover part of a floor.
2 A **mat** is also a small piece of cloth or other material that you put on a table to protect it.

match

matches
1 A **match** is a short, thin stick of wood with a special tip. It produces a flame when you rub its tip on a strip on the side of the matchbox.
2 A **match** is a game played by two players or two teams. *A football match.*

match

matches matching matched
If two or more things **match**, they look the same in some way. *Jessica's hat, scarf and gloves all match.*

material

materials
1 **Material** is a name for anything used to make something else. Bricks, wood and glass are all building materials.
2 **Material** is also a name for wool, cotton and other kinds of cloth. *Sienna's dress is made from thick material.*

maths

When you study **maths**, you learn about numbers, amounts and shapes.

matter to medal

matter
matters mattering mattered
If something **matters** to you, you care a lot about it and think that it is important. *It matters to me that you come to my party.*

mattress
mattresses
A **mattress** is the thick, soft part of a bed that you lie on. Mattresses often have springs inside them.

may
might
1 If something **may** happen, there is a chance that it will happen. *Susie may come round today.*
See also **might**
2 If you **may** do something, you are allowed to do it. *Please may I use the computer?*

meadow
meadows
A **meadow** is a field of grass.

meal
meals
A **meal** is the food you eat at certain times of the day. Breakfast, lunch and dinner are meals.

mean
means meaning meant
1 When you say what something **means**, you explain it. *William told us what the signs meant.*
2 If you **mean** to do something, you plan to do it. *I didn't mean to hurt my brother.*

mean
meaner meanest
Someone who is **mean** is not generous or kind.

measure
measures measuring measured
When you **measure** something, you find out how big it is.

meat
Meat is a kind of food that comes from animals. Beef, lamb and chicken are types of meat.

medal
medals
Medals are given to people as prizes or rewards. They often look like a coin hanging from a ribbon.

medicine

medicines
▲ say **med-ih-suhn**
Medicine is something that sick people take to make them better.

medium

Medium means between large and small in size.

meet

meets meeting met
When you **meet** someone, you both go to the same place and you see each other. *I **met** Lucy outside the museum.*

melt

melts melting melted
When something **melts**, it gets warmer and turns into a liquid. *My snowman **melted** in the sunshine.*

member

members
If you are a **member** of a group, you are one of the people in it.

memory

You use your **memory** to remember things. If you have a good memory, you remember things. If you have a bad memory, you f...

mend

mends mending mended
If you **mend** something that is broken, you put it right so that it can be used again.

*Dylan is **mending** his kite.*

menu

menus
A **menu** is a list of food that you can buy in a restaurant or a café.

mermaid

mermaids
In stories, **mermaids** are magical creatures that look like beautiful women with fish tails instead of legs.

mess

If something is a **mess**, it is very untidy and sometimes dirty. *Your bedroom is a **mess**!*

message

messages
A **message** is a piece of information that you send to someone or leave for someone.

met

Met comes from the word **meet**. *Our club meets every week. Last term, it met on Fridays.*

metal

metals
A **metal** is a hard material that is found in the ground. Metals are used to make things such as machines, vehicles and jewellery. Iron and gold are metals.

microphone

microphones
You use a **microphone** to make your voice sound louder.

microscope

microscopes
A **microscope** makes small things look much bigger, so that you can see and study them. *We looked at leaves and petals through a microscope.*

midday

Midday is 12 o'clock in the middle of the day.

middle

middles
1 The **middle** of something is the place that is the same distance away from all of its sides. *There's a tree in the middle of our garden.*
2 If you are **in the middle of** something, you have started it but aren't close to finishing it yet. *Alice is in the middle of watching her favourite programme.*

midnight

Midnight is 12 o'clock in the middle of the night.

might

Might comes from the word **may**. *We may go out today. Sarah said she might come too.*

milk

Milk is a white liquid that mothers feed to their babies. People often drink cows' milk.

mime

mimes
When using being

mind
minds
Your **mind** is the part of you that thinks, remembers and imagines.

mind
minds minding minded
If you **mind** something, it bothers you. *Do you mind if I turn up the TV?*

mine
mines
A **mine** is a place where things, such as coal or diamonds, are dug out of the ground.

mine
If something belongs to me, then it is **mine**. *Don't touch that chocolate. It's mine!*

minus
Minus means take away. The sign for minus is –. *Ten minus four is six.*

- opposite **plus**

minute
minutes
▲ *say **min**-it*
A **minute** is an amount of time. There are 60 seconds in a minute, and 60 minutes in an hour.

mirror
mirrors
A **mirror** is a special piece of glass that you can see yourself in. *Nat is looking at himself in the mirror.*

mischievous
▲ *say **miss**-chiv-us*
Someone who is **mischievous** is lively and naughty. *The mischievous children helped themselves to the cake.*

miserable
Someone who is **miserable** feels sad and unhappy. *Robin is miserable because it is raining.*

miss
misses missing missed
1 If you **miss** someone, you are unhappy because they are not with you.
2 If you **miss** a train or a bus, you do not manage to catch it.
3 If you **miss** a target, you do not manage to hit it.

missing
If something is **missing**, it isn't where it should be.

mist

Mist is a cloud that is close to the ground. When there is a mist, you cannot see very far.

mistake

mistakes
If you make a **mistake**, you do or say something that is wrong.

mix

mixes mixing mixed
1 When you **mix** things, you put them together to make one thing. *Joe **mixed** red and yellow paint to make orange paint.*
2 If you **mix** things **up**, you get them the wrong way round.

mixture

mixtures
A **mixture** is something you make by mixing things together. *Mud is a **mixture** of earth and water.*

moan

moans moaning moaned
1 If you **moan**, you make a long, low sound because you are unhappy or hurt.
2 If you **moan** about something, you say that you are unhappy about it. *Robin was **moaning** because it was too wet to go outside.*

mobile phone

mobile phones
A **mobile phone** is a small telephone that you can carry around with you.

model

models
A **model** is a small copy of something. *Jake has a **model** of a sailing boat inside a bottle.*

mole

moles
A **mole** is a small animal with strong front claws that lives under the ground.

moment

moments
A **moment** is a very short amount of time. *Wait a **moment** while I shut the door.*

money

Money is the name for the coins and notes that you use to buy things.

monkey

monkeys
A **monkey** is an animal with long arms and legs, a very long tail and a furry body. Monkeys live in trees in hot countries.

monster
monsters
In stories, a **monster** is a strange and horrible creature that is very dangerous. Monsters are often very large, like dragons.

month
months
1 There are twelve **months** in a year. May and July are months.
2 A **month** is also any period of about four weeks.

mood
moods
Your **mood** is the way that you feel. *Matilda is in a good mood because she is on holiday.*

Moon
The **Moon** is the big, bright ball of rock you often see in the sky at night. It takes a month to go round the Earth.

more
More means larger in size or number. *My brother ate more lunch than I did.*
■ opposite **less** or **fewer**

morning
mornings
The **morning** is the part of the day before midday.

most
Most means the largest amount. *My brother ate more than I did, but my father ate most of all.*
■ opposite **least** or **fewest**

moth
moths
A **moth** is an insect with four large wings. Moths usually come out at night.

mother
mothers
A **mother** is a woman who has a child.

motorbike
motorbikes
A **motorbike** is a large, heavy bicycle with an engine.

motorway
motorways
A **motorway** is a wide road where vehicles travel fast. People drive long distances on motorways.

mountain to muscle

mountain
mountains
A **mountain** is a very high piece of land. Mountains are higher than hills.

mouse
mice
1 A **mouse** is a small, furry animal with a long tail and sharp teeth. *The **mouse** climbed up the wheat stalk.*
2 A **mouse** is also something that you use to move things on a computer screen.

mouth
mouths
Your **mouth** is the part of your face that you use to eat and talk.

move
moves moving moved
▲ *say moov*
1 When things **move**, they change position and do not stay still. *The leaves **moved** in the breeze.*
2 When people **move**, they go from one place to another. *Andy **moved** to a more comfortable chair.*
3 **Move** also means to stop living in one place and start living somewhere else. *Amy **moved** to Wales.*

movie
movies
▲ *say moo-vee*
A **movie** is a film.

much
Much means a large amount. *Tilly doesn't eat **much**.*

mud
Mud is earth that is wet and sticky.

mug
mugs
A **mug** is a large cup with tall, straight sides.

multiply
multiplies multiplying multiplied
When you **multiply** numbers, you add the same number to itself several times. *Four **multiplied** by three is twelve.*

■ opposite **divide**

mum
mums
Mum is a name for your mother.

muscle
muscles
A **muscle** is a part of your body. Muscles are fixed to bones and pull on them to make them move.

museum

museums
A **museum** is a place where you can see a collection of interesting things.

mushroom

mushrooms
A **mushroom** is a plant-like thing with a rounded top on a stalk. You can eat some mushrooms.

music

Music is a pattern of sounds. People make music by playing musical instruments or by singing.

musical instrument

musical instruments
A **musical instrument** is something that you use to make music. You can play musical instruments by blowing into them or hitting them, or by pulling their strings.

recorder   guitar

xylophone

must

If you **must** do something, you have to do it. *I **must** go now.*

mustn't

Mustn't is a short way of saying must not. *You **mustn't** forget to take your umbrella.*

myself

Myself means me and nobody else. *I have hurt **myself**.*

mysterious

▲ say mist-**ear**-ee-us
Something that is **mysterious** is difficult to understand or explain. *We heard a **mysterious** sound.*

Nn

nag

nags nagging nagged
If someone **nags** you, they keep telling you to do something. *Mum keeps **nagging** me to do up my laces.*

nail

nails
1 A **nail** is a piece of metal with a point at one end. You use nails to join pieces of wood together.
2 Your **nails** are the hard parts at the ends of your fingers and toes.

naked

▲ say **nay**-kid
Someone who is **naked** is not wearing any clothes.

name

names
A **name** is what you call a person or a thing. *My friend's name is Angus.*

nap

naps
If you have a **nap**, you sleep for a short time.

napkin

napkins
A **napkin** is a piece of cloth or paper that you use to protect your clothes when you eat.

nappy

nappies
A **nappy** is a pad of cloth or tissue that covers a baby's bottom.

narrow

narrower narrowest
If something is **narrow**, its sides are not far apart. *A narrow path wound between the hills.*
■ opposite **wide**

nasty

nastier nastiest
Someone who is **nasty** is cruel and unkind. *A nasty witch.*

natural

Something that is **natural** has not been made by people or machines. Wood is a natural material.

nature

Nature is everything in the world that has not been made by people. Plants, animals and the weather are all parts of nature.

naughty

naughtier naughtiest
Someone who is **naughty** behaves badly. *Sophie was very naughty today. She threw her lunch out of the window.*

near

nearer nearest
If something is **near**, it is only a short distance away. *The park is very near our house.*
■ opposite **far**

nearly

Nearly means almost, but not quite. *Ruth is nearly 140 centimetres high. I nearly won the race today.*

neat

neater neatest
Something that is **neat** is very tidy. *Please make your handwriting neat so I can read it. Chloe has tidied her bedroom so that it looks really neat.*

neck

necks
Your **neck** is the part of your body that joins your head to your shoulders.

necklace

necklaces
A **necklace** is a string of beads or a chain that you wear round your neck.

necklace

Some words that begin with an "n" sound, such as **knee, knife, knock** and **know**, are spelt "kn".

need

needs needing needed
If you **need** something, you must have it. *Human beings need food and water to live.*

needle

needles
1 A **needle** is a very thin, pointed piece of metal used for sewing. You put thread through a hole in the needle.
2 **Knitting needles** are long sticks made of plastic or metal. People use knitting needles to knit clothes out of wool.

neighbour

neighbours
A **neighbour** is someone who lives near you.

neither

Neither means not one or the other. *Neither of the boys knew the way home.*

nephew

nephews
Someone's **nephew** is the son of their brother or sister.

nervous

1 If you are **nervous** about something, you are worried or excited about it. *Tom is nervous about his first trip on a plane.*
2 A **nervous** person or animal is easily frightened. *Don't scare the kittens. They're very nervous.*

nest

nests
A **nest** is a home made by birds and some animals. Birds keep their eggs and babies in a nest.

nest

net to nickname

net
nets
1 A **net** is a bag made of knotted thread or rope. Nets are used to catch fish. *Jon caught some fish in his net and then put them back in the water.*
2 When you play tennis, you hit the ball over a **net**. Tennis nets are made of knotted rope.
3 The **net** is a short way of saying the **internet**.

never
Never means not at any time. *I've never climbed a mountain.*
■ opposite **always**

new
newer newest
1 If something is **new**, it has just been made or it has just been bought. *Ruby has a new bicycle.*
2 **New** can also mean different. *There is a new family next door.*
■ opposite **old**

news
1 **News** is information about things that are happening in the world. *Dad always listens to the news on the radio.*
2 **News** is also information about things that have happened to you. *I've had some good news. I'm in the school team.*

newspaper
newspapers
A **newspaper** is made of several sheets of paper with stories and pictures about the news. Most newspapers come out every day.

newt

newts
A **newt** is a small creature with short legs and a long tail. Newts live on land and lay their eggs in water.

next
1 **Next** means the one after this. *We're all going on holiday next week.*
■ opposite **last**
2 **Next to** means nearest. *Jason sits next to me at school.*

nice
nicer nicest
If you think that something is **nice**, you like it. *A nice meal. A nice day.*

Some other words for **nice** are **beautiful, pleasant, good, lovely** and **enjoyable**.

nickname
nicknames
A **nickname** is a name that you give to a friend. *Finn's nickname is Fish because he swims so well.*

niece

nieces
Someone's **niece** is the daughter of their brother or sister.

night

Night is the time when it is dark outside. People sleep at night.
■ *opposite* **day**

nightie

nighties
A **nightie** is a loose dress that girls and women wear in bed.

Rowena has a purple nightie.

nightmare

nightmares
A **nightmare** is a horrible, frightening dream.

nobody

Nobody means no person. *There was nobody in the house.*

nod

nods nodding nodded
When you **nod**, you move your head up and down. People often nod to show that they agree.

noise

noises
A **noise** is a sound. *We heard a noise coming from the cellar.*

noisy

noisier noisiest
If something is **noisy**, it is very loud. *I wish that Rupert's drums were not quite so noisy.*

none

None means not one or not any. *Jonathan went to buy some doughnuts, but there were none left.*

nonsense

Something that is **nonsense** is silly and does not mean anything. *Katy is talking nonsense again.*

noon

Noon is 12 o'clock in the middle of the day.

no one

No one means no person. *There was no one in when I got home.*

normal

Something that is **normal** is ordinary and usual. *I got up at the normal time.*

north to nut

north
North is a direction. If you face the Sun when it rises, north is on your left.
■ opposite **south**

nose
noses
Your **nose** is the part of your face that you use to smell and breathe.

note
notes
1 A **note** is a sound that you make when you sing or play a musical instrument.
2 A **note** is also a sign that stands for a musical note.
3 A **note** is also a short message that you write down.
4 A **note** is also a piece of paper money. *A £5 note.*

nothing
Nothing means not a thing. *There was nothing left in Pepper's bowl.*

notice
notices noticing noticed
If you **notice** something, you see it and pay attention to it. *Melina noticed that Fiona looked pale.*

now
Now means at this time. *It's raining now, so let's go out later.*

nowhere
Nowhere means no place. *There was nowhere we could hide.*

number
numbers
A **number** is a word or a sign that shows you how many there are. Four and thirty-three are numbers. 9 and 27 are also numbers.

nurse
nurses
A **nurse** is someone who looks after people who are ill or hurt. Nurses often work in hospitals.

nursery
nurseries
A **nursery** is a place where young children are looked after while their parents are at work.

nut
nuts
A **nut** is a seed with a hard shell. Many nuts can be eaten.

cashews
walnuts
hazelnuts

Oo

oar
oars
An **oar** is a long pole with a wide end. You use oars to row a boat.

obey
obeys obeying obeyed
When you **obey** someone, you do what they tell you. *Connor is teaching his puppy to **obey** him.*
- opposite **disobey**

object
objects
An **object** is a thing that you can touch and see. Objects are not alive. Computers, toys, books and furniture are all objects.

obvious
If something is **obvious**, it is easy to see or easy to understand.

ocean
oceans
An **ocean** is a very large sea. There are five oceans in the world.

o'clock
You use the word **o'clock** when you say what time it is. O'clock is short for of the clock. *It is now seven **o'clock**.*

octopus
octopuses
An **octopus** is a sea creature with a soft body and eight long legs.

odd
odder oddest
1 An **odd** number cannot be divided exactly by two. 1, 3, 5 and 7 are odd numbers.
- opposite **even**

2 If something is **odd**, it is strange or unusual. *Oscar has the **odd** habit of scratching his knees when he's nervous.*

3 **Odd** things are not part of a pair or a set. *Ben was wearing **odd** socks.*

off
1 **Off** means away from something. *Take the plates **off** the table.*

2 When you turn a machine **off**, you make it stop working.
- opposite **on**

offer

offers offering offered

1 If you **offer** to do something, you say that you will do it without being asked. *Adam offered to make the tea.*
2 If you **offer** someone something, you ask them if they would like it. *Tilly offered a sandwich to her aunt.*

office

offices

An **office** is a room or a building where people work at desks.

often

If you do something **often**, you do it a lot. *We often go skating.*

oil

oils

Oil is a thick liquid. Some oil comes from the ground and is used to help machines run, or to make heat. Some oil comes from plants and is used for cooking.

old

older oldest

1 Someone who is **old** has lived for a long time. *An old man.*
▪ opposite **young**
2 Something that is **old** has been used for a long time. *Old clothes.*
▪ opposite **new**

on

1 On means touching the surface of something. *Put the plates on the table.*
2 When you turn a machine **on** you make it start working.
▪ opposite **off**
3 On also means about. *Louise bought a book on cats.*
4 You use **on** to say when something happens. *We went out for lunch on Friday.*

once

▲ say **wunce**

1 If something happens **once**, it happens one time. *I've only been to London once.*
2 Once also means after. *Once we've had lunch, we can go out.*

onion

onions

An **onion** is a round vegetable with a strong taste and smell. Onions grow under the ground.

online

Online means on the internet. *I read about it online.*

only

▲ say **own-lee**

Only means just that and not any more. *There's only one cake left.*

onto

To move **onto** something is to get on it, or on top of it. *Get **onto** the bus. He threw his coat **onto** the chair.*

open

opens opening opened
1 If you **open** a door, you move it so that you can go through it.
2 If you **open** a box, you take its lid off, so that you can put things in or take things out of it.
■ *opposite* **close**

open

If something is **open**, people can go through it or into it. *The door is **open**. The shop is **open** all day.*
■ *opposite* **closed**

operation

operations
When someone has an **operation**, part of their body is repaired, replaced or removed.

opposite

opposites
The **opposite** of something is the thing that is most different from it. *The **opposite** of day is night.*

day
night

opposite

If two people are **opposite** one another, they face each other. *My friend sat **opposite** me, on the other side of the table.*

orange

oranges
1 **Orange** is the colour that you make when you mix red and yellow. Carrots are orange.
2 An **orange** is a round, juicy fruit with a thick, orange skin.

orchard

orchards
An **orchard** is a piece of land where fruit trees are grown.

orchestra

orchestras
An **orchestra** is a large group of people who play different musical instruments together. *The **orchestra** gave a concert.*

order

Order is the way that things are arranged. *Elsa arranged her dolls in **order** of size, from the smallest to the biggest.*

order

orders ordering ordered
1 If someone **orders** you to do something, they tell you to do it.
2 If you **order** food in a restaurant, you say that you want it.

ordinary

If something is **ordinary**, it is usual and not special.
*It was just an **ordinary** day.*

organ

organs
1 An **organ** is a musical instrument with keys like a piano and lots of pipes of different sizes. When you press the keys, air is pushed through the pipes to make notes.
2 An **organ** is also a part of your body that does a particular job. Your heart and lungs are organs.

organize

organizes organizing organized
When you **organize** something, you plan it so that it happens in the way that you want it to.
*We are **organizing** a party.*

ornament

ornaments
An **ornament** is a small object that you put in a room because it looks nice. *Imogen arranged the **ornaments** on a shelf.*

ostrich

ostriches
An **ostrich** is a very large bird with a long neck and long legs. Ostriches can run very fast, but cannot fly.

other

1 **Other** means different. *Do you have any **other** games?*
2 **Other** also means the second of two things. *I can't find my **other** shoe.*

otter

otters
An **otter** is an animal with brown fur and a long tail. Otters live near water, and catch fish to eat.

ought

If you **ought to** do something, it is the right thing for you to do.
*You **ought to** practise the piano.*

our

Our means belonging to us. *Have you met **our** new dog?*

ours

If something belongs to us, then it is **ours**. *Your house is so tidy. **Ours** is falling apart.*

out

1 **Out** means not inside, or from inside. *We went **out** for some fresh air. We took the books **out** of the box.*
■ opposite **in**
2 If a light or a fire **goes out**, it stops shining, or stops burning.

outdoors

If you are **outdoors**, you are not in a building. *In the summer, we play **outdoors**.*
■ opposite **indoors**

outing

outings
If you go on an **outing**, you visit somewhere, usually for a day. *Our class went on an **outing** to the zoo.*

outline

outlines
An **outline** is a line around the edge of something. *Rosa drew the **outline** of a leaf.*

outside

1 If something is **outside** a thing, it is close to it but not in it. *I left my shoes **outside** my bedroom.*
2 **Outside** also means outdoors. *We went **outside** as soon as it stopped raining.*

oval

ovals
An **oval** is a shape like an egg.

oven

ovens
An **oven** is the part of a cooker that you use for baking or roasting food.

over

1 **Over** means above or on top of something. *Tim wore a jumper **over** his shirt.*
2 **Over** also means more than. *Lexi owns **over** 20 pairs of sunglasses.*
■ opposite **under**
3 If something is **over**, it is finished. *When the party was **over**, we went home.*
4 **Over** also means down. *Jake fell **over**.*

overboard

If someone falls **overboard**, they fall off a boat into the water.

overtake

overtakes overtaking overtook overtaken
When one vehicle **overtakes** another, it goes past it in the same direction. *Dad **overtook** a lorry on the motorway.*

owe

owes owing owed
If you **owe** someone money, you have to pay them what you have borrowed.

owl

owls
An **owl** is a bird with large eyes. Owls hunt at night.

own

1 If something is your **own**, it is yours. *He bought it with his **own** money.*
2 If you are **on your own**, there is no one else with you.

own

owns owning owned
If you **own** something, it belongs to you. *Richard **owns** two goldfish and three mice.*

pack

packs packing packed
When you **pack** a bag or a suitcase, you put things in it.

package

packages
A **package** is a small parcel.

packet

packets
A **packet** is a small container made from paper, card or plastic. *A **packet** of seeds.*

pad

pads
1 A **pad** has many pages joined together at one side. You can write or draw on a pad.
2 A **pad** is also a thick piece of soft material.

paddle

paddles paddling paddled
When you **paddle**, you walk in shallow water. *Pete and Lucy **paddled** in the sea.*

page

pages
A **page** is a piece of paper in a book or a pad.

paid

Paid comes from the word **pay**. *You must pay for your ticket before the show starts. We have already paid for ours.*

pain

Pain is what you feel when you are hurt.

painful

If something is **painful**, it hurts. *A painful knee.*

paint

paints
Paint is a liquid that you use to put colour on things.

paint

paints painting painted
1 When you **paint**, you use a brush and paints to make a picture.
2 If you **paint** a room, you put paint on its walls.

pair

pairs
A **pair** is the name for two things that go together. *A pair of socks.*

palace

palaces
A **palace** is a very large house where kings, queens or other very important people live.

pale

paler palest
Pale colours have a lot of white in them. *Leona painted her room pale blue.*

palm

palms
1 Your **palm** is the flat, inside surface of your hand. Your palm has many lines on it.
2 A **palm** is also a tall tree with large leaves at the top of its trunk. Palms grow in hot countries.

pancake

pancakes
A **pancake** is a kind of thin, flat cake. You make pancakes by frying a mixture of milk, eggs and flour.

panda

pandas
A **panda** is a black and white bear. Pandas live in China and eat bamboo.

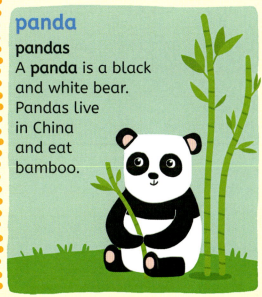

panic to park

panic
panics panicking panicked
If you **panic**, you have a sudden feeling of fear. *Emma panicked when she couldn't find her mum.*

pant
pants panting panted
When you **pant**, you breathe quickly and loudly because you are out of breath. *Jay was panting after his run.*

panther
panthers
A **panther** is a leopard, usually a black one.

pantomime
pantomimes
A **pantomime** is a play with songs and jokes. A pantomime usually tells the story of a fairy tale. *We went to see the pantomime Aladdin.*

pants
Pants are underwear that cover your bottom.

paper
papers
1 **Paper** is the material that is used for writing on, making books and wrapping things.
2 **Paper** is short for **newspaper**.

parachute
parachutes
A **parachute** is a large piece of cloth with strings attached to it. Parachutes are used to drop people or things safely to the ground from a plane.

parcel
parcels
A **parcel** is something wrapped in paper. Parcels are usually sent through the post.

parent
parents
A **parent** is a mother or a father.

park
parks
A **park** is a large piece of land where people can walk or play.

park
parks parking parked
When someone **parks** their car, they leave it on the street or in a car park.

parrot

parrots
A **parrot** is a brightly coloured bird with a curved beak. Some parrots can talk.

part

parts
A **part** of a thing belongs to that thing. *Wheels and pedals are parts of a bicycle.*

particular

Particular means this one and not any others. *This particular book is very helpful.*

partner

partners
A **partner** is someone you do something with. *Darren is my dancing partner.*

party

parties
If you have a **party**, you invite your friends to eat and have fun with you. *A birthday party.*

pass

passes passing passed
1 If you **pass** someone or something, you go past them. *We passed you as we drove home.*
2 If you **pass** something to someone, you hand it to them.
3 If you **pass** a ball to someone, you throw it or kick it to them.
4 If you **pass** a test, you do well in it.

passage

passages
A **passage** is a narrow path, usually between two buildings.

passenger

passengers
A **passenger** is someone who travels in a vehicle and is not the driver.

past

The **past** is the period of time that has already happened. *This story is set in the past when no one had televisions or telephones.*

past

Past means by or beside. *The main road goes past our house.*

paste

Paste is a soft, sticky mixture that you can spread. *Toothpaste.*

pastry to pea

pastry

Pastry is a food made from flour, butter and water. You roll it flat and use it for making pies and tarts.

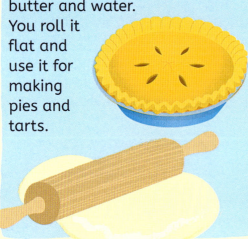

pat

pats patting patted
If you **pat** something, you hit it gently with your hand. *Liam patted Fido on the back.*

patch

patches
A **patch** is a small piece of cloth that you sew on clothes to cover a hole. *Jemima has a patch on her jeans.*

path

paths
A **path** is a narrow road for people to walk along. *This path goes through the wood.*

patient

patients
A **patient** is someone who is ill or hurt and is looked after by a doctor or a nurse.

patient

Someone who is **patient** can wait for a long time without getting annoyed.
■ *opposite* **impatient**

pattern

patterns
A **pattern** is the way that lines, shapes and colours are arranged. *I like the pattern on your curtains.*

pause

pauses pausing paused
When you **pause**, you stop what you are doing for a short time.

pavement

pavements
A **pavement** is a hard path beside a road. You walk on the pavement.

paw

paws
A **paw** is an animal's foot. Dogs and cats have paws.

pay

pays paying paid
If you **pay** someone, you give them money for something.

pea

peas
A **pea** is a small, round, green vegetable. Peas grow in pods.

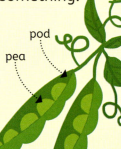

peaceful
When it is **peaceful**, it is quiet.

peach
peaches
A **peach** is a soft, round fruit with a furry skin. A peach has a stone in the middle of it.

peacock
peacocks
A **peacock** is a large bird with long, colourful tail feathers.

peak
peaks
1 The **peak** of a mountain is the point at its top.
2 The **peak** of a cap is the part at the front that sticks out.

peanut
peanuts
A **peanut** is a small, oval nut. Peanuts have shells and grow under the ground.

pear
pears
A **pear** is a juicy fruit. Pears are rounded at the bottom and get narrower towards the top.

pebble
pebbles
A **pebble** is a smooth, round stone. You find pebbles on beaches.

peculiar
If something is **peculiar**, it is unusual or strange. *Aunt Dottie has a **peculiar** habit of talking to flowers.*

pedal
pedals
A **pedal** is a part of a bicycle. You press the pedals with your feet to make the bicycle move.

peel
peels peeling peeled
When you **peel** a fruit or a vegetable, you remove the skin from it. *Ruth is **peeling** an apple.*

peep
peeps peeping peeped
If you **peep** at something, you have a quick look at it. *Sophie **peeped** at the sleeping baby.*

peg to perfume

peg
pegs
1 A **peg** is a hook that you use to hang things on.
2 You also use **pegs** to hold clothes on a washing line. Pegs are made from wood or plastic.

pen
pens
You use a **pen** to write or draw in ink. Pens are made from plastic or metal.

pencil
pencils
A **pencil** is a long, thin piece of wood with a black stick in the middle of it, called a lead. You use a pencil to write or draw.

penguin
penguins
▲ say **pen**-gwin
A **penguin** is a black and white bird that lives in very cold places. Penguins cannot fly. They use their wings to swim.

penny
pennies or **pence**
A **penny** is a coin. In Britain, there are 100 pennies in a pound.

people
▲ say **pee**-pull
People are men, women and children.

pepper
You shake **pepper** over your food to give it more flavour. Pepper tastes hot.

perch
perches perching perched
Perch means to sit or stand on the edge of something. *The bird **perched** on the branch.*

perfect
If something is **perfect**, it has nothing wrong with it at all. *Victoria practised the tune on her recorder until it was **perfect**.*

performance
performances
A **performance** is something that you do in front of lots of people, such as singing, acting or playing an instrument.

perfume
perfumes
Perfume is a liquid that smells nice. People put perfume on their skin.

perhaps

You say **perhaps** when you mean that something is possible, but not certain. *Perhaps we'll see you this weekend.*

period

periods
A **period** is a length of time. *Robert left the room for a short period.*

permission

If you have **permission** to do something, you are allowed to do it. *Lisa was given permission to leave school early.*

person

people
A **person** is a man, a woman or a child.

persuade

persuades persuading persuaded
If you **persuade** someone to do something, you make them agree to do it. *Amy persuaded me to wait for her.*

pest

pests
A **pest** is a person or an animal that causes trouble. *Wasps can be terrible pests.*

pet

pets
A **pet** is an animal that lives with you at home. Cats and dogs are common pets. *Joel keeps rabbits as pets.*

petal

petals
Petals are the colourful parts of a flower. *This daisy has pink petals.*

petal

petrol

Petrol is a liquid that you put into a vehicle to make it run.

phone

phones
Phone is short for **telephone**.

photograph

photographs
A **photograph** is a picture that you take with a camera. Photo is short for photograph.

piano to pigeon

piano
pianos
A **piano** is a large musical instrument with a row of black and white keys. You press the keys with your fingers to play different notes.

pick
picks picking picked
1 When you **pick** something, you choose it. *Pick any cake you want.*
2 If you **pick** fruit or flowers, you take them from a plant or a tree.
3 If you **pick up** something, you lift it up. *Kim picked up the kitten.*

picnic
picnics
A **picnic** is a meal that you take with you to eat outdoors.

picture
pictures
A **picture** is a painting, a drawing or a photograph.

pie
pies
A **pie** is a pastry case filled with meat, vegetables or fruit. Pies are baked in an oven.

piece
pieces
A **piece** of something is a part of it. *A piece of the jigsaw is missing.*

pier
piers
A **pier** is a long platform that is built out over the sea. Piers often have games and rides on them.

pig
pigs
A **pig** is a farm animal with a fat body and short legs. Pigs are kept for their meat.

pigeon
pigeons
▲ say **pij**-in
A **pigeon** is a grey bird with a rounded body and a small head.

pile
piles
A **pile** is a lot of things that have been put on top of each other. *A **pile** of clothes.*

pill
pills
A **pill** is a small, dry piece of medicine. People swallow pills when they are ill to help them get better.

pillow
pillows
A **pillow** is a kind of cushion that you rest your head on when you are lying in bed.

pilot
pilots
A **pilot** is someone who flies a plane. *The **pilot** flew his plane over the woods and fields.*

pin
pins
A **pin** is a small, thin piece of metal with a point at one end. You use pins to hold things together.

pinch
pinches pinching pinched
If you **pinch** someone, you squeeze their skin between your thumb and finger.

pineapple
pineapples
A **pineapple** is a large, oval fruit with a tough skin and pointed leaves at the top.

pink
Pink is the colour that you make when you mix red and white. Strawberry ice cream is pink.

pipe
pipes
A **pipe** is a long tube that carries gas or liquids.

pirate
pirates
A **pirate** is someone who attacks ships at sea and steals things from them.

pit
pits
A **pit** is a deep hole in the ground.

pitch to plank

pitch
pitches
A **pitch** is an area of ground where people play sports such as football.

pity
pities pitying pitied
If you **pity** someone, you feel sorry for them.

pizza
pizzas
▲ say **peet**-sah
A **pizza** is a flat piece of bread with tomatoes and cheese on top. You can also have vegetables, meat or fish on pizzas. Pizzas are usually round and are baked in an oven.
A slice of pizza.

place
places
A **place** is somewhere. Places can be very big, like a country, or very small, like a cupboard. *Africa is a very hot place. Can you find a place to put your mug?*

place
places placing placed
If you **place** a thing somewhere, you put it there. *Place the vase in the middle of the table.*

plain
plainer plainest
1 Something that is **plain** is ordinary, or not decorated. *Rory prefers plain food. I have plain curtains in my room.*
2 If something is **plain**, it is clear and easy to understand. *Gareth made it plain that he did not like peas.*

plan
plans planning planned
If you **plan** something, you decide how you will do it. *We planned the treasure hunt carefully.*

plane
planes
Plane is short for **aeroplane**.

planet
planets
A **planet** is a huge, round object that moves around the Sun. *The Earth is a planet.*

plank
planks
A **plank** is a long, flat piece of wood.

plant

plants
A **plant** is a living thing that grows in soil or in water. Trees and flowers are plants.

plaster

plasters
1 A **plaster** is a sticky strip with a soft pad in the middle, that you use to protect a cut.
2 A **plaster** is also a hard case that holds the parts of a broken bone together until they are mended.

plastic

Plastic is a material that can be shaped to make bottles, buckets and many other things.

plastic bucket

plate

plates
A **plate** is a flat dish that you put food on.

platform

platforms
1 A **platform** is the place where you stand to wait for a train.
2 A **platform** is also a raised area, often used as a stage.

play

plays
A **play** is a story that you act out.

play

plays playing played
1 When you **play**, you do something for fun. *The boys are playing in the park.*
2 If you **play** a sport, you take part in it. *Alex is playing football.*
3 If you **play** a musical instrument, you use it to make music.

Charlotte plays the recorder.

playground

playgrounds
A **playground** is a place where you can play outdoors. Playgrounds often have swings and other play equipment.

pleasant

If something is **pleasant**, you enjoy it. *We had a pleasant walk.*

please to pod

please
pleases pleasing pleased
If you **please** someone, you make them happy. *Carlo **pleased** his mother by tidying his room.*

please
You say **please** when you ask for something in a polite way. ***Please** may I have an apple?*

plenty
If there is **plenty** of something, there is more than enough of it. *We have **plenty** of food for our picnic.*

plough
ploughs
▲ rhymes with **cow**
A **plough** is a set of sharp blades that is pulled by a tractor. Ploughs are used to dig up earth in fields.

pluck
plucks plucking plucked
When you **pluck** something, you pull on it with your fingers. *Amy **plucked** the guitar string. Suzy **plucked** her eyebrows.*

plug
plugs
1 A **plug** is a round piece of plastic or rubber used to keep water in a sink or a bath.
2 A **plug** is also a small object that connects a machine to the electric power.

plum
plums
A **plum** is a soft fruit with yellow, red or purple skin. A plum has a stone in the middle of it.

plus
Plus means add. The sign for plus is **+**. *Three **plus** four equals seven.*

■ opposite **minus**

pocket
pockets
A **pocket** is a small bag that is sewn into clothes. You can keep things in your pockets.

pocket money
Pocket money is money that your parents give you to spend.

pod
pods
A **pod** is a part of a plant that contains seeds. Peas and most beans grow in pods.

poem

poems
A **poem** is a piece of writing. Poems usually have short lines and often have words that rhyme.

> There was an old man
>   with a beard
> Who said, "It is just as I feared!
> Two owls and a hen,
>   Four larks and a wren,
> Have all built their nests
>   in my beard!"
>   — Edward Lear

point

points
1 A **point** is the sharp end of something. *A pencil point.*
2 A **point** is also part of a score in a game or a competition. *Our team got seven points.*

point

points pointing pointed
If you **point at** something, you use your finger to show where it is. *Karma pointed at the squirrels in the bushes.*

poisonous

If you eat something **poisonous**, it can make you very ill or even kill you.

polar bear

polar bears
A **polar bear** is a large, white bear that lives near the North Pole.

pole

poles
A **pole** is a long, thin piece of wood or metal. *A flagpole.*

police

▲ *say puh-**leece***
The **police** protect people and make sure that the law is obeyed.

polish

polishes polishing polished
When you **polish** something, you rub it to make it shiny. *Jayden polished his dad's car.*

polite

politer politest
A **polite** person has good manners and thinks about other people's feelings.
■ *opposite* **rude**

pollution to possession

pollution

Pollution is damage to the environment. Traffic fumes and litter are types of pollution.

pond
ponds
A **pond** is a small area of water.

pony
ponies
A **pony** is a type of horse that is small even when it is fully grown.

pool
pools
A **pool** is a small area of water.

paddling pool

poor
poorer poorest
1 People who are **poor** do not have much money.
▪ opposite **rich**
2 If something is **poor**, it is not very good. *Poor handwriting.*

pop
pops popping popped
If something **pops**, it explodes with a small bang. *The balloon popped when the cat jumped on it. She had such a fright!*

popular
Someone who is **popular** is liked by many people. *Jodie is very popular. She has lots of friends.*

pork
Pork is a type of meat that comes from a pig.

porridge
Porridge is a thick, sticky food made from oats cooked in milk or water.

port
ports
A **port** is a town with a harbour.

position
positions
1 The **position** of something is the place where it is. *Sarah's house is in a wonderful position, just next to the park.*
2 Someone's **position** is the way that they are standing or sitting.

possession
possessions
A **possession** is something that you own. *Don't leave any of your possessions on the coach.*

possible

If something is **possible**, it can happen or it can be done. *It is **possible** to reach Mars, but it will be hard to get there.*
■ opposite **impossible**

post

posts
A **post** is a long, thick piece of wood, metal or concrete that is fixed in the ground.

post

posts posting posted
1 If you **post** a letter, you put it in a postbox to be sent to someone.
2 If you **post** a comment or a picture on the internet, you put it on a website where lots of people can see it.

postcard

postcards
A **postcard** is a card that you post without an envelope. Postcards usually have a picture on one side.

poster

posters
A **poster** is a large picture or notice that is stuck on a wall. *Callum has covered his bedroom wall with **posters**.*

post office

post offices
A **post office** is a place where you can buy stamps and post letters and parcels.

pot

pots
1 A **pot** is a deep, round container. People use pots for cooking food.
2 A **pot** is also a container for a plant.

potato

potatoes
A **potato** is a rounded vegetable that grows under the ground.

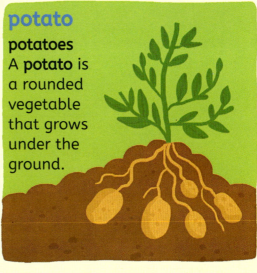

pottery

Pottery is a name for objects that are made out of clay, such as bowls and mugs.

pound

pounds
A **pound** is a unit of money. In Britain, a pound is made up of 100 pennies. The sign for a pound is £.

pour

pours pouring poured
When you **pour** a liquid, you tip it carefully out of its container.

powder

powders
Powder is made up of lots of very tiny grains. Flour is a powder.

power

1 **Power** is the strength and ability to do something. *The truck had the power to tow our car out of the mud.*
2 If someone has **power** over other people or things, they control them.
3 **Power** is another name for electricity. *Our power was cut off in the storm.*

practise

practises practising practised
If you **practise** something, you do it again and again so that you get better at it. *Abby practises the trumpet every day.*

precious

1 A **precious** object is worth a lot of money. *Princess Aurora has a chest of precious jewels.*
2 Something that is **precious** is very important or special to you.

prefer

prefers preferring preferred
If you **prefer** something, you like it better than another thing. *I prefer apples to oranges.*

prepare

prepares preparing prepared
If you **prepare**, you get ready. *Lydia is preparing for her holiday.*

present

presents
1 A **present** is something special that you give to someone.
2 The **present** is the time now. *The story begins in the present.*

president

presidents
A **president** is someone who runs a country.

press

presses pressing pressed
If you **press** something, you push it with your finger. *Press this button to turn on the television.*

pretend

pretends pretending pretended
When you **pretend**, you act as if something were true, even though it is not. *Sam pretended that he was asleep. Ella is pretending to be a frog.*

pretty

▲ rhymes with **pity**
prettier prettiest
Something or someone that is **pretty** is nice to look at.

prevent

prevents preventing prevented
If you **prevent** something, you stop it from happening. *Jessica acted quickly to prevent an accident.*

prey

Prey is a name for the creatures that birds and animals hunt and eat. *The tiger chased after its prey.*

price

prices
The **price** of something is how much money it costs. *What's the price of this bag?*

prick

pricks pricking pricked
If you **prick** yourself, something sharp makes a tiny hole in your skin. *Coral has pricked her finger.*

prince

princes
A **prince** is the son of a king or a queen.

princess

princesses
A **princess** is the daughter of a king or a queen.

print

prints printing printed
1 When someone **prints** something, they use a machine called a printer to put words or pictures onto paper. *Mrs Parsnip printed my story for me.*
2 When you **print**, you write with letters that are not joined up.

prison

prisons
A **prison** is a place where people are kept as a punishment because they have not obeyed the law.

private

If something is **private**, it is only for particular people. *A **private** letter.*
■ opposite **public**

prize

prizes
You win a **prize** as a reward for doing something well. *Carl won a cup as his **prize** for coming first in the race.*

probably

If something will **probably** happen, there is more chance that it will happen than it won't. *It will **probably** rain again tomorrow.*

problem

problems
A **problem** is something difficult that you need to find an answer to. *We have a **problem** with our kitten. She keeps running away.*

produce

produces producing produced
1 When you **produce** something, you make it. *The chocolate factory **produces** all kinds of sweets.*
2 If you **produce** something, you get it out so that people can see it. *Ginger **produced** a mouse from his pocket.*

program

programs
A **program** is a set of instructions that tells a computer how to work.

programme

programmes
1 A **programme** is something that you watch on television or hear on the radio. *A nature **programme**.*
2 A **programme** is also a small book or list that tells you about a play or a concert.

progress

When you **make progress**, you get better or move forwards. *Lucy is **making** good **progress** at school. The explorers **made** slow **progress** through the jungle.*

project

projects
When you do a **project**, you find out about a subject.

*Ewan and Ravi are doing a **project** on sound.*

promise

promises promising promised
When you **promise**, you say that you will really do something. *Molly **promised** to be on time.*

proper

Proper means right or correct. *Is this the **proper** way to get on a horse?*

protect

protects protecting protected
When you **protect** someone or something, you keep them safe.

*Jo **protected** her puppy from the rain.*

proud

prouder proudest
If you feel **proud**, you feel pleased about what you have done. *Jessie is **proud** of her cake.*

prove

proves proving proved
When you **prove** something, you show that it is true.

provide

provides providing provided
When you **provide** something, you give people what they need. *The hotel **provides** lunch.*

public

If something is **public**, everyone can use it. *A **public** park.*
■ opposite **private**

pudding

puddings
A **pudding** is a sweet food that you eat at the end of a meal.

puddle

puddles
A **puddle** is a small pool of water. You see puddles on the ground when it has been raining.

puddle

pull

pulls pulling pulled
If you **pull** something, you move it towards you. *Richard **pulled** his suitcase out of the cupboard.*

pump

pumps
You use a **pump** to push air or liquid into something. *A bicycle **pump**.*

punch

punches punching punched
If you **punch** something, you hit it with your fist.

punish

punishes punishing punished
If someone **punishes** you, they do something to you because you have been naughty. *Mum **punished** me for being rude by sending me to bed.*

pupil

pupils
A **pupil** is someone who learns something, usually in a school. *There are 30 **pupils** in my class.*

puppet

puppets
A **puppet** is a doll that can be made to move. Some puppets are like gloves and you move them with your fingers. Others have strings that you can pull.

puppy

puppies
A **puppy** is a young dog.

purple

Purple is the colour that you make when you mix red and blue.

purpose

▲ say *pur-pus*
If you do something **on purpose**, you mean to do it. *Matt kicked his sister **on purpose** to see if she would cry.*

purr

purrs purring purred
When a cat **purrs**, it makes a low sound in its throat to show that it is happy.

purse

purses
A **purse** is a small bag that you keep money in.

push

pushes pushing pushed
If you **push** something, you move it in front of you or away from you. *Daniel **pushed** his bike up the hill.*

put

puts putting put
When you **put** a thing somewhere, you move it to that place. *Please **put** the milk in the fridge.*

puzzle

puzzles

A **puzzle** is a type of game where you have to work out an answer.

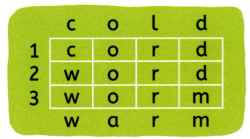

Can you get from cold to warm in three words?

Answer the clues and fill in the boxes. For each answer, change just one letter from the word above.

CLUES
1. A type of string
2. A group of letters
3. A creature that lives in the ground

pyjamas

Pyjamas are the matching shirt and trousers that some people wear in bed.

quack

quacks quacking quacked

When a duck **quacks**, it opens its beak and makes a loud sound.

quantity

quantities

A **quantity** is an amount or a number. *A large **quantity** of sand.*

quarrel

quarrels quarrelling quarrelled

When people **quarrel**, they argue and get angry with each other. *The boys **quarrelled** over who should go first.*

quarry

quarries

A **quarry** is a place where stone is dug out of the ground.

quarter

quarters

If something is cut into **quarters**, it is cut into four pieces of the same size.

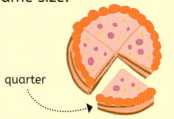

quarter

queen

queens

A **queen** is a woman who rules a country. Queens come from royal families and are not chosen by the people.

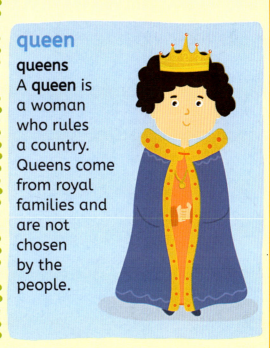

question to radiator

question
questions
A **question** is what you ask when you want to know something.

queue
queues
▲ *say kyoo*
A **queue** is a line of people who are waiting for something. *We waited in the queue for the bus.*

quick
quicker quickest
1 Something that is **quick** moves at a great speed.
2 If something is **quick**, it only lasts for a short time. *Miranda had a quick look round the house.*

quiet
quieter quietest
Someone who is being **quiet** does not make much noise.
■ *opposite* **loud**

quite
1 **Quite** means a bit. *It's quite warm outside.*
2 **Quite** also means completely. *I haven't quite finished my book.*

quiz
quizzes
A **quiz** is a game or a test to find out how much you know. You have to answer questions in a quiz.

Rr

rabbit
rabbits
A **rabbit** is a small, furry animal with long ears and a short tail. Wild rabbits live in holes under the ground called burrows.

race
races
A **race** is a competition to find out who can go fastest. *A relay race.*

racket
rackets
A **racket** is a bat with strings stretched across it. *A tennis racket.*

radiator
radiators
A **radiator** is used to heat a room. Radiators are made of metal and are usually filled with hot water.

radio

radios
A **radio** is a machine that receives signals through the air and sends out sounds. You can listen to music and news on a radio.

raft

rafts
A **raft** is a kind of flat boat. Rafts are often made from planks of wood that are fixed together.

rag

rags
A **rag** is a piece of old cloth. You use rags to clean things.

raid

raids
A **raid** is a sudden attack. *An air raid.*

rail

rails
1 A **rail** is a bar that you can hold on to. *Hold on to the rail as you climb the stairs.*
2 **Rails** are long metal bars that trains and trams run on.
3 If you go somewhere **by rail**, you travel on a train.

railway

railways
A **railway** is a track for trains to travel along.

rain

rains raining rained
When it **rains**, drops of water fall from the clouds.

rainbow

rainbows
A **rainbow** is a curved band of different colours that you sometimes see in the sky. Rainbows appear when the Sun shines while it is raining.

raise

raises raising raised
If you **raise** something, you lift it up. *Laura raised her hand to answer the question.*

rake

rakes
A **rake** is a garden tool with a long handle and metal teeth. You use a rake to collect leaves.

ran

Ran comes from the word **run**. *Kitty runs for the school team. She ran in five races last month.*

rare to really

Some words that begin with an "r" sound, such as **wrap**, are spelt "**wr**".

rare

rarer rarest
If something is **rare**, you do not see it very often.
*A **rare** butterfly.*
■ opposite **common**

raspberry

raspberries
A **raspberry** is a small, red fruit. Raspberries are soft and juicy and grow on bushes.

rat

rats
A **rat** is a small animal with a long tail and sharp teeth. Rats sometimes spread disease.

rather

1 If you would **rather** do something, you want to do it more than something else. *I'd **rather** go to the beach than do my homework.*
2 **Rather** means more than a little. *Henrietta is **rather** clever.*

raw

Food that is **raw** has not been cooked.
Raw carrots.

reach

reaches reaching reached
1 When you **reach** for something, you stretch out your hand to touch it. *Tia **reached** for the light.*
2 When you **reach** a place, you arrive there. *It was very late when we **reached** the hotel.*

read

reads reading read
1 When you **read**, you look at words and understand what they mean. *Jack **read** his new book.*
2 When you **read** something to someone, you say it out loud. *Skye is **reading** to her brother.*

ready

If you are **ready**, you can do something now. *I'm **ready** to go.*

real

1 Something that is **real** is true.
2 Something that is **real** is not a copy. *A **real** diamond.*

really

1 **Really** means that something is true. *Men **really** have walked on the Moon.*
2 **Really** also means very. *Georgia was **really** annoyed that she'd missed the bus.*

reason

reasons

The **reason** for something is why it has happened. *The reason I'm late is that my alarm clock didn't work.*

receive

receives receiving received

If you **receive** something, you get something that is given to you or sent to you. *I received your present this morning.*

recent

Something that is **recent** happened a short time ago.

recipe

recipes

▲ say **ress**-ippy

A **recipe** is a set of instructions that tells you how to make something to eat or drink.

recite

recites reciting recited

When you **recite** something, such as a poem, you remember it and say it aloud.

recognize

recognizes recognizing recognized

If you **recognize** someone, you see them and know who they are. *I recognized Dylan easily.*

record

records recording recorded

If you **record** some music or a television programme, you make a copy of it.

recorder

recorders

A **recorder** is a musical instrument. You blow into a recorder and cover the holes with your fingers to make different notes.

recover

recovers recovering recovered

When you **recover**, you feel better again.

rectangle

rectangles

A **rectangle** is a shape with four sides and four corners. It has two long sides of the same length and two short sides of the same length.

recycle to rehearse

recycle
recycles recycling recycled
If you **recycle** something, you use it again, or you use it to make something new. *Our class is collecting rubbish to recycle.*

red
Red is a colour. Blood and tomatoes are red.

reduce
reduces reducing reduced
If you **reduce** something, you make it smaller. *The toy shop has reduced its prices.*

referee
referees
A **referee** makes sure that the players obey the rules of a game.

The referee blew his whistle.

reflection
reflections
You see a **reflection** when you look in a mirror.

refreshments
Refreshments are food and drink. *There will be refreshments after the concert.*

refuse
refuses refusing refused
If you **refuse** to do something that someone has asked you to, you say that you will not do it.
■ opposite **agree**

register
registers
A **register** is a list of names. Registers are used in schools to check that everybody is there.

rehearse
rehearses rehearsing rehearsed
When you **rehearse**, you practise something before a performance. *We have been rehearsing for the concert all week.*

reindeer

reindeer
A **reindeer** is a kind of deer. Reindeer have large horns called antlers. They live in very cold places.

reins

Reins are the leather straps that you use to control a horse.

relative

relatives
A **relative** is a member of your family.

relax

relaxes relaxing relaxed
When you **relax**, you rest and stop worrying. *Ben relaxes by listening to music.*

remain

remains remaining remained
If you **remain** in a place, you stay there. *Clare remained at home while we went to the park.*

remember

remembers remembering remembered
When you **remember** something, it comes back into your mind. *Simon has remembered where he left his jacket.*
■ opposite **forget**

remind

reminds reminding reminded
If you **remind** someone about something, you help them to remember it. *Joshua reminded me to send Emily's birthday card.*

remote control

remote controls
You use a **remote control** to control a machine such as a television from a distance.

remove

removes removing removed
When you **remove** something, you take it away. *I didn't recognize Sue until she removed her mask.*

rent

rents renting rented
If you **rent** a house, you pay money to its owner so that you can live in it.

repair

repairs repairing repaired
When you **repair** something, you mend it so that it can be used again.

repeat to responsible

repeat
repeats repeating repeated
If you **repeat** something, you say it again or do it again. *Please **repeat** your name so that I can write it down.*

replace
replaces replacing replaced
1 If you **replace** something, you put another thing in its place. *Kian **replaced** the broken vase with a new one.*
2 **Replace** also means to put something back where it came from. *Shazia **replaced** the book on the shelf.*

reply
replies replying replied
When you **reply**, you give an answer. *Thomas **replied** to Lucy's invitation.*

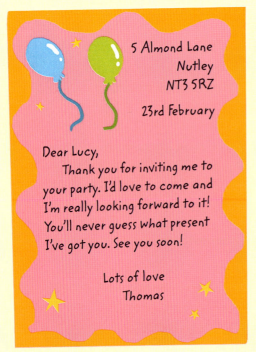

5 Almond Lane
Nutley
NT3 5RZ

23rd February

Dear Lucy,
   Thank you for inviting me to your party. I'd love to come and I'm really looking forward to it! You'll never guess what present I've got you. See you soon!

Lots of love
Thomas

reptile
reptiles
A **reptile** is an animal with dry, scaly skin. Most reptiles lay eggs. Crocodiles, snakes and lizards are reptiles.

lizard

require
requires requiring required
If you **require** something, you need it. *You will **require** paper, scissors and glue to make this model boat.*

rescue
rescues rescuing rescued
If you **rescue** someone, you help them to escape from danger.

*The helicopter crew **rescued** the boys from the sea.*

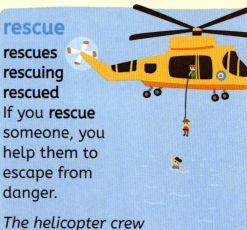

responsible
1 If you are **responsible** for something, you are the one who has to do it. *I am **responsible** for feeding Tinkerbell.*
2 A **responsible** person is sensible and can be trusted.

rest

The **rest** is what is left. *I ate **the rest** of the pizza the next day.*

rest

rests resting rested
When you **rest**, you sit down or lie down because you are tired.

restaurant

restaurants
A **restaurant** is a place with tables and chairs, where you buy and eat meals.

> Some words that begin with an "r" sound, such as **wrestle**, **wrist** and **write**, are spelt "**wr**".

result

results
A **result** is something that happens because of something else. *I got lost and I was late as a **result**.*

return

returns returning returned
1 If you **return** to a place, you come back to it.
2 If you **return** something, you give it back. *Theo **returned** the books that he had borrowed.*

reverse

reverses reversing reversed
When someone **reverses** a car, they drive it backwards.

revolting

If something is **revolting**, it makes you feel sick.
*A **revolting** smell.*

reward

rewards
A **reward** is something that you are given because you have done something good.

rhinoceros

rhinoceroses
A **rhinoceros** is a large, heavy animal with thick, wrinkled skin. Rhinoceroses have one or two horns on their noses.

rhyme

rhymes rhyming rhymed
Words that **rhyme** end with the same sound. Fight, kite and might all rhyme.

rhythm

rhythms
A **rhythm** is a repeated pattern of sound. Music and poems have rhythm.

rib to ring

rib
ribs
A **rib** is one of the bones that curve round from your back to your chest. Your ribs protect your heart and your lungs.

ribbon
ribbons
A **ribbon** is a long piece of material that you tie around things. *Alice tied a ribbon around the parcel.*

rice
Rice is a food that comes from a type of grass plant. Rice grains can be cooked and eaten.

rich
richer richest
People who are **rich** have a lot of money.
■ opposite **poor**

riddle
riddles
A **riddle** is a question with a surprising and clever answer.

ride
rides
1 A **ride** is a journey in a vehicle or on an animal. *It's a long car ride to my uncle's house.*
2 A **ride** at the fair is a machine that spins you round or turns you upside down.

ride
rides riding rode ridden
If you **ride** a bicycle or a horse, you sit on it and move along.

ridiculous
Something that is **ridiculous** is very silly. *Andrew looks ridiculous in his mum's hat.*

right
1 Something that is **right** is correct and does not have any mistakes in it.
■ opposite **wrong**
2 If you do something that is **right**, you do something good or fair.
■ opposite **wrong**
3 You have a **right** hand and a left hand. Most people draw with their right hand.
■ opposite **left**

ring
rings
A **ring** is a band that you wear on your finger.

ring to roar

ring
rings ringing rang rung
1 When you **ring** someone, you call them on the telephone.
2 When a bell **rings**, it makes a loud noise.

ringtone
ringtones
A **ringtone** is the sound or tune a mobile phone makes when someone calls it.

rink
rinks
A **rink** is a place where you can ice-skate or roller-skate.

rinse
rinses rinsing rinsed
When you **rinse** something, you clean it in water.

rip
rips ripping ripped
If you **rip** something, you tear it. *Evan **ripped** his trousers on the fence.*

ripe
riper ripest
If food is **ripe**, it is ready to be eaten. ***Ripe** tomatoes.*

rise
rises rising rose risen
When something **rises**, it moves up. *The balloon **rose** into the air.*

risk
risks
If you take a **risk**, you do something that you know could be dangerous. *Robert took a **risk** when he jumped backwards into the pool.*

river
rivers
A **river** is a large amount of water running across land. Rivers have banks on either side. They run into lakes or seas.

road
roads
A **road** is a hard strip of ground that goes from one place to another. Vehicles travel on roads.

roar
roars roaring roared
When an animal **roars**, it makes a loud, low sound in its throat. *The lion **roared**.*

roast to roller skate

roast

roasts roasting roasted

When you **roast** food, you cook it in a hot oven. *Mum has **roasted** a chicken for lunch.*

rob

robs robbing robbed

If you **rob** someone, you steal things from them. *Three men **robbed** the bank yesterday. We were **robbed**.*

robin

robins

A **robin** is a small bird with a red chest.

robot

robots

A **robot** is a machine that can do some jobs that people do. Some robots look a bit like people.

rock

rocks

1 **Rock** is the very hard part of the Earth. Mountains are made of rock.
2 A **rock** is a large stone.

rock

rocks rocking rocked

When you **rock**, you move gently backwards and forwards or from side to side.

rocket

rockets

1 A **rocket** is a spacecraft that travels very fast. Rockets take astronauts into space.
2 A **rocket** is also a type of firework.

rode

Rode comes from the word **ride**. *Lucy rides her pony every day. She **rode** for hours yesterday.*

roll

rolls

1 A **roll** is a small, round piece of bread. *A cheese **roll**.*
2 A **roll** is also a long piece of paper or tape wrapped around itself many times.

roll

rolls rolling rolled

When something **rolls**, it moves by turning over and over. *The ball **rolled** down the hill.*

roller skate

roller skates

Roller skates are boots with wheels on, used for skating.

Some words that begin with an "r" sound, such as **wrong** and **wrote**, are spelt "**wr**".

roof
roofs
A **roof** is the top of a building.

room
rooms
1 A **room** is an area inside a building. Rooms usually have four walls and a door.
2 If there is **room** for something, there is enough space for it.

root
roots
A **root** is the part of a plant that grows under the ground. Water travels up the root to the rest of the plant.

rope
ropes
A **rope** is made of lots of threads twisted together. Ropes are often used for pulling things.

rose
roses
A **rose** is a flower with thorns on its stem. Roses often smell nice.

rose
Rose comes from the word **rise**. *Laura watched the balloon rise. It rose high into the sky.*

rough
rougher roughest
▲ *rhymes with* **stuff**
1 If something is **rough**, it is not smooth. *Rough skin.*
2 Someone who is **rough** is not gentle. *Don't be so rough, you're hurting me!*
3 A **rough** answer is not exactly correct.

round
rounder roundest
Something that is **round** has a shape like a circle or a ball.

row
rows
1 A **row** is a line of people or things. *A row of chairs.*
▲ *rhymes with* **go**
2 A **row** is an argument.
▲ *rhymes with* **how**

row
rows rowing rowed
▲ *rhymes with* **go**
When you **row**, you use oars to make a boat move through water.

royal to rule

royal
Someone who is **royal** is part of the family of a king or a queen.

rub
rubs rubbing rubbed
If you **rub** something, you move your hand or a cloth backwards and forwards over it. You often rub things to make them clean.

rubber
rubbers
1 **Rubber** is a strong material that can bend and stretch. Rubber is used to make tyres, balls, boots and rubber bands.

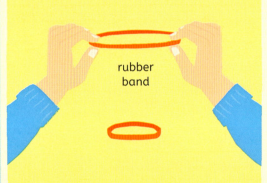
rubber band

2 A **rubber** is a soft block that you rub over pencil marks to remove them.

rubbish
1 **Rubbish** is the name for things that you throw away because you don't want them any more.
2 If you say that something is **rubbish**, you think it is very bad or isn't true. *That painting is rubbish. Don't talk rubbish, George.*

rude
ruder rudest
Rude people have bad manners and are not polite. *It is rude to speak with your mouth full of food.*
■ opposite **polite**

rug
rugs
A **rug** is a small carpet that covers part of a floor.

rugby
Rugby is a game with an oval ball played by two teams. Each team tries to carry the ball across a line or kick it over a bar.

ruin
ruins ruining ruined
If you **ruin** something, you spoil it completely. *My brother has ruined my picture by scribbling on it.*

rule
rules
A **rule** tells you what you can or cannot do. Games have rules that you must obey.

rule
rules ruling ruled
Someone who **rules** a country is in charge of it.

174

ruler to saddle

ruler
rulers
1 A **ruler** is a flat piece of plastic, wood or metal with straight edges. You use a ruler to draw straight lines or to measure things.

2 A **ruler** is also someone who is in charge of a country.

run
runs running ran run
1 When you **run**, you move quickly, using your legs.

Luke ran for the bus.

2 When water **runs**, it moves. *The river runs into the sea.*
3 When a machine **runs**, it works. *This radio runs on batteries.*
4 If someone **runs** something, they are in charge of it.

rung
Rung comes from the word **ring**. *Tim wants you to ring him. He has rung you twice today already.*

runway
runways
A **runway** is a strip of land where planes take off and land.

rush
rushes rushing rushed
When you **rush**, you hurry or you do something quickly. *We're late, so we'll have to rush.*

Ss

sack
sacks
A **sack** is a large bag made from strong cloth or plastic. Sacks are used for carrying and storing things.

sad
sadder saddest
If you are **sad**, you feel unhappy. *Ollie was sad when his fish died.*
■ opposite **happy**

> Some other words for **sad** are **unhappy, depressed, upset, miserable** and **glum**.

saddle
saddles
A **saddle** is a seat for a rider on a horse or a bicycle.

175

safe to sandal

safe
safer safest
1 If you are **safe**, nothing bad can happen to you.
2 If something is **safe**, it cannot hurt you. *Dad mended my bike so that it was **safe** to ride.*

said
▲ rhymes with **bed**
Said comes from the word **say**. *Mum asked us to say what we wanted. I **said** I would like some ice cream.*

sail
sails
A **sail** is a large piece of cloth that is fixed to a boat. When the wind blows into the sail, it makes the boat move.

sail

sail
sails sailing sailed
If you **sail** somewhere, you travel in a boat or a ship.

sailor
sailors
A **sailor** is someone who is part of a ship's crew.

salad
salads
A **salad** is a mixture of raw vegetables, such as lettuce and tomato.

sale
sales
1 When a shop has a **sale**, it sells things for less than their usual price.
2 If something is **for sale**, people can buy it.

salt
People use **salt** to give food flavour. You can add salt when you cook or you can shake it over your food.

same
Things that are the **same** are just like each other. *Freddie's dogs look the **same**.*
■ opposite **different**

sand
Sand is tiny pieces of rock and shell. Some beaches and deserts are covered with sand.

sandal
sandals
A **sandal** is a light shoe with straps that go over your foot. People wear sandals when it is hot.

sandwich to saucepan

sandwich
sandwiches
A **sandwich** is made from two pieces of bread with another food between them.
*Sam had cheese and salad **sandwiches** for lunch.*

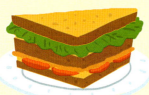

sang
Sang comes from the word **sing**.
*Aled often sings in concerts. He **sang** three songs last night.*

sank
Sank comes from the word **sink**.
*The ship hit the rocks and began to sink. It **sank** to the bottom of the sea.*

sari
saris
A **sari** is a long piece of light cloth that you wear wrapped round your body. Indian women and girls often wear saris.

sat
Sat comes from the word **sit**.
*Jane could not find anywhere to sit. In the end, she **sat** on the floor.*

satellite
satellites
1 A **satellite** is a machine that travels around the Earth or another planet.

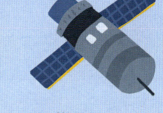

2 A **satellite** is also a natural object that travels around a planet. The Moon is a satellite of the Earth.

satellite dish
satellite dishes
A **satellite dish** is attached to a building to pick up TV signals from a satellite.

satnav
satnavs
A **satnav** is a small computer that uses satellite signals to help drivers find their way. Satnav is short for satellite navigation.

sauce
sauces
A **sauce** is a thick liquid that you eat with other food.

saucepan
saucepans
A **saucepan** is a metal pot with a handle that is used for cooking.

sausage to scarf

sausage
sausages
A **sausage** is made from chopped meat inside a special skin.

save
saves saving saved
1 If you **save** someone, you rescue them. *Lauren jumped into the water to **save** the child.*
2 If you **save** money, you keep it to use later. *Amelia is **saving** to buy some paints.*
3 If you **save** what you are doing on a computer, it is stored in the computer and you can look at it again later.

saw
saws
A **saw** is a tool with a handle and a blade. You use a saw to cut wood.

saw
Saw comes from the word **see**. *I see my cousin most weeks. I **saw** her twice last week.*

say
says saying said
If you **say** something, you speak words. *Mark **said** "Hello" to me.*

scale
scales
1 A **scale** is a set of musical notes that are played or sung in order.
2 A **scale** is also one of the small pieces of skin that cover the body of a fish or a reptile.

scales
You use **scales** to find out how much something weighs. *Weigh the sugar on the **scales**.*

scar
scars
A **scar** is a mark on your skin where a wound used to be.

scare
scares scaring scared
If you **scare** someone, you make them feel frightened. *Jessica **scared** me with a toy spider.*

scarf
scarves
A **scarf** is a piece of cloth that you wear round your neck. People wear scarves to keep warm.

scatter

scatters scattering scattered

When you **scatter** things, you throw them over a large area.

Tom scattered seeds for the birds to eat.

school

schools

A **school** is a place where children go to learn.

science

When you study **science**, you find out about the Earth, space, people, animals or plants. You do experiments to help you learn about science.

scientist

scientists

A **scientist** is someone who does experiments to find out more about the world.

scissors

You use a pair of **scissors** to cut paper or cloth. Scissors have two handles and two blades.

score

scores

A **score** is the number of points or goals that each side gets in a game. *What was the score in the football match?*

score

scores scoring scored

When you **score** a goal, you make a ball go into a net.

George scored three times in today's match.

scrap

scraps

A **scrap** is a small piece of something. *A scrap of paper. A scrap of food.*

scrapbook

scrapbooks

A **scrapbook** is a book with plain pages. You stick pictures and photos in a scrapbook.

scrape

scrapes scraping scraped

If you **scrape** something, you remove some of its surface by dragging something sharp across it. *Jacob scraped the potatoes with a knife. Amy scraped her knee on a rock.*

scratch to seagull

scratch
scratches scratching scratched
1 If you **scratch** something, you make a small cut in it. *William scratched his arm in the bushes. Jo scratched her name with a pin.*
2 If you **scratch** yourself, you rub a part of you that itches.

scream
screams screaming screamed
When you **scream**, you make a loud, high sound. People scream when they are very frightened, hurt or excited.

screen
screens
A **screen** is a flat surface used for showing pictures. Computers and televisions have screens.

screw
screws
A **screw** is a piece of pointed metal with a flat top. You twist screws into things to hold them together.

scribble
scribbles scribbling scribbled
If you **scribble**, you write or draw quickly and carelessly. *Matt scribbled on the notepad.*

scrub
scrubs scrubbing scrubbed
If you **scrub** something, you rub it hard to clean it. *Rosie scrubbed the carpet to get rid of the stains.*

sea
seas
A **sea** is a very large area of salty water.

sea creature
sea creatures
A **sea creature** is an animal that lives in the sea.

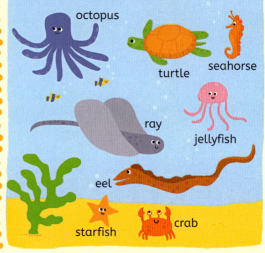

octopus, turtle, seahorse, ray, jellyfish, eel, starfish, crab

seagull
seagulls
A **seagull** is a large bird that lives near the sea. Seagulls are usually grey and white.

seal
seals
A **seal** is an animal with smooth fur that lives in the sea and on land. Seals eat fish and swim very well.

seal
seals sealing sealed
When you **seal** something, you close it tightly. *Seal the envelope and put it in the post.*

search
searches searching searched
If you **search** for something, you look for it. *We searched the house for our hamster, but we couldn't find it.*

search engine
search engines
A **search engine** is a website that helps you find things on the internet.

seaside
The **seaside** is a place by the sea where people go for their holidays. *We love going to the seaside because we can swim and play on the beach.*

season
seasons
A **season** is a part of the year. The four seasons are spring, summer, autumn and winter.

seat
seats
A **seat** is a place where you can sit. *There were only two seats left on the bus.*

seaweed
Seaweed is a name for many types of plants that grow in the sea.

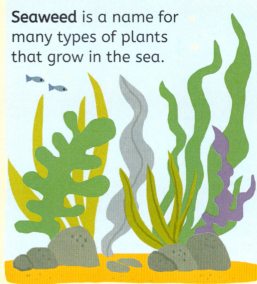

second
seconds
A **second** is a very short amount of time. There are 60 seconds in a minute.

secret
secrets
A **secret** is something that you keep hidden and do not tell people about. *We kept Cary's birthday present a secret.*

see to sent

see

sees seeing saw seen
1 When you **see**, you notice things with your eyes.
2 When you **see** someone, you meet them. *I saw Daisy in town.*

seed

seeds
A **seed** is a part of a plant. When you put seeds into the ground, new plants grow.

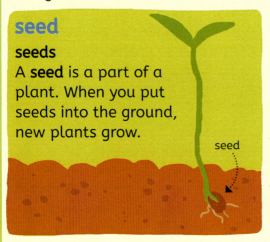

seed

seem

seems seeming seemed
If something **seems** to be a particular way, that is the way it looks or feels. *The journey seemed longer than usual.*

seen

Seen comes from the word **see**. *I want to see Vijay. I haven't seen him for weeks.*

> Some words with an "**s**" sound begin with "**ce**" or "**ci**", like **ceiling** or **city**.

selfish

Selfish people think about themselves rather than others.

sell

sells selling sold
Someone who **sells** things gives them to people for money.
■ *opposite* **buy**

send

sends sending sent
If you **send** something, you make it go somewhere. *Josie sent a postcard to her auntie.*

sense

senses
1 Your **senses** help you to find out about the things around you. Your five senses are sight, hearing, touch, taste and smell.
2 If something **makes sense**, you can understand it.

sensible

A **sensible** person thinks carefully and does not do stupid things.

sent

Sent comes from the word **send**. *I must send a letter to Marc. He sent me two postcards last month.*

sentence

sentences
A **sentence** is a group of words that makes sense. When you write down a sentence, you start with a capital letter and end with a full stop.

separate

If things are **separate**, they are not joined together.

*Lewis put the bottles and tins in **separate** boxes.*

series

A **series** is a group of things that follow each other. *A TV **series**.*

serious

1 If something is **serious**, it is important and should be thought about carefully. *We must have a **serious** talk about your work.*
2 A **serious** person does not laugh and joke very much.

serve

serves serving served
If someone **serves** you in a shop or a restaurant, they help you to buy what you want.

set

sets
A **set** is a group of things that belong together. *A chess **set**.*

set

sets setting set
1 When something is **set**, it is arranged or put in place. *Please set your watch to the right time.*
2 When the Sun **sets**, it goes out of sight in the evening.

several

Several means a small number, usually more than three. *Dan has **several** pairs of jeans.*

sew

sews sewing sewed sewn
▲ *rhymes with* **low**
When you **sew**, you join pieces of cloth together, using a needle and thread.

sex

sexes
The **sexes** are the two groups that humans and animals are divided into. One sex is male and the other is female.

shade

Shade is an area that is hidden from sunlight. *Lily sat in the **shade** because it was too hot.*

shadow to shark

shadow

shadows
A **shadow** is a dark shape made by something blocking out the light.

shadow

shake

shakes shaking shook shaken
If you **shake** something, you move it up and down or from side to side quite hard. *Shake the bottle before you open it.*

shall

should
1 **Shall** means will. *I shall call you tomorrow.*
2 You also use **shall** to make suggestions. *Shall we get ice cream?*

shallow

shallower shallowest
Something that is **shallow** does not go down very far. *A shallow pool.*
■ opposite **deep**

shampoo

Shampoo is a liquid that you use to wash your hair. You rub it into your hair and then rinse it out.

shape

shapes
The **shape** of something is its outline, or the way it looks on the outside.

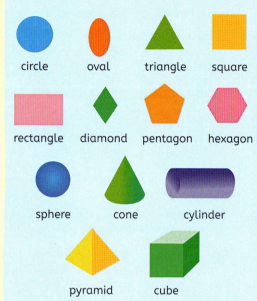

circle   oval   triangle   square
rectangle   diamond   pentagon   hexagon
sphere   cone   cylinder
pyramid   cube

share

shares sharing shared
1 If you **share** something, you let others use it or have some of it. *Joe shared his photo online. Mary shared her sweets.*
2 **Share** also means to use something with other people. *I share the computer with my family.*

shark

sharks
Sharks are big fish with sharp teeth. Sharks live in the sea.

sharp

sharper sharpest
Something that is **sharp** has a very thin edge or a point that can cut or prick you. A **sharp** knife. A **sharp** pencil.
■ opposite **blunt**

shave

shaves shaving shaved
When people **shave**, they cut hair from their skin. *Grandpa shaves every day.*

she'd

1 **She'd** is a short way of saying **she had**. *She'd never been to Rome before.*
2 **She'd** is also a short way of saying **she would**. *Ask Zoe if she'd like some cake.*

shed

sheds
A **shed** is a small, wooden building. People often keep tools in their sheds.

sheep

sheep
A **sheep** is a farm animal with a woolly coat. Sheep are kept for their wool and their meat.

sheet

sheets
1 A **sheet** is a large piece of cloth that you use to cover a mattress.
2 A **sheet** is also a flat piece of paper, glass or plastic.

shelf

shelves
A **shelf** is a flat piece of wood, metal or plastic that is fixed to a wall. You keep things on shelves.

she'll

She'll is a short way of saying **she will**. *Mel is finishing her lunch. She'll be here soon.*

shell

shells
A **shell** is a hard cover around something. Eggs, nuts, snails and some sea creatures have shells.

shelter to shop

shelter
shelters
A **shelter** is a place where you can stay dry and safe.

she's
1 **She's** is a short way of saying **she is**. *I'm waiting for Victoria to arrive. **She's** coming at 10 o'clock.*
2 **She's** is also short for **she has**. ***She's** brought gifts for everyone.*

shine
shines shining shone
If something **shines**, it gives off a bright light. *Hold the torch so that it **shines** on your face.*

ship
ships
A **ship** is a large boat that carries people and things over the sea.

shirt
shirts
A **shirt** is a piece of clothing that people wear on the top part of their bodies. Shirts often have a collar and fasten down the front.

shiver
shivers shivering shivered
When you **shiver**, your body shakes because you are cold or frightened.

shoe
shoes
▲ rhymes with **too**
A **shoe** is something that you wear to cover your foot. Shoes can be made of leather, plastic or cloth.

shone
Shone comes from the word **shine**. *We hoped that the Sun would shine all day, but it only **shone** for a few hours.*

shook
Shook comes from the word **shake**. *We told Andy to shake the orange juice, but he **shook** it too hard and the lid came off.*

shoot
shoots shooting shot
1 **Shoot** means to use a gun.
2 When you **shoot** in a game such as football, you try to score a goal.

shop
shops
A **shop** is a place where you can buy things.

shore

shores
The **shore** is the land at the edge of a sea, lake or wide river. *We searched for shells along the shore.*

short

shorter shortest
1 If something is **short**, it is not very long. *Short hair. A short time.*
■ opposite **long**
2 Someone who is **short** is not very tall.
■ opposite **tall**

shorts

Shorts are short trousers. People wear shorts when it is hot or when they are playing sport.

shot

Shot comes from the word **shoot**. *It's Danny's turn to shoot. Wayne has shot three times already in this match.*

should

If you **should** do something, you ought to do it. *You should brush your teeth every day.*

shoulder

shoulders
Your **shoulder** is the part of your body between your neck and your arm.

shouldn't

Shouldn't is a short way of saying **should not**. *If you're that sick, you shouldn't go out at all.*

shout

shouts shouting shouted
When you **shout**, you talk very loudly. *Jessie shouted to Nat to pass her the ball.*

show

shows
A **show** is a performance that you usually see in a theatre. Shows often have music.

show

shows showing showed shown
1 If you **show** something, you let people see it. *Sophie showed everyone her new watch.*
2 If you **show** someone how to do something, you do it and explain what you are doing. *Anna showed me how to knit.*

shower to sight

shower

showers
1 A **shower** is a piece of equipment that sends out a spray of water. You wash yourself by standing under it.
2 A **shower** is also a short fall of rain.

shown

Shown comes from the word **show**. *Asha wants to show her photographs to the class. She has already shown them to her family.*

shrink

shrinks shrinking shrank shrunk
If something **shrinks**, it gets smaller. *My T-shirt shrank when it was washed.*

shut

shuts shutting shut
1 If you **shut** a door, you move it so that it blocks a space in the wall.
2 If you **shut** a box, you put a lid on it.

shut

If something is **shut**, people or things cannot go into it or through it. *The shop is shut on Sundays. The door was shut and locked.*

shy

shyer shyest
If someone is **shy**, they are quiet and find it hard to talk to people they do not know.

sick

1 If you feel **sick**, you do not feel well.
2 When you are **sick**, you bring up food from your stomach through your mouth.

Kelly is feeling sick.

side

sides
1 A **side** is a surface of an object. *Use both sides of the paper. A cube has six sides.*
2 A **side** is also an edge. *Milly stayed at the side of the pool.*
3 A **side** is also a team. *Which side won the match?*

sigh

sighs sighing sighed
When you **sigh**, you breathe out noisily. People usually sigh because they are sad or bored.

sight

sights
1 A **sight** is something that you see. *A beautiful sight.*
2 **Sight** is the sense of seeing.

sign

signs
1 A **sign** is a shape that means something. *The **sign** for a pound is £.*
2 A **sign** is also a set of words or pictures that tell you what to do or where to go.

*Picnic places are often marked with a **sign**.*

sign

signs signing signed
When you **sign** something, you write your name on it.

signal

signals
1 A **signal** is a message that does not use any words. *The climbers waved their arms as a **signal** to the rescue helicopter.*
2 An electrical **signal** carries information through the air. *A television **signal**.*

silly

sillier silliest
If you are being **silly**, you are not behaving in a sensible way.

silver

Silver is a shiny, grey metal that is valuable. Some jewellery and coins are made of silver.

similar

If two things are **similar**, they are alike in some ways, but not exactly the same. *Leon and his brother look **similar**, but Leon has freckles.*

simple

simpler simplest
If something is **simple**, it is very easy to do. *A **simple** sum.*

since

1 **Since** means after. *I haven't seen Mandy **since** Friday.*
2 **Since** also means because. ***Since** you've been so good, you can stay up to watch the film.*

sing

sings singing sang sung
When you **sing**, you use your voice to make music. *Toby loves **singing** along to the radio.*

single

Single means only one. *There was a **single** rose in the vase.*

sink to skeleton

sink
sinks
A **sink** is something that you wash things in. Sinks have taps and a plug. *Tom is washing the plates in the sink.*

sink
sinks sinking sank sunk
If something **sinks**, it moves downwards, usually under water.

Tim's shoe sank.

sip
sips sipping sipped
When you **sip** a drink, you drink a small amount at a time. *Becky sipped her hot chocolate.*

sister
sisters
Your **sister** is a girl who has the same mum and dad as you.

sit
sits sitting sat
When you **sit**, you rest your bottom on something. *We sat on the steps to wait for Jack.*

size
sizes
The **size** of something is how big or small it is. *What size are your feet?*

skate
skates
Skates are special boots that you wear to move smoothly on ice. Skates have a metal blade fixed to the bottom of them.

ice skate

skate
skates skating skated
When you **skate**, you move along smoothly, wearing ice skates or roller skates.

skateboard
skateboards
A **skateboard** is a narrow board with wheels fixed to the bottom of it. You ride a skateboard by standing on it and pushing off with one foot.

skeleton
skeletons
A **skeleton** is all the bones in the body of a person or an animal.

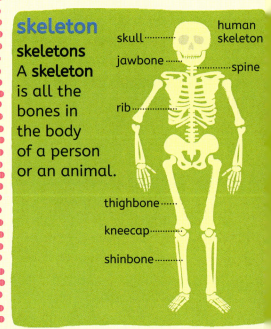

human skeleton — skull, jawbone, spine, rib, thighbone, kneecap, shinbone

sketch

sketches sketching sketched
When you **sketch**, you make a quick drawing. *Lucy **sketched** her brothers while they were eating tea.*

ski

skis
Skis are long, narrow strips of wood, metal or plastic. You fix skis to boots and use them to travel fast over snow.

ski

skis skiing skied
When you **ski**, you travel fast over snow, wearing skis. *Jessica **skied** down the mountain.*

skid

skids skidding skidded
If you **skid**, you slide on slippery ground. *Max **skidded** on the icy pavement.*

skill

skills
If you have a **skill**, you are able to do something well. *Sarah's special **skill** is drawing.*

skin

skins
1 Your body is covered with **skin**. *Babies have very smooth **skin**.*
2 The **skin** of a fruit or a vegetable is its outside layer.

banana skin

skip

skips skipping skipped
1 When you **skip**, you move by hopping first on one foot and then on the other.
2 When you **skip** with a skipping rope, you keep swinging the rope over your head and jumping over it.

skirt

skirts
A **skirt** is a piece of clothing worn by women and girls. Skirts hang from the waist.

skull

skulls
Your **skull** is the bony part of your head. Your brain is inside your skull.

sky

skies
The **sky** is the air that surrounds the Earth. On a sunny day, it is blue.

slam to slide

slam
slams slamming slammed
When you **slam** a door, you shut it with a bang.

slap
slaps slapping slapped
If you **slap** something, you hit it with the palm of your hand.

sledge
sledges
A **sledge** is a small vehicle that you use to ride over snow.

sleep
sleeps sleeping slept
When you **sleep**, you close your eyes and rest your whole body. Most people sleep at night.

sleet
Sleet is icy rain. It looks like wet snow.

sleeve
sleeves
A **sleeve** is the part of a piece of clothing that covers your arm. This shirt has long **sleeves**.

sleigh
sleighs
A **sleigh** is a sledge that is pulled by a horse or a reindeer.

slept
Slept comes from the word **sleep**. *Anna doesn't usually sleep well, but she **slept** for hours last night.*

slice
slices
A **slice** is a piece of food that has been cut from a larger piece. *A **slice** of cake.*

slide
slides
A **slide** is something that you play on in playgrounds. You climb up steps and then slide down.

slide
slides sliding slid
When something **slides**, it moves smoothly over something else. *Leah **slid** the book across the table.*

slimy

slimier slimiest
Something that is **slimy** is slippery and sticky.
Slimy green goo.

slip

slips slipping slipped
If you **slip**, you slide by accident and often fall over.

Jacob slipped on the wet floor.

slipper

slippers
A **slipper** is a soft, comfortable shoe that you wear indoors.

slippery

If something is **slippery**, it is difficult to grip or to walk on.

slope

slopes sloping sloped
If something **slopes**, it is higher at one end than the other. *The lawn slopes down to the gate.*

slot

slots
A **slot** is a small, narrow space that you put something in. *Put a coin in the slot.*

slow

slower slowest
Something that is **slow** takes a long time to go somewhere or to do something. *A slow train.*
■ opposite **fast**

slug

slugs
A **slug** is a slimy little animal with no legs and a soft body.

smack

smacks smacking smacked
If you **smack** someone, you hit them with the palm of your hand.

small

smaller smallest
Something that is **small** is little.
■ opposite **big**

> Some other words for **small** are **little**, **tiny** and **titchy**.

smartphone

smartphones
A **smartphone** is a mobile phone that has apps, and that can use the internet.

smash to snap

smash
smashes smashing smashed
If something **smashes**, it breaks into lots of pieces because it has been dropped or hit. *The cup* **smashed** *when Robert dropped it.*

smell
smells smelling smelt
1 When you **smell** something, you find out about it by using your nose. *Kate* **smelt** *the flowers.*
2 If something **smells**, you notice it by using your nose. *That cake* **smells** *good.*

smile
smiles smiling smiled
When you **smile**, the corners of your mouth turn up. You smile when you are happy or when you think that something is funny.

smoke
Smoke is made when something burns. Smoke usually looks like a white or grey cloud.

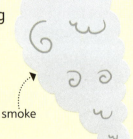
smoke

smooth
smoother smoothest
Something that is **smooth** does not have any bumps or lumps in it. *Smooth skin. A* **smooth** *sauce.*

snack
snacks
A **snack** is a small meal that you can eat quickly. *We had a* **snack** *when we got home from school.*

snail
snails
A **snail** is a small animal with no legs and a soft body. Snails have shells on their backs.

snake
snakes
A **snake** is a long, thin reptile with no legs. Snakes move by sliding their bodies along the ground. Some snakes have poisonous bites.

snap
snaps snapping snapped
When something **snaps**, it breaks with a sudden noise. *The twig* **snapped** *when Tom bent it.*

snatch

snatches snatching snatched
If you **snatch** something, you take it quickly and roughly. *Benjamin **snatched** the letter out of my hands.*

sneeze

sneezes sneezing sneezed
When you **sneeze**, air rushes out of your nose and mouth with a loud noise. You often sneeze when you have a cold.

sniff

sniffs sniffing sniffed
When you **sniff**, you breathe in hard through your nose.

*Jemimah **sniffed** the flower.*

snore

snores snoring snored
If you **snore**, you breathe noisily through your mouth while you are asleep.

snow

snows snowing snowed
When it **snows**, soft, white pieces of ice, called snowflakes, fall from the sky.

soak

soaks soaking soaked
When water **soaks** into something, it makes it very wet. *The rain has **soaked** my trousers.*

soap

soaps
You mix **soap** with water to wash and clean things.

sock

socks
Socks are clothes that you wear on your feet, inside your shoes.

*A pair of **socks**.*

sofa

sofas
A **sofa** is a long, comfortable seat for two or more people.

soft

softer softest
1 If something is **soft**, it is not hard or firm. Soft things change shape easily. *A **soft** pillow.*
▪ opposite **hard**
2 **Soft** also means quiet and gentle. *A **soft** voice.*

soil

Soil is the ground that plants grow in.

sold

Sold comes from the word **sell**. *Jasmine decided to sell her books. She had soon **sold** them all.*

soldier

soldiers

A **soldier** is a member of an army.

solid

Something that is **solid** does not change shape easily. Wood and metal are solid.

some

Some means an amount. *We had **some** soup for lunch.*

somebody

Somebody means a person. *Can **somebody** help me, please?*

someone

Someone means a person. *I saw **someone** that looked like you.*

somersault

somersaults

When you do a **somersault**, you roll over forwards so that your feet go over your head. You can do somersaults on the ground or in the air.

something

Something means a thing. *I want to show you **something** amazing.*

sometimes

Sometimes means at some times. *We **sometimes** hear the dog next door howling.*

somewhere

Somewhere means a place. *I put my book down **somewhere**.*

son

sons

A **son** is someone's male child.

song

songs

A **song** is a piece of music with words that you sing.

soon

sooner soonest

If something will happen **soon**, it will begin in a short time. *It will **soon** be bedtime.*

sore

sorer sorest

If part of your body is **sore**, it hurts. *A **sore** knee.*

sorry

1 If you feel **sorry** about something, you feel sad about it. *I am **sorry** that you are not well.*
2 You say **sorry** when you are upset that you have done something wrong.

sort

sorts

Things of the same **sort** belong to the same group. *What **sort** of dog do you like best?*

sound

sounds

A **sound** is something that you hear. *Bees make a buzzing **sound**.*

soup

soups

Soup is a liquid food that you usually eat hot. Soup is made from meat or vegetables and water.

sour

If something is **sour**, it has a taste like lemons or vinegar. *These apples are really **sour**!*

south

South is a direction. If you face the Sun when it rises, south is on your right.

■ opposite **north**

sow

sows sowing sowed sown

▲ *rhymes with* **low**

When you **sow** seeds, you put them in soil so that they can grow.

space

spaces

1   A **space** is an empty place or area. *We found a **space** to park the car.*
2   **Space** is the area outside the Earth. The stars and planets are in space.

spacecraft

spacecraft

A **spacecraft** is a vehicle that travels into space. Spacecraft carry astronauts and their equipment.

spade

spades

A **spade** is a tool that you use to dig. A spade has a long handle and a flat metal end.

spare

Spare means left over. *What do you do in your **spare** time?*

speak

speaks speaking spoke spoken
When you **speak**, you use your voice to make words. *Henry **speaks** loudly.*

special

1 If something is **special**, it is important or better than usual. *A **special** meal.*
2 Something that is **special** is made to do a particular job. *You need to take **special** equipment when you go camping.*

speed

The **speed** of something is how fast it moves. *Cheetahs run at an amazing **speed**.*

spell

spells spelling spelt
When you **spell** a word, you write or say its letters in the right order. *Can you **spell** my name?*

spend

spends spending spent
1 When you **spend** money, you use it to buy things. *Izzy **spent** all her pocket money on sweets.*
2 If you **spend** time doing something, you use that time to do it. *I **spent** half an hour practising the piano.*

spider

spiders
A **spider** is an animal with eight legs. Spiders make webs to catch insects.

spike

spikes
A **spike** is a sharp point.

spill

spills spilling spilt
If you **spill** a liquid, you let it fall out of its container by accident. *Joel has **spilt** the milk.*

spin

spins spinning spun
When something **spins**, it keeps turning round quickly. *Eleanor started **spinning** the top as fast as she could.*

splash

splashes splashing splashed
When someone **splashes**, they throw water around. *Sarah **splashed** in the waves.*

split

splits splitting split
If something **splits**, it tears or comes apart. *Ryan's shirt has **split** down the side.*

spoil

spoils spoiling spoilt
If you **spoil** something, you damage it or make it worse. *Amy **spoilt** the soup by adding too much salt.*

spoilt

Spoilt children have too many things and are allowed to do what they like too often.

spoke

Spoke comes from the word **speak**. *Aidan usually speaks very quietly, but he **spoke** loudly to the class.*

sponge

sponges
Sponge is a soft material with lots of holes in it. Sponges can soak up water and are used for cleaning and for washing yourself.

spoon

spoons
You use a **spoon** to stir things and to eat with. Spoons have a handle and a rounded end for holding food.

sport

sports
A **sport** is a kind of game that you do to exercise. Football and tennis are sports.

spot

spots
1 A **spot** is a round mark or shape. *Lara's dress has yellow **spots** on it.*
2 A **spot** is also a small lump on your skin.

spot

spots spotting spotted
If you **spot** something, you notice it with your eyes. *Jack **spotted** some toadstools in the wood.*

spout

spouts
A **spout** is a kind of tube on a kettle or a teapot. You pour liquid out of a spout.

spray

Spray is lots of tiny drops of water or another liquid. *The waves crashed against the rocks and covered us in **spray**.*

spread

spreads spreading spread
1 If you **spread** something **out**, you lay or stretch it out over a surface. *Nella **spread** the map **out** on the table.*
2 If you **spread** something soft, you put a layer of it on something else. ***Spread** some butter on your bread.*
3 When you **spread** some news, you tell lots of people about it.

spring

springs
1 A **spring** is a piece of wire that is wound into circles. Springs jump back into shape when you press them.
2 **Spring** is also one of the four seasons. It comes between winter and summer. In the spring, the weather gets warmer and plants begin to grow.

spun

Spun comes from the word **spin**. *The skater began to spin around. She **spun** seven times.*

spy

spies
A **spy** is someone who secretly watches other people to get information.

square

squares
A **square** is a shape with four corners, and four sides of equal length.

squash

squashes squashing squashed
If you **squash** something, you press it and make it flatter. *Nat stood on a tomato and **squashed** it.*

squeal

squeals squealing squealed
When you **squeal**, you make a long, high sound because you are excited or frightened.

squeeze

squeezes squeezing squeezed
When you **squeeze** something, you press its sides together. *Malik **squeezed** the toothpaste tube.*

squirrel

squirrels
A **squirrel** is a small animal with a big, furry tail. Squirrels live in trees and are very good at climbing.

stable

stables
A **stable** is a building where horses are kept.

stack

stacks stacking stacked
If you **stack** things, you put them one on top of another. *Oliver stacked his comics on the table.*

stage

stages
A **stage** is an area in a theatre or a hall where plays and concerts are performed.

stain

stains
A **stain** is a mark that is hard to remove.

stairs

Stairs are a set of steps that you use to walk up and down, usually inside a building.

stalk

stalks
A **stalk** is the long, central part of a plant. Leaves, flowers and fruit grow from the stalk. Stalk is another word for **stem**.

stamp

stamps
A **stamp** is a small piece of paper with a picture printed on it. You stick stamps on letters and parcels to show that you have paid to post them.

stamp

stamps stamping stamped
If you **stamp** your foot, you put it down hard on the ground.

stand

stands standing stood
When you **stand**, you are on your feet and upright. *Stand up straight!*

stank

Stank comes from the word **stink**. *My brother's feet stink. After his run, they stank even more than usual.*

star

stars
1 A **star** is a huge ball of burning gases in space. At night, stars look like tiny points of light in the sky.
2 A **star** is also a shape with points.
3 A **star** is also a famous person, such as an actor or a singer.

stare to steel

stare
stares staring stared
If you **stare** at something, you look at it for a long time with your eyes wide open.

start
starts starting started
When you **start** to do something, you do the first part of it. *Maria started to tidy her room.*

starve
starves starving starved
If someone **starves**, they become very ill or die because they do not have enough to eat.

station
stations
1 A **station** is a place where trains stop.
2 A **station** is also a building where police or firefighters work.
3 A **station** is also a company that provides television or radio programmes.

statue
statues
A **statue** is a large model of a person or an animal. Statues are made from stone, metal or some other hard material.

Statue of Liberty

stay
stays staying stayed
1 If you **stay** in a place, you do not leave it. *We stayed at home all day.*
2 If you **stay** with someone, you live with them for a short time. *We are staying with my uncle for a week.*

steady
steadier steadiest
If something is **steady**, it does not move about or shake. *You need a steady hand to hold the camera still.*

steal
steals stealing stole stolen
People who **steal** take things that do not belong to them.

steam
Steam is water that has boiled and turned into a cloud of tiny water drops.

steel
Steel is a hard, strong metal that is made mostly from iron.

steep

steeper steepest
Something that is **steep** slopes a lot.

Natalie climbed the steep hill.

steer

steers steering steered
When you **steer** a bicycle or a car, you make it go in the direction you want.

stem

stems
A **stem** is the long, central part of a plant.

stem

step

steps
1 When you take a **step**, you move your foot forward and then put it down.
2 A **step** is a flat surface that you put your foot on when you climb up or down. *There are three steps outside our front door.*

stick

sticks
A **stick** is a long, thin piece of wood.

stick

sticks sticking stuck
1 If you **stick** two things together, you use glue to join them.
2 If you **stick** a pin or a needle into something, you push it in. *Susannah stuck a needle into her finger by accident.*

sticker

stickers
A **sticker** is a sticky piece of paper with pictures or writing on it. *Lucy has stuck animal stickers all over her bedroom door.*

sticky

stickier stickiest
If something is **sticky**, it sticks to things.

stiff

stiffer stiffest
Something that is **stiff** is hard to bend or move. *The handle was stiff. Stiff cardboard.*

stile to stool

stile
stiles
A **stile** is a kind of step that you use to climb over a wall or a fence. Stiles are made of wood or stone.

still
1 Something that is **still** is not moving. *Everything was **still** and silent.*
2 If something is **still** happening, it has not stopped. *Maggie was **still** asleep when Lisa arrived.*

sting
stings stinging stung
If an insect **stings** you, it pricks your skin and leaves some poison in your body.

stink
stinks stinking stank stunk
If something **stinks**, it smells horrible. *This cheese **stinks**!*

stir
stirs stirring stirred
If you **stir** a liquid or a mixture, you move it around with a spoon or a stick. *Louie **stirred** all the ingredients together in a bowl.*

stitch
stitches
A **stitch** is a loop of thread on a piece of cloth. You use a needle and thread to make stitches.

stole
Stole comes from the word **steal**. *Mum told us never to steal. Dan **stole** a pencil and she was cross.*

stomach
stomachs
▲ say **stum**-uck
Your **stomach** is the part of your body where your food goes after you have eaten it.

stone
stones
1 **Stone** is very hard and is found under the ground. Stone is used for building.
2 A **stone** is a small piece of rock that you find on the ground.
3 A **stone** is also the hard seed in the middle of fruits such as plums or peaches.

stood
Stood comes from the word **stand**. *We had to stand in a queue for the cinema. We **stood** there for half an hour.*

stool
stools
A **stool** is a seat without a back.

stop

stops stopping stopped
1 If something **stops**, it no longer happens. *It has stopped snowing.*
2 When something **stops**, it no longer moves. *The bus stopped.*

store

stores storing stored
When you **store** things, you put them away until you need them. *James stores his toys in a chest.*

storm

storms
When there is a **storm**, it rains hard and the wind blows very strongly. Sometimes there is also thunder and lightning.

story

stories
A **story** tells you about something that has happened. Stories can be true or made up.

straight

straighter straightest
Something that is **straight** does not bend or curve. *Use a ruler to draw a straight line.*
■ **opposite** bent

strange

stranger strangest
Strange things are unusual, or are different from what you expect. *A strange dream.*

stranger

strangers
A **stranger** is someone you do not know.

strap

straps
A **strap** is a strip of leather or other material. Straps are often used to hold things together.

straw

straws
1 **Straw** is the name for dry stalks of plants, such as corn and wheat. Farm animals often sleep on straw.
2 A **straw** is a thin plastic tube that you use to suck drink into your mouth.

strawberry

strawberries
A **strawberry** is a soft, red fruit with tiny, yellow seeds on its skin.

stream

streams
A **stream** is a small river.

street to stripe

street

streets

A **street** is a road. Streets usually have buildings on both sides.

strength

The **strength** of something is how strong it is.

stretch

stretches stretching stretched

1 If you **stretch** something, you make it longer or bigger. *Simon stretched the rubber band until it snapped.*
2 When you **stretch**, you push your arms up or out as far as they will go.

Miriam stretched up high.

stretcher

stretchers

A **stretcher** is a narrow bed that is used to carry someone who is hurt or ill.

strict

stricter strictest

A **strict** person makes you behave and do what you are told. *Our teacher is very strict.*

strike

strikes striking struck

1 If you **strike** something, you hit it.
2 When you **strike** a match, you light it.
3 When a clock **strikes**, it makes a sound to tell you what time it is. *The clock strikes every hour.*

string

strings

1 **String** is thin rope. People use string to tie things together.
2 Some musical instruments have **strings**. You pluck the strings or rub them with a bow to make notes.

harp strings

strip

strips

A **strip** is a narrow piece of something, like paper or material.

stripe

stripes

A **stripe** is a line of colour. *Ali's shirt has red and white stripes on it.*

stroke

strokes stroking stroked
When you **stroke** an animal, you move your hand over it gently. *Rachel stroked the cat.*

strong

stronger strongest
1 A **strong** person can lift heavy things and has a lot of energy. *Keith is very strong.*
2 Something **strong** does not break easily. *A strong box.*
■ opposite **weak**

struck

Struck comes from the word **strike**. *Our clock strikes every hour. It has just struck seven.*

struggle

struggles struggling struggled
If you **struggle**, you find something difficult to do. *Bill is struggling with his homework.*

stuck

Stuck comes from the word **stick**. If you are **stuck**, you can't move or carry on. *The cat got stuck in the hole. My dad helped me with my homework because I was stuck.*

student

students
A **student** is someone who is learning something, usually at school or college.

study

studies studying studied
When you **study** something, you learn about it.

stuff

Stuff means things or possessions. *There's so much stuff to do. Lily took all my stuff.*

stuff

stuffs stuffing stuffed
If you **stuff** something into a bag, you push it in roughly.

stung

Stung comes from the word **sting**. *Chloe is scared that the bee might sting her. She has been stung twice before.*

stupid

stupider stupidest
If you are being **stupid**, you do silly things and are not sensible.

subject

subjects
A **subject** is something that you learn about. Science and art are subjects.

submarine to sum

submarine
submarines
A **submarine** is a ship that can travel under water.

subtract
subtracts subtracting subtracted
When you **subtract**, you take one number away from another. Hannah **subtracted** seven from twelve.

■ *opposite* **add**

successful
Someone who is **successful** has done well at something. A **successful** writer.

suck
sucks sucking sucked
1 When you **suck**, you pull in liquid through your mouth. Alice **sucked** her juice through a straw.
2 If you **suck** a sweet, you roll it around in your mouth without chewing it.

sudden
Something **sudden** happens very quickly and is not expected. We heard a **sudden** shout.

sugar
You put **sugar** in food or drink to make it taste sweet. Sugar grains are white or brown.

suggest
suggests suggesting suggested
If you **suggest** something, you give someone an idea that might help them. Holly **suggested** that we should try the other path.

suit
suits
A **suit** is a set of clothes that are meant to be worn together. Suits are made up of a jacket and trousers or a jacket and a skirt.

suitable
Something that is **suitable** is right for a particular job. Wear **suitable** clothes for painting.

suitcase
suitcases
You use a **suitcase** to carry your clothes when you travel.

sum
sums
A **sum** is a maths question. I have some **sums** for homework.

208

summer

Summer is one of the four seasons. It comes between spring and autumn. Summer is the warmest season.

Sun

The **Sun** is the very big, bright light that you see in the sky in the daytime. It gives us heat and light. The Earth takes a year to go round the Sun.

sunflower

sunflowers
A **sunflower** is a very tall flower with a large centre and yellow petals.

*Giant **sunflowers** are taller than grown-ups.*

sung

Sung comes from the word **sing**. *Maria loves to sing. She has **sung** in several concerts.*

sunk

Sunk comes from the word **sink**. *Some things float and others sink. The stone has **sunk** to the bottom of the bucket.*

sunlight

Sunlight is the light that comes from the Sun. Most plants need sunlight to grow.

sunny

sunnier
sunniest
When it is **sunny**, the Sun is shining.

sunshine

Sunshine is the light and warmth that comes from the Sun. *Go out and play in the **sunshine**!*

supermarket

supermarkets
A **supermarket** is a large shop that sells food and other things that you need at home.

supper

suppers
Supper is a meal or a snack that you eat in the evening.

support

supports supporting supported
1 If you **support** something, you hold it so that it does not fall. *Support the baby's head when you hold her.*
2 When you **support** people, you help them. *We **supported** Carly when she got into trouble.*
3 When you **support** a team, you want them to win.

suppose

supposes supposing supposed
1 If you **suppose** something will happen, you expect that it will. *I **suppose** Justin will be late.*
2 If you are **supposed to** do something, you are meant to do it. *I'm **supposed to** make my bed every morning.*

sure

▲ say **shore**
If you are **sure** about something, you know that it is right. *Alistair was **sure** that he had seen the film before.*

surface

surfaces
A **surface** is the outer part, or top of something. *The **surface** of the table is very scratched.*

surname

surnames
Your **surname** is your last name or your family name.

surprise

surprises
A **surprise** is something that you do not expect. *The party was a **surprise**.*

surround

surrounds surrounding surrounded
If something **surrounds** you, it is all around you. *The juggler was **surrounded** by a crowd.*

swallow

swallows swallowing swallowed
When you **swallow** food, it goes down your throat into your stomach.

swam

Swam comes from the word **swim**. *Katherine tries to swim as often as she can. She **swam** every day last week.*

swan

swans
A **swan** is a large, white bird with a long neck. Swans swim on rivers and lakes.

swap

swaps swapping swapped
▲ rhymes with **top**
If you **swap** with someone, you give them something of yours and they give you something of theirs. *Jack and Jill **swapped** comics.*

sway

sways swaying swayed
If you **sway**, you move slowly from side to side. *Tamsin **swayed** to the music.*

swear

swears swearing swore sworn
1 If you **swear**, you use rude words.
2 If you **swear** to do something, you promise to do it. *Leo made Rick swear to keep silent.*

sweat

sweats sweating sweated
When you **sweat**, water comes out of tiny holes in your skin. You sweat when you are hot or nervous.

sweater

sweaters
A **sweater** is a knitted piece of clothing that covers the top part of your body. Sweaters are often made from wool and are worn over other clothes.

sweet

sweets
A **sweet** is a small type of food that tastes sweet. *James has chosen all his favourite sweets.*

sweet

sweeter sweetest
1 Food that is **sweet** tastes as though it has sugar in it.
2 If something is **sweet**, it is lovely. *A sweet kitten.*
3 If someone is **sweet**, they are kind. *It was sweet of Emily to give me a present.*

swim

swims swimming swam swum
When you **swim**, you move through water using your arms and legs.

Milo swims every day.

swing

swings
A **swing** is a seat that hangs from ropes or chains. You sit on a swing and make it move backwards and forwards. *We have a swing hanging from our apple tree.*

swing

swings swinging swung
If something **swings**, it moves backwards and forwards while hanging from something.

switch

switches
You turn or press a **switch** to make something electrical start or stop. *A light switch.*

swollen to tail

swollen
Something that is **swollen** is larger than usual. *Pete has a **swollen** ankle.*

sword
swords
▲ say **sord**
A **sword** is a weapon with a handle and a long, sharp blade. In the past, soldiers fought with swords. *A toy **sword**.*

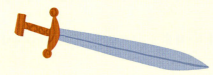

swore
Swore comes from the word **swear**. *Sam made me swear to keep his secret. I **swore** not to tell anyone.*

swum
Swum comes from the word **swim**. *I always swim on holiday. I have **swum** every day so far.*

swung
Swung comes from the word **swing**. *Elsa started to swing from the tree. She **swung** higher and higher each time.*

syrup
Syrup is a thick, sweet liquid that is made from sugar. *Paul bought some **syrup** to make flapjacks.*

table
tables
A **table** is a piece of furniture with legs and a flat top.

tablet
tablets
1 A **tablet** is a small, dry piece of medicine. People swallow tablets when they are ill to make them feel better again.
2 A **tablet** is also a small, light computer with a touch screen.

tadpole
tadpoles
A **tadpole** is a small creature that will grow into a frog or a toad. Tadpoles hatch from eggs and live in water.

tail
tails
A **tail** is the part at the end of an animal's body.

take

takes taking took taken
1 **Take** means to remove something or steal something. *Keith has **taken** my pen.*
2 **Take** also means to bring something with you. *Don't forget to **take** your umbrella.*
3 If something **takes** an amount of time, that is how long it goes on for. *The journey **took** an hour.*

takeaway

takeaways
A **takeaway** is a meal that you buy and take away to eat somewhere else.

tale

tales
A **tale** is a story. *A fairy **tale**.*

talent

talents
If you have a **talent** for something, you can do it very well. *Craig has a **talent** for drawing.*

talk

talks talking talked
When you **talk**, you speak to people.

tall

taller tallest
If something is **tall**, the top of it is high above the ground. *A **tall** tower.*
■ opposite **short**

tame

tamer tamest
A **tame** animal is not wild and will not hurt people. Tame animals can be kept as pets.
■ opposite **wild**

tangerine

tangerines
A **tangerine** is a small, sweet orange that you can peel easily.

tangle

tangles
A **tangle** is a bunch of knots that has been made by accident.

*The wool is full of **tangles**.*

tank

tanks
1 A **tank** is a large container for liquids. *A water **tank**.*
2 A **tank** is also a large, heavy vehicle with a gun. Tanks are used by soldiers.

tap

taps
A **tap** is something that you turn to make water run or stop. Sinks and baths have taps.

tap to teabag

tap
taps tapping tapped
If you **tap** something, you hit it gently. *Jonathan tapped the table with his fingers.*

tape
Tape is a long, thin strip of paper, cloth or plastic. *Sticky tape.*

tape measure
tape measures
A **tape measure** is a long, thin strip, marked with centimetres or inches. You use a tape measure to measure things.

target
targets
A **target** is something that people aim at. *Robin aimed his arrow at the centre of the target.*

tart
tarts
A **tart** is a pie with no pastry on top. *A strawberry tart.*

taste
tastes tasting tasted
When you **taste** food or drink, you put it in your mouth to find out what it is like. *Leo tasted the soup to see if he liked it.*

tasty
tastier tastiest
Food that is **tasty** has a lovely flavour. *A tasty pie.*

taught
Taught comes from the word **teach**. *My dad teaches people to swim. He taught me when I was small.*

taxi
taxis
A **taxi** is a car that you pay to ride in. *We took a taxi to the station.*

tea

teas
1 **Tea** is a drink. People make tea by pouring boiling water onto the chopped, dried leaves of the tea plant.
2 **Tea** is a meal that you eat in the afternoon or the early evening.

teabag
teabags
A **teabag** is a small bag of chopped, dried leaves from the tea plant. People pour boiling water onto teabags to make tea.

teach

teaches teaching taught
When people **teach** you something, they help you to understand it, or they show you how to do it. *Monica is **teaching** me how to play the piano.*

teacher

teachers
A **teacher** is someone whose job is to teach other people. Teachers usually work in schools. *Mrs Parsnip is our class **teacher**.*

team

teams
A **team** is a group of people who work together or play a sport together. *Alex plays in the school football **team**.*

teapot

teapots
A **teapot** is a container that people use to make and pour tea. A teapot has a handle, a lid and a spout.

tear

tears
▲ rhymes with **deer**
Tears are drops of water that come from your eyes when you cry. ***Tears** poured down her face.*

tear

tear tearing tore torn
▲ rhymes with **bare**
When you **tear** something, you pull one part of it away from the rest. *Fraser **tore** his shirt on a nail.*

tease

teases teasing teased
If you **tease** someone, you make jokes about them, either in a playful way, or in a cruel way.

teddy bear

teddy bears
A **teddy bear** is a soft, furry toy that looks like a bear.

teenager

teenagers
A **teenager** is someone who is between 13 and 19 years old.

telephone

telephones
A **telephone** is a machine that you use to speak to someone in another place.

telescope to test

telescope
telescopes
A **telescope** makes things that are far away look larger and closer. People use telescopes to look at the stars.

television
televisions
A **television** is a machine that shows pictures and sends out sounds. Televisions receive signals through the air and turn them into pictures and sounds. TV is short for television.

tell
tells telling told
1 If you **tell** someone something, you let them know about it. *Laura **told** me about her holiday.*
2 When someone **tells** you **to** do something, they say that you must do it. *Mum **told** me **to** go to bed.*
3 If you **can tell** something, you know it without being told. *I **can tell** that Sam is sad.*

temperature
temperatures
The **temperature** of something is how hot or cold it is.

tennis
Tennis is a game played by two or four players with rackets and a ball. The players hit the ball to each other over a net.

tent
tents
A **tent** is a shelter made of strong material and held up by poles and ropes. You sleep in a tent when you go camping.

term
terms
A **term** is one part of the school year. There are usually three terms in a year.

terrible
If something is **terrible**, it is very bad. *A **terrible** film.*

test
tests
You take a **test** to show how much you know about something. *A maths **test**.*

test

tests testing tested
When you **test** something, you try it to see if it works properly. *Ella **tested** the new recipe.*

text

texts
A **text** is a message that you can send from one mobile phone to another.

thank

thanks thanking thanked
When you **thank** someone, you tell them you are pleased about something they have done. *I **thanked** Jay for helping me.*

that's

1 **That's** is a short way of saying **that is**. *Evie, **that's** a lovely dress.*
2 **That's** is also a short way of saying **that has**. ***That's** been bothering me all day.*

theatre

theatres
A **theatre** is a building where you go to see plays or shows.

their

Their means belonging to them. *Do all the children have **their** tickets with them?*

them

You use **them** to mean more than one person or thing. *I baked two cakes yesterday. Today I will decorate **them**.*

themselves

Themselves means them and no one else. *The children dressed **themselves**.*

then

1 **Then** means afterwards. *Eat your tea, **then** you can go out.*
2 **Then** also means at that time. *I did this painting last year. I wasn't as good **then** as I am now.*

there

1 **There** means to or at that place. *Have you been **there** before? Put them down **there**.*
■ opposite **here**
2 You also use the word **there** to make someone notice something. ***There** is a cat in the tree.*

there's

1 **There's** is a short way of saying **there is**. *There's lots of food left.*
2 **There's** is also a short way of saying **there has**. *There's been an accident.*

thermometer

thermometers
You use a **thermometer** to find out how hot or cold something is. *We hung a **thermometer** in the garden and looked at it every day.*

they

You use the word **they** when you talk about more than one person. *Rosa and Robin are best friends. **They** go everywhere together.*

they'd

1 **They'd** is a short way of saying **they had**. *The boys were late because **they'd** lost their way.*
2 **They'd** is also a short way of saying **they would**. *The girls promised **they'd** return.*

they'll

They'll is a short way of saying **they will**. *The boys have said that **they'll** be here soon.*

they're

They're is a short way of saying **they are**. *The girls are very excited because **they're** going on holiday.*

they've

They've is a short way of saying **they have**. *The Robinsons are away. **They've** gone on holiday for a week.*

thick

thicker thickest
1 If something is **thick**, it is deep or wide. *A **thick** book.*
2 A **thick** liquid does not pour easily.
■ opposite **thin**

*Lydia loves **thick** syrup.*

thief

thieves
Thieves take things that do not belong to them.

thigh

thighs
Your **thigh** is the part of your leg between your knee and your hip.

thin

thinner thinnest
1 If something is **thin**, it is narrow. *A **thin** belt.*
■ opposite **thick**
2 **Thin** people are not fat and do not weigh very much.
■ opposite **fat**

thing

things
A **thing** is an object or an action. *Take your **things** off the table. There are lots of **things** to do.*

think

thinks thinking thought
1 When you **think**, you use your mind. *Try to **think** of the answer.*
2 If you **think** something, you believe it. *My brother **thinks** that hats are in fashion.*

thirsty

thirstier thirstiest
When you are **thirsty**, you want to drink something.

thorn

thorns
A **thorn** is a sharp point on the stem of a flower or a bush.

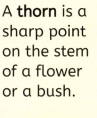

thorn

thought

thoughts
A **thought** is something that you think. *Megan's mind was full of happy **thoughts**.*

thought

Thought comes from the word **think**. *We tried to think of things to do. We **thought** very hard.*

thread

threads
A **thread** is a long, thin length of cotton or wool. Thread is used for making cloth or for sewing.

thread

threads threading threaded
When you **thread** a needle, you pass a thread through the hole in its end.

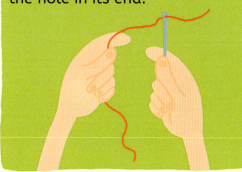

threw

Threw comes from the word **throw**. *Throw the ball to me. Last time you **threw** it to Sarah.*

throat

throats
1 Your **throat** is the front part of your neck.
2 Your **throat** is also the part inside your body that you use to swallow.

throne

thrones
A **throne** is a special chair for a king or a queen.

The queen sat on her golden throne.

through

When something goes **through**, it goes in one side and out the other. *We wandered through the woods.*

throw

throws throwing threw thrown
When you **throw** something, you use your hand to send it through the air. *Tilly has thrown a stick for Fido.*

thumb

thumbs
Your **thumb** is the short, thick finger on the side of each hand.

thunder

Thunder is a loud, low sound that you sometimes hear when there is a storm.

tick

ticks
1 A **tick** is a sign that shows that something is correct.
2 A **tick** is also the sound that a clock or a watch makes.

ticket

tickets
A **ticket** is a small piece of paper or card that shows that you have paid for something. *A bus ticket.*

tickle

tickles tickling tickled
If you **tickle** someone, you keep touching them with your fingers to make them laugh.

tidy

tidier tidiest
A **tidy** room is neat, with everything in its proper place.

tie

ties
1 A **tie** is a long strip of material that you wear knotted round your neck.
2 If a game is a **tie**, it is a draw.

tie
ties tying tied
Tie means to hold things together by putting string, rope or ribbon around them, joined with a knot. *Jill **tied** a ribbon round the parcel. Dan **tied** the boat to the post.*

tiger
tigers
A **tiger** is a very large wild cat. Tigers have orange fur with black stripes.

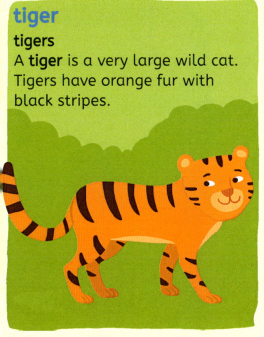

tight
tighter tightest
1 Something that is **tight** is fastened firmly. *A **tight** knot.*
2 Clothes that are **tight** fit closely to your body. ***Tight** trousers.*
■ opposite **loose**

tights
Tights cover your bottom, legs and feet. They are made out of stretchy material and fit very closely.

time
times
1 **Time** is how long something takes to happen. Time is measured in seconds, minutes and hours. *It took a long **time** to walk home.*
2 The **time** is a particular moment, shown on a clock or a watch. *What **time** is it now?*

timid
Someone who is **timid** is shy and easily frightened.

tin
tins
1 **Tin** is a silver-coloured metal.
2 A **tin** is a small metal container. *A **tin** of beans.*

tiny
tinier tiniest
Something that is **tiny** is very small. *A **tiny** insect.*

tip
tips
1 The **tip** of something is the end of it. *The **tip** of a pen.*
2 A **tip** is also somewhere that you take your rubbish.

tip
tips tipping tipped
When you **tip** something, you turn it over. *Henry **tipped** a bucket of water over Harriet's head.*

tiptoe to together

tiptoe
tiptoes tiptoeing tiptoed
When you **tiptoe**, you walk very quietly without putting your heels down. *Stephen **tiptoed** across the hall.*

tired
When you are **tired**, you want to rest or sleep.

tissue
tissues
A **tissue** is a piece of soft, thin paper that you use to wipe your nose.

title
titles
A **title** is the name by which something is known, such as a book, film or television programme.

toad
toads
A **toad** is a small creature similar to a frog. Toads have rough, dry skin and live on land.

toadstool
toadstools
A **toadstool** is a poisonous plant-like thing with a rounded top on a stalk.

toast
Toast is bread that has been heated until it turns brown.

today
Today is the day that is happening now. *I'm going to a birthday party **today**.*

toddler
toddlers
A **toddler** is a young child who has just begun to walk.

toe
toes
Your **toes** are the parts at the ends of your feet. You have five toes on each foot.

toffee
toffees
A **toffee** is a chewy sweet that is made from butter and sugar.

together
If people do something **together**, they do it with each other. *Zara and Luke played a game **together**.*

toilet

toilets

A **toilet** is a bowl with a seat. When you go to the toilet, you get rid of waste food and liquid from your body and they are washed away with water.

told

Told comes from the word **tell**. *Can you tell Skye to come inside? I've already told her twice.*

tomato

tomatoes

A **tomato** is a soft, juicy fruit with a red skin. You use tomatoes to make salads.

tomorrow

Tomorrow is the day after today. *We're going to the beach tomorrow.*

tongue

tongues

▲ *say tung*

Your **tongue** is the long, soft part inside your mouth. You use your tongue to taste, eat and talk.

tongue

tongue-twister

tongue-twisters

A **tongue-twister** is a sentence that is very hard to say quickly.

The big black bug bit the big black bear, but the big black bear bit the big black bug back!

tonight

Tonight is the evening or night of this day. *We're staying in tonight.*

too

1 **Too** means also. *Is Ed here, too?*
2 **Too** also means more than enough. *That's too sweet for me.*

took

Took comes from the word **take**. *Mum said we could take a biscuit. Liam took four!*

tool

tools

A **tool** is something that you use to do a job.

tooth

teeth

1 A **tooth** is one of the hard, white things inside your mouth. You use your teeth to bite and chew food.
2 A **tooth** is also one of a row of thin parts on a comb, a saw, a zip or a rake.

toothbrush

toothbrushes
A **toothbrush** is a small brush with a long handle. You use a toothbrush to clean your teeth.

toothpaste

Toothpaste is a thick paste that you use to clean your teeth.

top

tops
1 The **top** is the highest point of something. *Carlos climbed to the top of the mountain.*
▪ opposite **bottom**
2 The **top** of an object is also a kind of lid that fits over its end.
3 A **top** is also an item of clothing that covers the top part of your body.

topic

topics
A **topic** is the name of something that you study. Children work on topics at school. *This term, our topic is weather.*

torch

torches
A **torch** is a small lamp that you can carry around with you. Torches run on batteries.

tore

Tore comes from the word **tear**. *Patrick must try not to tear his trousers. He tore his last pair when he went exploring.*

tortoise

tortoises
A **tortoise** is an animal with thick, scaly skin and a shell on its back. Tortoises move very slowly.

toss

tosses tossing tossed
If you **toss** something, you throw it into the air. *Aimee tossed the pancake and caught it in the pan.*

total

totals
The **total** of a sum is its answer or its result. *Four is the total of two plus two.*

touch

touches touching touched
If you **touch** something, you put part of your body against it.

touch screen

touch screens
A **touch screen** is a screen on a computer or smartphone that you control by touching it instead of pressing buttons.

tough

tougher toughest
▲ rhymes with **stuff**
1 Something that is **tough** is hard to break or damage. *You'll need tough boots for this climb.*
2 Someone who is **tough** is strong and is not afraid of getting hurt.

tow

tows towing towed
When one vehicle **tows** another, it pulls it along. *The truck towed our car away.*

towards

Towards means in the direction of something. *Abigail ran towards the castle.*

towel

towels
A **towel** is a thick, soft piece of cloth that you use to dry your body.

tower

towers
A **tower** is a tall, narrow building or part of a building.

town

towns
A **town** is a place where many people live and work. Towns have houses, offices, schools and shops. Towns are smaller than cities.

toy

toys
A **toy** is something that you play with.

trace

traces tracing traced
When you **trace** a picture, you put a thin piece of paper over it and draw over its outline.

track

tracks
1 A **track** is a path.
2 **Tracks** are marks left by the feet of a person or an animal. *We followed the fox's tracks into the wood.*

tractor

tractors
A **tractor** is a strong vehicle with very large back wheels. Tractors are used on farms to pull machinery or heavy loads.

traffic to travel

traffic

Traffic is the name for all the vehicles travelling on the roads at the same time. *There's a lot of **traffic** in the centre of town.*

traffic lights

Traffic lights are a set of lights that show traffic when to stop and go. Traffic lights are red, yellow and green.

train

trains
A **train** is a vehicle that travels along a railway track.

trainer

trainers
Trainers are soft shoes with rubber bottoms. People often wear them to play sports.

tram

trams
A **tram** is a kind of bus that travels on rails in the road.

trampoline

trampolines
A **trampoline** is a large piece of strong material attached to a frame with springs. You jump up and down on a trampoline.

transparent

If something is **transparent**, it is clear and you can see through it. Glass and water are transparent.

transport

Transport is the name for all the kinds of vehicles that take people or things from one place to another. *What kind of **transport** do you use to travel to school?*

trap

traps trapping trapped
If you **trap** something, you catch it and stop it from escaping.

travel

travels travelling travelled
When you **travel**, you go from one place to another. *We **travel** to school by car.*

tray

trays
A **tray** is a flat piece of wood, metal or plastic that you use to carry food and drink.

tread

treads treading trod trodden
When you **tread**, you put your foot down on something. *Don't **tread** on the flowers!*

treasure

Treasure is a name for valuable things, such as gold and jewels. *The pirates buried a chest full of **treasure**.*

treat

treats
A **treat** is a special present or a trip to somewhere nice. *Mum took us to the cinema as a **treat**.*

treat

treats treating treated
1 The way you **treat** someone is the way you behave towards them. *Darvesh **treats** his little sister very well.*
2 When doctors **treat** people who are ill, they try to make them better.

tree

trees
A **tree** is a very large plant with leaves, branches and a trunk.

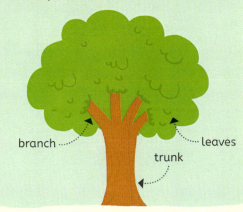

branch · · · · · · · · · · · · leaves
trunk

triangle

triangles
1 A **triangle** is a shape with three straight sides.
2 A **triangle** is also a musical instrument that is made of metal and shaped like a triangle. You play a triangle by hitting it with a metal stick.

trick

tricks
1 If you do a **trick**, you do something clever and surprising.
2 If you **play a trick** on someone, you make them believe something that is not true.

tricycle

tricycles
A **tricycle** is like a bicycle, but has two wheels at the back and one at the front.

tried

Tried comes from the word **try**. *Lewis will try to move the box. He has tried twice already.*

trip

trips
When you go on a **trip**, you travel to a place and then come back. *We went on a trip to the zoo.*

trip

trips tripping tripped
If you **trip**, you hit your foot on something and fall or nearly fall. *Natasha tripped over the toys on the floor.*

troll

trolls
1 In stories, a **troll** is a big, ugly, stupid monster.
2 A **troll** is someone who posts nasty comments on the internet to upset people or start arguments.

trolley

trolleys
A **trolley** is a large basket on wheels. *A supermarket trolley.*

trophy

trophies
A **trophy** is a prize that you are given to show that you did well at something. *This year, our team won the swimming trophy.*

trouble

1 **Trouble** is something that is difficult or dangerous. *The farmer had trouble rescuing his sheep.*
2 If you are **in trouble**, you have done something wrong and someone is angry with you.

trousers

trousers
Trousers are clothes that cover your legs.

truck

trucks
A **truck** is a large vehicle that carries things from place to place.

true

1 If something is **true**, it is correct or right.
■ opposite **false**
2 If a story is **true**, it really happened.

trumpet

trumpets
A **trumpet** is a musical instrument made of metal. You play a trumpet by blowing into it.

trunk

trunks
1 A **trunk** is the thick stem of a tree.
2 An elephant's **trunk** is its long nose. Elephants use their trunks to suck up water and to pick things up.

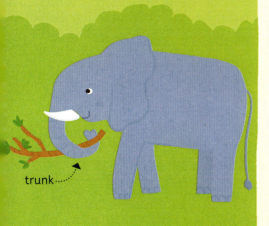

trunk

3 A **trunk** is also a large, strong box that you keep things in.

trust

trusts trusting trusted
If you **trust** someone, you think that they are honest and will keep their promises.

truth

If you tell the **truth**, what you say is true.

try

tries trying tried
1 When you **try** to do something, you do it as well as you can. *Mel **tried** to climb the wall.*
2 If you **try** something, you test it to see what it is like. *Daisy **tried** the rice to see if it was cooked.*

T-shirt

T-shirts
A **T-shirt** is a piece of clothing that you wear on the top part of your body. T-shirts usually have short sleeves and round necks with no collar.

tube

tubes
1 A **tube** is something that is long, round and hollow. *A **tube** of sweets.*
2 A **tube** is also a container for soft mixtures, such as toothpaste. You squeeze the tube to get the mixture out.

tug

tugs tugging tugged
If you **tug** something, you pull it hard.

tune to twig

tune
tunes
A **tune** is a group of musical notes arranged in a special order. Tunes are usually pleasant to listen to.

tunnel
tunnels
A **tunnel** is a long passage under the ground.

turban
turbans
A **turban** is a long piece of cloth that some men and boys wear wrapped round their heads.

turkey
turkeys
1 A **turkey** is a large bird that is kept on a farm.
2 **Turkey** is also a kind of meat that comes from turkeys.

turn
turns
If it is your **turn** to do something, it is your time to do it. *It's Tom's **turn** to use the computer.*

turn
turns turning turned
1 When you **turn**, you move in a different direction. *The car **turned** left.*
2 If something **turns**, it moves around in a circle.
3 If you **turn** a machine **on** or **off**, you make it start or stop.
4 If a thing **turns into** something else, it changes into it. *The frog **turned into** a handsome prince.*

turtle
turtles
A **turtle** is an animal with thick, scaly skin and a shell on its back. Turtles live in water.

tusk
tusks
An elephant's **tusks** are its two long, pointed teeth on either side of its trunk.

twice
If something happens **twice**, it happens two times.

twig
twigs
A **twig** is a small, thin branch of a tree or a bush.

twin

twins
Twins are two children who have the same parents and were born on the same day. Twins often look alike.

twist

twists twisting twisted
When you twist something, you turn part of it while holding the rest of it still.

tying

Tying comes from the word tie. *Kim is learning to tie knots. She has been tying knots for hours.*

type

types
Things of the same type belong to the same group. *Poppies are a type of flower.*

type

types typing typed
When you type, you write something using a keyboard.

tyre

tyres
A tyre is a circle of strong rubber that fits round a wheel. Tyres are usually full of air.

Uu

ugly

uglier ugliest
Something that is ugly is not nice to look at. *An ugly building. An ugly monster.*

umbrella

umbrellas
You hold an umbrella over your head to keep the rain off. An umbrella is made of a piece of cloth or plastic stretched over a frame.

Many words are given the opposite meaning by adding un to the start. For example: able – unable; do – undo.

unable

If you are unable to do something, you cannot do it. *Leo is unable to come tonight.*

uncle

uncles
Your uncle is the brother of your mum or dad.

uncomfortable
If something is **uncomfortable**, it does not feel good. *Uncomfortable shoes. An uncomfortable chair.*

under
1 If something is **under** another thing, it is lower than it, or underneath it. *Amy checked for monsters under her bed.*
2 **Under** also means less than. *Josh ran the race in under three minutes.*
■ opposite **over**

underline
underlines underlining underlined
If you **underline** something, you draw a line under it.

underneath
If one thing is **underneath** another thing, it is in the space under it. *My toys are underneath my bed.*

understand
understands understanding understood
If you **understand** something, you know what it means or how it works.

underwear
Underwear is the name for the clothes that you wear under your other clothes. Vests and pants are kinds of underwear.

undress
undresses undressing undressed
When you **undress**, you take off your clothes.

unemployed
Someone who is **unemployed** does not have a job.

unhappy
unhappier unhappiest
If you are **unhappy**, you are sad or upset.

uniform
uniforms
A **uniform** is a special set of clothes worn by all the members of a group. *A school uniform.*

unit
units
A **unit** is a fixed amount of something. Units are used for counting or for measuring things. *A minute is a unit of time. A pound is a unit of money.*

universe
The **universe** is everything that is in space. The Earth, Sun, Moon and stars are all parts of the universe.

unkind

unkinder unkindest
An **unkind** person is unpleasant and not helpful.

unlucky

unluckier unluckiest
If you are **unlucky**, bad things happen to you that are not your fault.

unpleasant

If something is **unpleasant**, it is horrible or nasty. *An **unpleasant** smell.*

untidy

untidier untidiest
If something is **untidy**, it is messy and not neat.

until

Until means up to the time that something happens.

*I am looking after Tom's fish **until** he comes back from holiday.*

unusual

If something is **unusual**, it is not normal, or is not what you would expect. *Jasmine was wearing an **unusual** hat. It's **unusual** for it to be so hot in February.*

up

When something moves **up**, it goes from a lower place to a higher place. *We pushed our bikes **up** the hill.*
■ opposite **down**

upon

Upon means on top of. *The cat sat **upon** the step.*

upright

Upright means standing up straight.

upset

If you are **upset**, you are unhappy or angry. *Rosie was very **upset** when her cat died.*

upside down

1 If you turn something **upside down**, you put its top where its bottom should be. *Leon turned the bucket **upside down** to make a seat.*
2 If you hang **upside down**, your head is below your feet.

*Anna loves hanging **upside down**.*

urgent to vase

urgent
If something is **urgent**, you need to do something about it quickly.

use
uses using used
▲ *rhymes with* **choose**
When you **use** something, you do a job with it. *Jayden **used** scissors to cut the card.*

useful
If something is **useful**, it helps you to do something.

usual
If something is **usual**, it is what you would expect. *I'll be home at the **usual** time.*

usually
If something **usually** happens, it happens most of the time.

Vv

vacuum cleaner
vacuum cleaners
A **vacuum cleaner** is a machine that you use to clean the floor. Vacuum cleaners suck up dirt and dust.

valley
valleys
A **valley** is an area of low ground between mountains or hills. Rivers often run through valleys.

valuable
1 Something that is **valuable** is worth a lot of money. *Mum has a **valuable** ring.*
2 **Valuable** also means important. ***Valuable** information.*

van
vans
A **van** is a vehicle that is used for carrying things.

vanish
vanishes vanishing vanished
If something **vanishes**, it disappears suddenly. *The rabbit **vanished** from the magician's hat.*

vase
vases
▲ *say* **varz**
A **vase** is a kind of jar. You can put flowers in a vase or you can use it as an ornament.

vase

vegetable

vegetables
A **vegetable** is a plant that you can eat. Potatoes, carrots and peas are all vegetables.

vegetarian

vegetarians
A **vegetarian** is someone who does not eat meat or fish.

vehicle

vehicles
▲ say **vee**-ickle
A **vehicle** is a machine that carries people or things from one place to another. Bicycles, cars and trains are all vehicles.

verse

verses
A **verse** is a part of a poem or a song. *We sang all five **verses** of the song.*

very

Very means a lot. *I am **very** excited about going on holiday.*

vest

vests
A **vest** is a piece of underwear that you wear on the top part of your body.

vet

vets
A **vet** is someone who helps sick animals to get better.

video

videos
When you watch a **video**, you see moving pictures with sound. People often watch videos on the internet.

view

views
1 A **view** is what you can see from a particular place.
*I have a **view** of the beach from my window.*
2 A **view** is also what you think about something. *What is your **view** of this book?*

village

villages
A **village** is a small group of houses and other buildings in the country.

vinegar

Vinegar is a liquid that you use to add flavour to food. Vinegar tastes sour.

violent

If something is **violent**, it is very strong and damages things. *A violent storm.*

violin

violins
A **violin** is a musical instrument with strings. You hold a violin under your chin and move a bow across its strings.

visit

visits visiting visited
If you **visit** someone, you go to see them. *I visited my granny yesterday afternoon.*

visitor

visitors
A **visitor** is someone who comes to your house to see you or to stay with you.

vital

If something is **vital**, it is very important. *Vital information.*

voice

voices
Your **voice** is the sound that you make when you talk or sing. *Ruth has a high voice.*

volcano

volcanoes or **volcanos**
A **volcano** is a mountain with a hole in the top. Sometimes hot, liquid rock and gas burst out of a volcano.

volume

volumes
1 The **volume** of a sound is how loud it is.
2 The **volume** of an object is how much space it takes up.
3 A **volume** is one of a set of books. *This set of encyclopedias has six volumes.*

volunteer

volunteers
A **volunteer** is someone who offers to do something.

vote

votes voting voted
1 When you **vote** for something, you show that you agree with it.
2 When you **vote** for a person, you show that you support them. *My dad says voting is important.*

vowel

vowels
A **vowel** is one of the letters a, e, i, o, u.

voyage

voyages
A **voyage** is a long journey, especially one by sea.

Ww

wade

wades wading waded
When you **wade**, you walk through quite deep water.

wagon

wagons
A **wagon** was a vehicle used in the past for carrying loads. Wagons had four wheels and were often pulled by horses.

waist

waists
Your **waist** is the narrow, middle part of your body, below your chest.

waistcoat

waistcoats
A **waistcoat** is a short jacket with no sleeves.

wait

waits waiting waited
When you **wait**, you stay in a place until something happens. *James **waited** for Charlotte to arrive at the station.*

waiter

waiters
A **waiter** is a man who serves people with food or drink in a restaurant or a café.

waitress

waitresses
A **waitress** is a woman who serves people with food or drink in a restaurant or a café.

wake

wakes waking woke woken
When you **wake up**, you stop sleeping. *Josiah **woke up** early.*

walk

walks walking walked
When you **walk**, you move along by putting one foot in front of the other. *Katie always **walks** to school.*

Some other words for **walk** are **stride, stroll, march** and **hike**.

wallpaper to wasn't

wallpaper

wallpapers

Wallpaper is paper that people stick to walls. Wallpaper sometimes has patterns on it.

wander

wanders wandering wandered

If you **wander**, you walk around without deciding where to go. *Jonathan **wandered** around the shops.*

want

wants wanting wanted

If you **want** something, you would like it. *Ella **wanted** some chocolate.*

war

wars

In a **war**, armies fight each other over a long period of time.

wardrobe

wardrobes

A **wardrobe** is a cupboard that you keep your clothes in. *Ed hung his jacket in the **wardrobe**.*

warm

warmer warmest

Something that is **warm** is quite hot. *A **warm** day.*

warn

warns warning warned

If you **warn** someone, you tell them about something dangerous or bad that may happen. *Phoebe **warned** us that the path was very steep.*

was

Was comes from the word **be**. *I will be at the swimming pool later. I **was** there yesterday, too.*

wash

washes washing washed

When you **wash** something, you clean it with soap and water.

*Millie and Dan **washed** their dad's car.*

washing machine

washing machines

A **washing machine** is a machine that washes clothes.

wasn't

Wasn't is a short way of saying **was not**. *Becky **wasn't** interested in playing the game.*

wasp

wasps
A **wasp** is an insect with black and yellow stripes. Wasps can sting.

waste

wastes wasting wasted
If you **waste** something, you use more of it than you need to, or you use it for something that isn't important. *Don't **waste** your money on sweets.*

watch

watches
A **watch** is a small clock that you wear on your wrist.

watch

watches watching watched
1 If you **watch** something, you look at it to see what happens.
2 You tell someone to **watch out** when you warn them to be careful. ***Watch out** for that step!*

water

Water is the clear liquid in rivers, seas and rain. Water also comes out of taps. People, animals and plants need water to live.

waterfall

waterfalls
A **waterfall** is a place where water from a river falls down over rocks.

wave

waves
A **wave** is the water that rises and falls on the surface of the sea. *The children jumped over the **waves**.*

wave

waves waving waved
When you **wave**, you move your hand from side to side. You wave to say hello or goodbye.

wax

Wax is a soft material that melts when it is heated. Wax is used to make candles and crayons.

way

ways
1 The **way** you do something is how you do it. *Is this the right **way** to spell your name?*
2 A **way** is how you get from one place to another. *Tell me the **way** home.*

weak to week

weak
weaker weakest
1 A **weak** person is not strong and does not have much energy.
2 Something that is **weak** breaks easily. *This chair has weak legs.*

weapon
weapons
A **weapon** is a tool for fighting. Guns and swords are weapons.

wear
wears wearing wore worn
1 When you **wear** clothes, they cover your body. *Max wore his green jacket.*
2 If something **wears out**, it becomes less useful because it has been used so much. *Grace's shoes are wearing out.*

weather
The **weather** is what it is like outside, such as hot or cold, rainy or sunny.

web
webs
1 A **web** is a very thin net that a spider makes to catch insects.
2 The **web** is also short for the world wide web, a huge collection of web pages on the internet that are linked to each other.

web page
web pages
A **web page** is an electronic page on the internet.

website
websites
A **website** is a group of web pages that are linked to each other.

we'd
1 **We'd** is a short way of saying we had. *We'd just reached the forest when it started to rain.*
2 **We'd** is also a short way of saying we would. *We'd love to come to your party.*

wedding
weddings
When two people have a **wedding**, they get married.

week
weeks
A **week** is a period of seven days. There are fifty-two weeks in a year.

weekend

weekends
The **weekend** is Saturday and Sunday. *We often go cycling at the weekend.*

weigh

weighs weighing weighed
When you **weigh** something, you find out how heavy it is. *Shauna weighed the sugar on the scales.*

weight

weights
Your **weight** is how heavy you are. *Do you know your weight?*

welcome

welcomes welcoming welcomed
If you **welcome** someone, you are friendly to them when they arrive. *We rushed to welcome our grandparents.*

we'll

We'll is a short way of saying we will. *We'll come and see you at the weekend.*

well

wells
A **well** is a deep hole in the ground. People dig wells to reach water, oil or gas.

well

better best
1 If you do something **well**, you are good at it. *Edward plays the violin well.*
2 If you are **well**, you are healthy or happy. *Bert is looking very well.*

went

Went comes from the word **go**. *Carolyn likes to go to the beach. She went there last week with some friends.*

we're

We're is a short way of saying we are. *We're going on holiday tomorrow.*

were

Were comes from the word **be**. *The children tried to be quiet. They were silent for almost two minutes.*

weren't

Weren't is a short way of saying **were not**. *We **weren't** allowed to stay up late.*

west

West is a direction. The Sun goes down in the west.
- opposite **east**

wet

wetter wettest
If something is **wet**, it has liquid on it. *A **wet** towel.*
- opposite **dry**

we've

We've is a short way of saying **we have**. *We've been to the park.*

whale

whales
A **whale** is a very big animal that lives in the sea. A whale breathes through a hole in the top of its head.

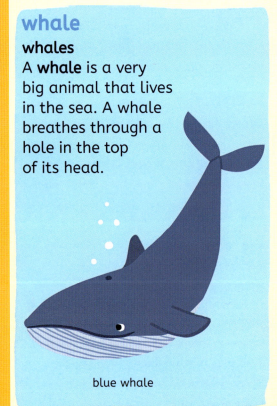

blue whale

what

You use the word **what** to find out more about something. ***What** is your name?*

what's

1 **What's** is a short way of saying **what is**. ***What's** the time?*
2 **What's** is also a short way of saying **what has**. ***What's** happened to your hair?*

wheat

Wheat is a plant that is grown on farms. Wheat is used to make flour.

wheel

wheels
A **wheel** is round and can turn in a circle. Cars, bicycles and roller skates use wheels to move along.

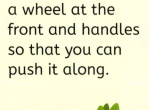

wheelbarrow

wheelbarrows
You use a **wheelbarrow** to carry things in a garden. A wheelbarrow has a wheel at the front and handles so that you can push it along.

wheelchair

wheelchairs
A **wheelchair** is a chair on wheels. People who cannot walk use a wheelchair to get from place to place.

when

You use the word **when** to talk or ask about the time of something. *When did you last see Marcus?*

where

You use the word **where** to talk or ask about a place. *Where are you?*

where's

1 **Where's** is a short way of saying **where is**. *Where's my football?*
2 **Where's** is also a short way of saying **where has**. *Where's Jacob gone?*

which

You use the word **which** to ask about one of a number of things. *Which shirt shall I wear?*

while

1 **While** means in the time that something is happening. *Sam fed my cat while I was away.*
2 **While** also means a period of time. *It's a long while since we first met.*

whiskers

Whiskers are the long hairs that grow near the nose of some animals, such as mice, cats and rabbits. *My pet mouse has very long whiskers.*

whisper

whispers whispering whispered
When you **whisper**, you talk very quietly.

whistle

whistles
A **whistle** is a small tube that makes a high, loud sound when you blow into it.

whistle

whistles whistling whistled
When you **whistle**, you make a sound or a tune by blowing through your lips.

white

White is a colour. Snow is white.

whiteboard

whiteboards

A **whiteboard** is a board that teachers write on, with special pens that can be wiped off.

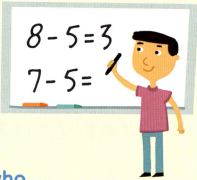

who

▲ Say *hoo*

You use the word **who** to talk or ask about someone. *Who won the race?*

who'd

1 **Who'd** is a short way of saying **who had**. *Rosa was the only one who'd seen the film.*
2 **Who'd** is also a short way of saying **who would**. *Who'd like to come?*

whole

Whole means all of something. *George has eaten a whole packet of biscuits.*

who'll

Who'll is a short way of saying **who will**. *Who'll come with me?*

who's

▲ Say *hooze*

1 **Who's** is a short way of saying **who is**. *Who's going to the fair?*
2 **Who's** is also a short way of saying **who has**. *Who's been eating my porridge?*

whose

▲ Say *hooze*

You use **whose** to talk or ask about who or what things belong to. *Whose gloves are these?*

why

You use the word **why** to talk or ask about the reason for something. *Why are you upset?*

wicked

Someone who is **wicked** is very bad. *The wicked witch waved her wand.*

wide

wider widest

If something is **wide**, it measures a lot from one side to the other. *A wide table.*

■ opposite **narrow**

width

widths
The **width** of something is how far it is from one side to the other.

wife

wives
Someone's **wife** is the woman they are married to.

wig

wigs
A **wig** is false hair that fits on someone's head.

wild

wilder wildest
Wild animals and plants are not looked after by people.
■ opposite **tame**

A wild bird.

wildlife

Wildlife is a name for wild animals, insects and plants.

will

would
If someone **will** do something, they are going to do it.
Jake will tidy up later.

willing

If you are **willing** to do something, you don't mind doing it.

win

wins winning won
If you **win** a race or a game, you come first.
■ opposite **lose**

wind

▲ *rhymes with* **tinned**
Wind is air that moves quickly. *The wind blew Hattie's hat off.*

wind

winds winding wound
▲ *rhymes with* **kind**
1 If you **wind** something **around** another thing, you put it around it several times. *Rollo wound his scarf around his neck.*
2 When you **wind up** a clock or a toy, you turn its key to make it work.
3 If a road or a river **winds**, it has lots of bends and turns.

windmill

windmills
A **windmill** is a tall building with large sails. When the wind turns the sails, a machine inside the windmill turns grain into flour.

window

windows
A **window** is a space in a wall or a vehicle that lets in light and air. Windows are usually filled with glass.

wing

wings
Wings make things able to fly. Birds, bats, insects and planes all have wings.

wink

winks winking winked
When you **wink**, you close and open one eye very quickly. You wink to show that something is a joke or a secret.

winner

winners
The **winner** of a race or a game is the person who comes in first place.

winter

Winter is one of the four seasons. It comes between autumn and spring. Winter is the coldest season.

wipe

wipes wiping wiped
When you **wipe** something, you rub it with a cloth to make it clean.

wire

wires
A **wire** is a long, thin piece of metal that bends easily. Wires can be used to carry electricity or to fasten things.

wise

wiser wisest
Wise people know the right thing to say and do.

wish

wishes wishing wished
If you **wish** that something would happen, you want it to happen very much.

witch

witches
A **witch** is a woman with magic powers who you read about in stories.

with

1 If you do something **with** someone, you both do it together.
2 You also use **with** to show that someone has something. *I know a boy* **with** *green eyes.*
3 The word **with** also shows what you use to do something. *Natasha loves eating chicken* **with** *her fingers.*

without

If you are **without** something, you do not have it. *Alex came to school **without** his packed lunch.*

wizard

wizards
A **wizard** is a man with magic powers who you read about in stories.

wobble

wobbles wobbling wobbled
If something **wobbles**, it moves from side to side. *The jelly **wobbled** on the plate.*

woke

Woke comes from the word **wake**. *Anna usually wakes up early, but today she **woke** up late.*

wolf

wolves
A **wolf** is a wild animal that looks like a large dog. Wolves have thick coats. They live in forests and hunt in groups.

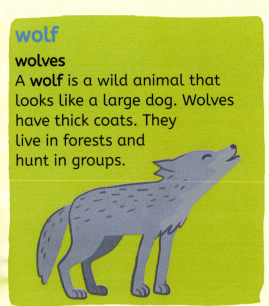

woman

women
A **woman** is an adult, female human being.

won

Won comes from the word **win**. *Our team hopes to win today. We have **won** our last five games.*

wonder

wonders wondering wondered
If you **wonder** what to do, you are not sure what you should do. *Jessie **wondered** which path she should take.*

won't

Won't is a short way of saying **will not**. *Meg **won't** let her brother come into her room.*

wood

woods
1 **Wood** comes from the trunks and branches of trees. It is used in building and to make things such as furniture.
2 A **wood** is a place where lots of trees grow close together. Woods are smaller than forests.

wooden

Something that is **wooden** is made from wood. *A **wooden** spoon.*

wool to worth

wool
Wool is the hair that grows on sheep. Wool is made into thread and used for knitting or making cloth.

word
words
A **word** is a group of sounds or letters that means something. You use words when you speak or write.

wore
Wore comes from the word **wear**. *Kim didn't know what to wear. In the end, she **wore** her jeans.*

work
works working worked
1 When people **work**, they do a job. *My mum **works** in a hospital.*
2 If you **work**, you use your energy to do something. *Zack is **working** hard at maths.*
3 If something **works**, it does what it is meant to do. *Our radio is **working** again.*

world
The **world** is the Earth, and everything that lives on it.

worm
worms
A **worm** is a small animal with a long, thin body and no legs. Worms live in the ground.

worn
Worn comes from the word **wear**. *Emily likes to wear big hats. She has **worn** a hat every day this week.*

worry
worries worrying worried
If you **worry**, you keep thinking about bad things that might happen.

worse
Worse means less good. *Your handwriting is **worse** than mine.*
■ opposite **better**

worst
Worst means worse than anything else. *This is the **worst** film I have ever seen.*
■ opposite **best**

worth
If something is **worth** an amount of money, it could be sold for that amount. *This painting is **worth** a lot of money.*

248

would

Would comes from the word **will**. *I will come to see you this week. I would have come last week, but I was busy.*

wouldn't

Wouldn't is a short way of saying **would not**. *Amy wouldn't lend her brother any money.*

wound

wounds
▲ rhymes with **spooned**
A **wound** is a cut in your skin. *Wounds are usually quite deep.*

wound

▲ rhymes with **sound**
Wound comes from the word **wind**. *Jo started to wind the wool. She wound it around her hand.*

wrap

wraps wrapping wrapped
When you **wrap** an object, you cover it with something, such as paper or cloth. *Ethan wrapped Kieran's present in red paper.*

wrapper

wrappers
A **wrapper** is a piece of paper or plastic that covers something. *A sweet wrapper.*

wreck

wrecks wrecking wrecked
If you **wreck** something, you completely destroy it. *My uncle was in a car accident. He's okay, but his car was wrecked.*

wrestle

wrestles wrestling wrestled
When people **wrestle**, they fight and try to throw each other to the ground.

wrinkle

wrinkles
A **wrinkle** is a line on someone's skin. *The old man's face was covered with wrinkles.*

wrist

wrists
Your **wrist** is the joint between your arm and your hand.

write

writes writing wrote written
1 When you **write**, you use a pen or pencil to put words or numbers on paper.
2 When you **write** a story, you make it up, then put it on paper or type it on a computer. *Amelia is writing a story about a dragon.*

writing to year

writing

Writing is anything that has been written.

written

Written comes from the word **write**. *Polly writes to Ali regularly. She has **written** every week since she moved house.*

wrong

1 Something that is **wrong** is not correct. *Some of my answers were **wrong**.*
2 If people do something **wrong**, they do something bad.
■ opposite **right**

wrote

Wrote comes from the word **write**. *William likes to write poems. Last week, he **wrote** a brilliant poem about a tiger.*

x-ray

x-rays
An **x-ray** is a kind of photograph that shows the inside of someone's body.

xylophone

xylophones
▲ *say **zy-loh-fone***
A **xylophone** is a musical instrument with a row of wooden bars. You play a xylophone by hitting the bars with small hammers.

yacht

yachts
▲ *say **yot***
A **yacht** is a boat with big sails. Most yachts also have engines.

yawn

yawns yawning yawned
When you **yawn**, you open your mouth wide and breathe in deeply. You yawn because you are tired or bored.

year

years
1 A **year** is the time from 1st January to 31st December.
2 A **year** is also any period of 12 months.

yell to yourself

yell
yells yelling yelled
If you **yell**, you shout or scream very loudly. *Felix **yelled** for help.*

yellow
Yellow is a colour. Lemons and butter are yellow.

yesterday
Yesterday means the day before today.

yet
Yet means up to this time. *Jon hasn't called **yet**.*

yogurt
Yogurt is a thick liquid food that is made from milk.

yolk
yolks
▲ *say yoke*
The **yolk** is the yellow part in the middle of an egg.

you
You is a word that you use when you speak to someone else, or to a group of people. *How are **you** feeling?*

you'd
1 **You'd** is a short way of saying **you had**. ***You'd** already left when I came round.*
2 **You'd** is also a short way of saying **you would**. ***You'd** have loved the museum.*

you'll
You'll is a short way of saying **you will**. ***You'll** get cold if you don't wear a coat.*

young
younger youngest
▲ *say yung*
Someone who is **young** has lived for only a short time.
■ opposite **old**

your
Your means belonging to you. *Please would you hang **your** coats in the hall.*

you're
You're is a short way of saying **you are**. ***You're** late again!*

yours
If something belongs to **you**, then it is **yours**. *I've lost my ruler. Can I borrow **yours**?*

yourself
Yourself means you and nobody else. *Help **yourself** to some food.*

you've to zoo

you've
You've is a short way of saying **you have**. *You've eaten far too much cake!*

yo-yo
yo-yos
A **yo-yo** is a toy that rolls up and down on a string that you loop round your finger.

Zz

zebra
zebras
A **zebra** is an animal with black and white stripes on its body. Zebras look like horses and live in herds, in Africa.

zigzag
zigzags
A **zigzag** is a line that goes up and down.

zip
zips
Zips are sewn into clothes and bags and are used to fasten them. A zip has two rows of metal or plastic teeth that fit together when you do it up.

zoo
zoos
A **zoo** is a place where animals are kept for people to see.

Numbers

0	zero or nought
1	one
2	two
3	three
4	four
5	five
6	six
7	seven
8	eight
9	nine
10	ten
11	eleven
12	twelve
13	thirteen
14	fourteen
15	fifteen
16	sixteen
17	seventeen
18	eighteen
19	nineteen
20	twenty
21	twenty-one
30	thirty
40	forty
50	fifty
60	sixty
70	seventy
80	eighty
90	ninety
100	hundred
1000	thousand

Order

1st	first
2nd	second
3rd	third
4th	fourth
5th	fifth
6th	sixth
7th	seventh
8th	eighth
9th	ninth
10th	tenth
11th	eleventh
12th	twelfth
13th	thirteenth
14th	fourteenth
15th	fifteenth
16th	sixteenth
17th	seventeenth
18th	eighteenth
19th	nineteenth
20th	twentieth
21st	twenty-first
30th	thirtieth
40th	fortieth
50th	fiftieth
60th	sixtieth
70th	seventieth
80th	eightieth
90th	ninetieth
100th	hundredth
1000th	thousandth

Days of the week
Monday
Tuesday
Wednesday
Thursday
Friday
Saturday
Sunday

Months of the year
January
February
March
April
May
June
July
August
September
October
November
December

Seasons
spring
summer
autumn
winter

Colours of the rainbow

red

orange

yellow

green

blue

indigo

violet

Measurements
Length
1 millimetre (mm)
1 centimetre (cm) = 10mm
1 metre (m) = 100cm
1 kilometre (km) = 1,000m

Volume
1 millilitre (ml)
1 centilitre (cl) = 10ml
1 litre (l) = 100cl
1 kilolitre (kl) = 1,000l

Weight
1 milligram (mg)
1 gram (g) = 1,000mg
1 kilogram (kg) = 1,000g
1 tonne (t) = 1,000kg

Temperature
°C = degrees Celsius
0°C = water freezes
37°C = body temperature
100°C = water boils

The planets
Mercury   Jupiter
Venus   Saturn
Earth   Uranus
Mars   Neptune

Directions
north
west
east
south

Continents and oceans

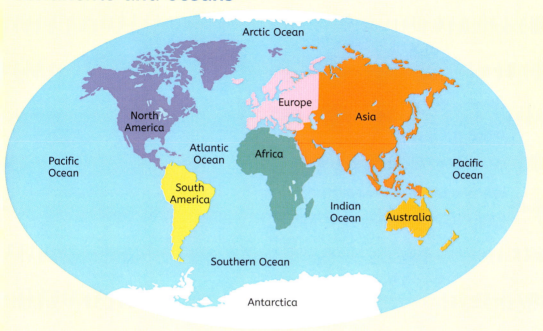

Spelling quiz

For each question, choose the correct spelling: **a** or **b**. You can check your answers on page 256.

1. a seperate   b separate
2. a arguement   b argument
3. a forty   b fourty
4. a foriegn   b foreign
5. a calendar   b calender
6. a receive   b recieve
7. a until   b untill
8. a sensable   b sensible
9. a beginning   b begining
10. a allmost   b almost
11. a freind   b friend
12. a library   b libary
13. a chello   b cello
14. a language   b languadge
15. a jewlerry   b jewellery
16. a Wednesday   b Wendsday
17. a raspberry   b rasberry
18. a rescueing   b rescuing
19. a rhinocerous   b rhinoceros
20. a appear   b appere
21. a thread   b thred
22. a disguise   b disgiuse
23. a musn't   b mustn't
24. a left   b leaved
25. a ammount   b amount
26. a believe   b beleive

Word hunt

Search the dictionary section for the answers to these questions. Check the answers below.

1. What does an **anchor** do?
2. What is the **capital** city of Japan?
3. What is **CD** short for?
4. What does **hibernate** mean?
5. What is **leather** made from?
6. What does a **microscope** do?
7. How long does the **Moon** take to go around the Earth?
8. When does an **owl** hunt?
9. What does a **panda** eat?
10. What does a **penguin** use its wings for?
11. What is **steel** mostly made of?
12. How long does the Earth take to go around the **Sun**?
13. What do you use a **thermometer** for?
14. How does a **whale** breathe?
15. What is a **xylophone**?

Answers

Page 255 Spelling quiz

1. b 2. b 3. a 4. b 5. a 6. a 7. a 8. b 9. a 10. b 11. b 12. a 13. b 14. a 15. b 16. a 17. a 18. b 19. b 20. a 21. a 22. a 23. b 24. a 25. b 26. a

Page 256 Word hunt

1. It stops a ship from moving. 2. Tokyo 3. compact disc 4. To sleep through the winter. 5. animal skin 6. It makes things look much bigger. 7. a month 8. at night 9. bamboo 10. swimming 11. iron 12. a year 13. To find out how hot or cold something is. 14. Through a hole in the top of its head. 15. a musical instrument

flutter
fly

scary
creepy

First Illustrated Thesaurus

noisy
loud

Illustrated by
Tjarda Borsboom
and Beatrice Tinarelli

gigantic
massive

Using your thesaurus	258
Thesaurus contents	260
Thesaurus	262
Word finder	352

speed
zoom

Using your thesaurus

A thesaurus groups together words with the same or similar meanings. You can use it to find words to make your writing and speaking more interesting. So you can change this:

My friends are nice. We went to a nice party and had a nice time.

to this:

My friends are lovely. We went to a fantastic party and had a wonderful time.

This thesaurus is divided into topics. You can search through the book to find a topic you want, or check the contents on pages 260 and 261.

Look at the words and pictures to give you ideas.

Find a range of words to make your writing more varied.

Discover striking phrases.

Choose from a list of interesting words to describe things.

Using the word finder

If you want to find other ways to say a particular word, use the word finder on pages 352 to 360. It is in alphabetical order, so to find the word 'nice', look under 'n'.

The word finder will help you choose a word.

nervous, 274

nice, 262

noise, 337

The word finder tells you to look on page 262 to find other words that mean 'nice'.

Choosing words

Each time you write or speak, you make choices about words. Here are some ways to use words to create dramatic effects.

Make people come to life by showing how they look, sound and act.

The pirate had <u>flowing hair</u> and a <u>menacing grin</u>. He gave an <u>evil cackle</u> as he <u>waved</u> his hook.

Describe how places look, sound, feel, and even smell.

Parrots <u>screeched</u> in the <u>dark</u>, <u>steamy</u> jungle, and the air was filled with the <u>scent</u> of flowers.

Create a sense of speed and movement by using lots of action words.

The spaceship <u>zoomed</u> through the clouds, <u>hurtled</u> past the planet and <u>raced</u> away.

Thesaurus contents

262	Good, bad, nice	285	Homes and gardens
263	Big and small	286	Building words
264	Colours	287	Tools and materials
265	Shapes and patterns	288	In a city
266	Describing faces	290	Going shopping
267	Hair and hairstyles	291	At a supermarket
268	Clothes and shoes	292	On the road
270	Talking and thinking	294	Ships and boats
271	Action words	296	Trains, planes and aircraft
272	All sorts of feelings		
274	All kinds of people	298	At an airport
276	Your body	300	Jobs people do
277	Your senses	301	Fun and hobbies
278	Feeling ill	302	Dance and theatre
279	Getting better	303	Film and TV
280	Food and drink	304	At a funfair
282	Eating and drinking	305	At a circus
283	In the kitchen	306	Music words
284	Inside a home	308	All sorts of sports

310	Cats and dogs	332	Words for weather
311	More pets	333	Ice, frost and snow
312	Horses and riding	334	Storm words
314	Bugs and insects	335	Night words
315	Animal words	336	Fire and fireworks
316	Bird words	337	Noisy words
318	Trees	338	Fairy-tale words
319	Bushes and flowers	340	Pirates and treasure
320	In the country	342	In space
321	On a farm	343	On a space adventure
322	Rivers, lakes and ponds	344	Ghosts and haunted houses
324	In the mountains	346	Monsters
326	In a desert	347	Dinosaurs
327	In a jungle	348	Adventure words
328	Grassland animals	350	Knights and castles
329	Under the sea	351	At a feast
330	At the seaside	352	Word finder
331	Sea and shore		

Good, bad, nice

A good artist
expert
gifted
skilful
talented

A good child
angelic
obedient
polite
well-behaved

A good book
brilliant
excellent
marvellous
wonderful

A bad person
cruel
evil
nasty
wicked

Bad behaviour
cheeky
disobedient
mischievous
naughty

A bad smell
disgusting
horrible
revolting
vile

A nice time
amazing
fantastic
great
wonderful

A nice view
beautiful
breathtaking
spectacular
stunning

A nice person
helpful
kind
lovely
warm-hearted

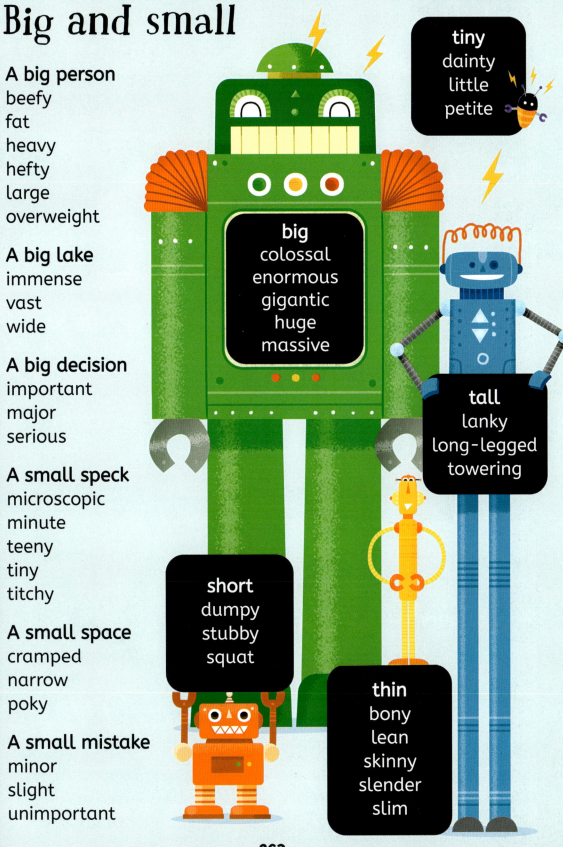

Big and small

A big person
beefy
fat
heavy
hefty
large
overweight

A big lake
immense
vast
wide

A big decision
important
major
serious

A small speck
microscopic
minute
teeny
tiny
titchy

A small space
cramped
narrow
poky

A small mistake
minor
slight
unimportant

tiny
dainty
little
petite

big
colossal
enormous
gigantic
huge
massive

tall
lanky
long-legged
towering

short
dumpy
stubby
squat

thin
bony
lean
skinny
slender
slim

Colours

Colours can be ...

dark
deep

light
pale

bright
bold
brilliant
fluorescent
garish
luminous
rich
vivid

dull
dingy
drab
dreary
faded
faint
muddy

More colours
beige
black
brown
cream
fawn
hazel
ivory
khaki

yellow
lemon
mustard

red
crimson
ruby
scarlet

pink
coral
rose pink
salmon pink

white

grey
charcoal
dove grey

blue
navy
royal blue
sky blue
turquoise

orange
amber
apricot
peach

green
bottle green
emerald green
lime green
olive green

violet
lavender
lilac
mauve

purple
maroon
plum

Shapes and patterns

Shapes can be ...
hexagonal
rectangular
square
triangular

round
circular
globular
spherical

flat
level
smooth

pointed
sharp
spiky

long
stretched-out

short
squat

Patterns can be ...
bold
delicate
eye-catching
floral
flowing
random
regular
swirling

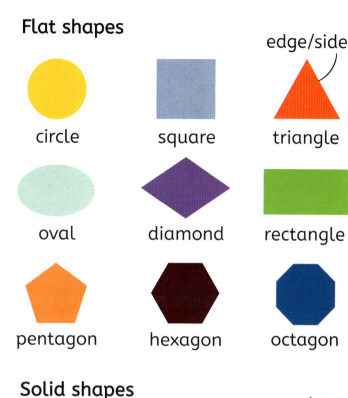

Flat shapes

circle · square · triangle
oval · diamond · rectangle
pentagon · hexagon · octagon

edge/side

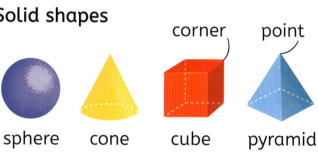

Solid shapes

sphere · cone · cube · pyramid

corner · point

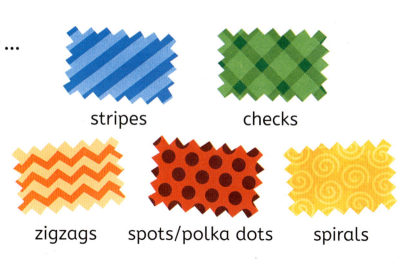

stripes · checks
zigzags · spots/polka dots · spirals

Describing faces

Faces can be ...
heart-shaped
long
round

good-looking
attractive
beautiful
handsome
pretty

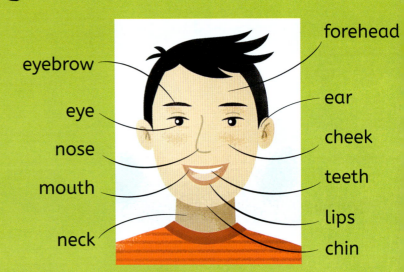

forehead
ear
cheek
teeth
lips
chin
eyebrow
eye
nose
mouth
neck

Faces can have ...

wrinkles

freckles

glasses

a beard

braces

stubble

spots

a moustache

dimples

People may ...

grin

smile

frown

blush

Hair and hairstyles

Hair can be…
curly
floppy
flowing
frizzy
greasy
lank
receding
shiny
sleek
spiky
straggly
straight
windswept
wiry

thick
bushy
shaggy

thin
fine
thinning
wispy

Hair may be…
bleached
dyed
gelled
layered
permed
scraped back
shaved
spiked
tinted

Hair colours
auburn
black
blonde
brown
chestnut
fair
ginger
grey
mousy
red
silver
white

Hairstyles
bob
bunches
crew cut
dreadlocks
mohican
ponytail
pudding bowl
quiff
ringlets
short back
  and sides
top knot

Other hair words
bald patch
hairband
hair clip
hair extension
hair slide
sideburns
wig

bun
fringe
parting
plait
pigtail
cornrows
tangled
wavy
braids

Clothes and shoes

vest — raincoat — T-shirt — tights — sweater/jumper — skirt
wool, pleats

Coats
anorak
cagoule
duffle coat
parka

Hats
baseball cap
beanie
beret
bobble hat
sunhat
top hat

Dresses
pinafore dress
sari
tunic

Trousers
jogging bottoms
leggings
shorts

Underwear
boxer shorts
bra
knickers
pants
underpants

Tops
cardigan
fleece
hoodie
shirt
sweatshirt

Nightclothes
dressing gown
nightdress/
  nightie
pyjamas
slippers

Other clothes
braces
gloves
mittens
onesie
scarf
socks
suit
tie
tracksuit
waistcoat

Shoes and boots

flip-flops — sandals — pumps (canvas) — wellingtons

collar, silk, denim, zip, puffed sleeve, cuff, pocket, frill

blouse, jeans, dungarees, dress

Clothes can be made from ...
corduroy
cotton
fur
lace
satin
velvet

Some clothes have ...
buttons
fringes
patches
ruffles
sequins
tassels

Clothes can be ...
smart
neat
tidy

scruffy
frayed
shabby
ragged

tight
clingy

loose
baggy

flowing
floating

dirty
grubby
muddy
stained

They can also be ...
comfortable
elegant
fancy
fashionable
fun
itchy
plain
sporty
trendy

shoelaces

leather

walking boots

trainers

slippers

shoes

Talking and thinking

Let's have a talk
chat
conversation
discussion
gossip
heart-to-heart

Please talk quietly
keep your voice down
talk softly
whisper

Don't talk so loudly
bawl
bellow
raise your voice
shout
yell

I think it's too late
believe
expect
feel
guess
imagine
reckon
suppose

Let's think about what to do
chew over
concentrate on
consider
contemplate
decide
focus on
weigh up
work out

I think you're wrong
believe
consider
reckon

We must think up a plan
come up with
create
dream up
invent

Amy likes to sit and think
brood
dream
imagine
ponder
reflect
wonder

Other words for 'say'...

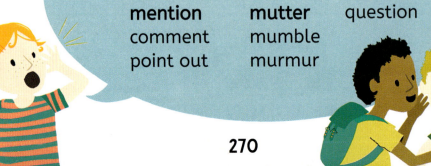

announce
declare
state

answer
reply
respond

ask
beg
demand
enquire
question

mention
comment
point out

mutter
mumble
murmur

Action words

walk
hike
march
plod
saunter
stagger
stomp
stride
stroll
trek
trudge
wander

climb
clamber
scale
scramble

jump
bound
hurdle
leap
spring

push
drive
force
press
prod
ram
shove

pull
drag
heave
tow
tug
yank

take
grab
help yourself
pick
seize
select
snatch

give
deliver
hand over
pass
present

hold
clasp
cling on to
clutch
grab
grasp
grip
hang on to
seize

carry
lift
lug
move
shift
transport

put
dump
lay
leave
place
plonk
rest
set
stand

squash
crumple
crush
flatten
squeeze

sit
perch
rest
sprawl
squat

run
sprint
race
dash
hurtle
gallop

All sorts of feelings

I'm feeling ...

proud, weary, delighted, energetic, uneasy

angry
cross
fuming
furious
irate
livid
seething

bored
fed-up
restless

confused
baffled
bewildered
dazed
flummoxed
muddled
puzzled

surprised
amazed
astonished
shocked
startled
stunned

happy
cheerful
chirpy
glad
overjoyed
over the moon

excited
eager
keen
thrilled
wound up

worried
anxious
distressed
fretful
on edge
tense
troubled

sad
depressed
devastated
down in the
   dumps
heartbroken
low
miserable
tearful
unhappy
wretched

contented
nervous
confident
flustered

Love and hate

I love ...
adore
am devoted to
am in love with
am very fond of
think the world of

I hate ...
can't bear
can't stand
despise
detest
loathe

tired
exhausted
shattered
sleepy
worn out

grumpy
annoyed
bad-tempered
cranky
cross
grouchy
irritable
peeved

upset
distressed
hurt
shaken

scared
afraid
frightened
panic-stricken
petrified
scared stiff
startled
terrified

When you're angry, you ...
clench your fists
grind your teeth
scream
shout
slam doors
stamp your foot
yell

When you're sad, you cry
burst into floods of tears
shed tears
snivel
sob
wail
weep
whimper

When you're happy, you smile
beam
grin
grin from ear to ear
smirk

All kinds of people

People can be …

young
babyish
childish
youthful

old
aged
ancient
elderly

strong
athletic
hefty
muscular
strapping

weak
delicate
feeble
helpless
puny

healthy
fine
fit
in good shape
well

cheerful
cheery
chirpy
happy
jolly
light-hearted
optimistic

calm
easy-going
laid-back
peaceful
relaxed

nervous
jittery
jumpy
on edge
tense

crazy
daft
foolish
idiotic
insane
mad
silly

honest
trustworthy
truthful

dishonest
deceitful
two-faced

polite
courteous
well behaved

rude
bad-mannered
cheeky
impolite

unkind
cruel
mean
nasty
spiteful

kind
caring
generous
helpful
warm-hearted

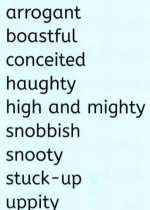

brave
bold
courageous
daring
fearless
plucky

clever
brainy
bright
gifted
intelligent
knowledgeable
smart
talented
wise

clumsy
awkward
bumbling
butter-fingered

funny
amusing
comical
hilarious
ridiculous
witty

fussy
choosy
hard-to-please
pernickety
picky

lively
bouncy
bubbly
chatty
confident
energetic
full of life
high-spirited

naughty
badly behaved
cheeky
disobedient
mischievous
wild

nosy
curious
inquisitive
interfering
prying
snooping

proud
arrogant
boastful
conceited
haughty
high and mighty
snobbish
snooty
stuck-up
uppity
vain

sensible
down-to-earth
level-headed
practical
wise

shy
bashful
quiet
self-conscious
timid

confident
calm
fearless
poised

Your body

Bodies can be…
bony
chubby
flexible
muscly
puny
skinny
strong
toned
weak

Inside your body

organs

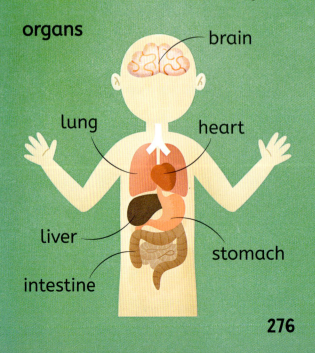

skeleton

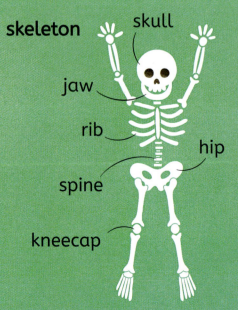

Your senses

I can smell roses.
scent
sense
sniff out
track down

Smell this perfume.
breathe in
inhale
sniff

Taste this treat.
nibble
sample
sip
try

Can you taste lime in this dish?
make out
notice
recognize

Did you hear that noise?
catch
notice
pick up

Please listen!
concentrate
pay attention
prick up your ears
take in

Did you see that star?
catch sight of
notice
spot

Please don't look.
gaze
peep
peer
watch

You won't feel any pain.
be aware of
experience
notice

Feel this scarf.
handle
run your hands over
touch

Feeling ill

I've got a...

bruise

cut

headache

lump

rash

tummy ache

temperature

toothache

Are you...?

coughing

shivering

sneezing

itching

I'm feeling...
awful
bad
faint
poorly
shaky
sick
unwell

You could have...
an allergy
a broken bone
a bug
a cold
a disease
an infection
a virus

Or you could have...
asthma
chickenpox
hay fever
flu
measles
mumps

Getting better

Hospital words
accident and
 emergency
clinic
operating theatre
ward

You may need...
an appointment
an examination
an injection
an operation
a prescription
an x-ray

porter
ambulance
wheelchair
crutches
cast
stethoscope
nurse
sling
doctor

In a medicine cabinet...

antiseptic spray
plasters
medicine
bandage
capsules
ointment
pills
throat lozenges
tablets

We need to look after Jess.	Then she'll get better.	Now she's feeling fine.
care for	get well	all right
cure	heal	better
nurse	improve	fit
take care of	recover	healthy

279

Food and drink

Food can taste ...
bitter
bland
fresh
mouldy
rich
salty
sour
stale
sweet

Food can feel ...
chewy
creamy
greasy
juicy
lumpy
rubbery
slimy
stringy

soft
gooey
mushy
sloppy
soggy
spongy
squishy

hard
crisp
crunchy
tough

Fruit
apple
cherries
grapes
lemon
lime
peach
strawberries

melon   pineapple
grapes   pear
orange
plum   bunch of bananas

Fish
cod
haddock
mackerel
plaice
salmon
sardines
tuna

Seafood
crab
lobster
mussels
oysters
prawns
scallops
shrimp

FISH FILLETS

SHELLFISH

Meat
bacon
duck
gammon
goose
ham
kidney
lamb
liver
offal
salami
steak
turkey

PORK CHOPS   CHICKEN DRUMSTICKS   SPICY SAUSAGES   MINCED BEEF

In a salad you may find ...
avocado
beetroot
celery
cucumber
lettuce
peppers
spring onions
tomatoes

Vegetables
aubergine
broad beans
cabbage
cauliflower
leeks
mushrooms
peas
runner beans
spinach

chillies
garlic
sweetcorn
onions
carrots
broccoli
potatoes

Takeaway food
burger
chips
curry
ice cream
noodles
pasta
pizza
sandwich

Bread and cakes
bagel
bread roll
brownie
bun
cupcake
doughnut
flapjack
muffin
naan
pitta

Dairy foods
butter
cheese
cottage cheese
cream
goat's cheese
margarine
milk
sour cream
yogurt

Drinks
coffee
juice
lemonade
milk shake
smoothie
squash
tea
water

Drinks can be ...
fizzy
sparkling
refreshing
thirst-quenching
warm
lukewarm
tepid

cold
chilled
freezing cold
ice-cold
hot
boiling hot
piping hot
scalding

Eating and drinking

eat
bite
chew
gnaw
gobble
munch
nibble

drink
gulp
slurp
suck

You eat quickly
fast
hurriedly
rapidly
swiftly

I eat slowly
carefully
steadily

Food can be ...
delicious
mouthwatering
scrumptious
tasty
yummy

disgusting
foul
revolting
vile

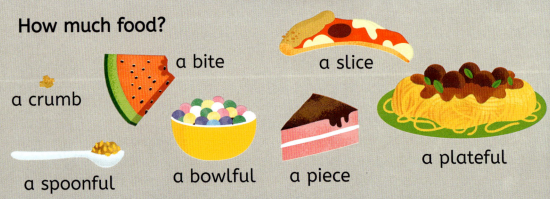

How much food?

In the kitchen

Ways to prepare food

beat
blend
grate
knead
mash
mix
peel

stir
whip

chop
cut up
dice
slice

Ways to cook food

bake
barbecue
boil
deep-fry
fry
grill
microwave

poach
roast
simmer
steam
stew
stir-fry
toast

Inside a home

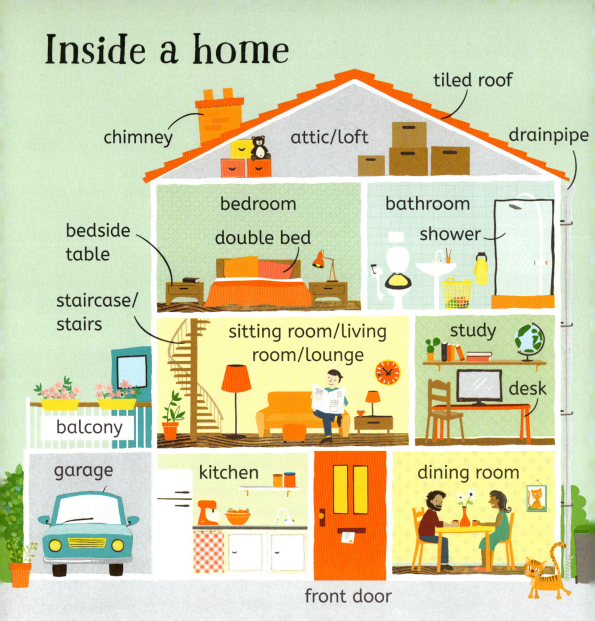

In the kitchen
cooker/oven/stove
cupboard/cabinet
dishwasher
kettle
microwave oven
mixer
sink
tumble dryer
washing machine

On the floor
carpet
floorboards
tiles
rugs

On the walls
paint
tiles
wallpaper

Types of furniture
armchair
bookcase
bunk bed
chest of drawers
dining table
rocking chair
single bed
sofa/couch
wardrobe

Homes and gardens

Homes can feel
airy
cosy
cramped
damp
dark
draughty
dusty
homely
luxurious
roomy
spacious
stuffy
welcoming

This house is ...

messy
cluttered
untidy

tidy
neat
well-organized

clean
immaculate
polished
scrubbed
spick-and-span

Different homes
apartment
bungalow
cottage
detached house
farmhouse
flat
houseboat
log cabin
mansion
mobile home
palace
semidetached house

In a garden
fishpond
flowerbed
paddling pool
path
patio
swimming pool

Gardens can be ...
blooming
colourful
neglected
overgrown
overrun by weeds
well kept

washing line
swing
slide
plant pot
greenhouse
vegetable patch
shed

Building words

build
construct
erect
put up

People on site
architect
builder
electrician
labourer
plasterer
plumber
site manager

Vehicles and machinery
excavator
front loader
pneumatic drill
rock breaker

Buildings can be made from...
brick
concrete
steel
timber

On a building site you can hear...
banging
crashing
hammering
sawing
shouting
shovelling
thumping

Tools and materials

nuts
bolt

Materials can be ...

soft
springy
squashy

hard
firm
rigid
solid
stiff

strong
sturdy
tough

weak
brittle
flimsy
fragile

clear
see-through
transparent

smooth
glossy
polished
silky
sleek

Different materials
glass
leather
metal
paper
plastic
rubber
stone
wood

Types of metal
aluminium
brass
bronze
copper
gold
iron
lead
silver
steel
tin

Types of wood
ash
beech
cedar
ebony
mahogany
oak
pine

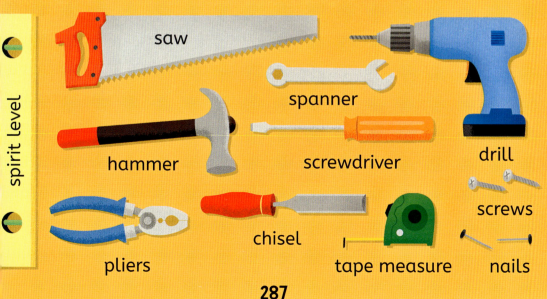

spirit level
saw
spanner
hammer
screwdriver
drill
pliers
chisel
tape measure
screws
nails

287

In a city

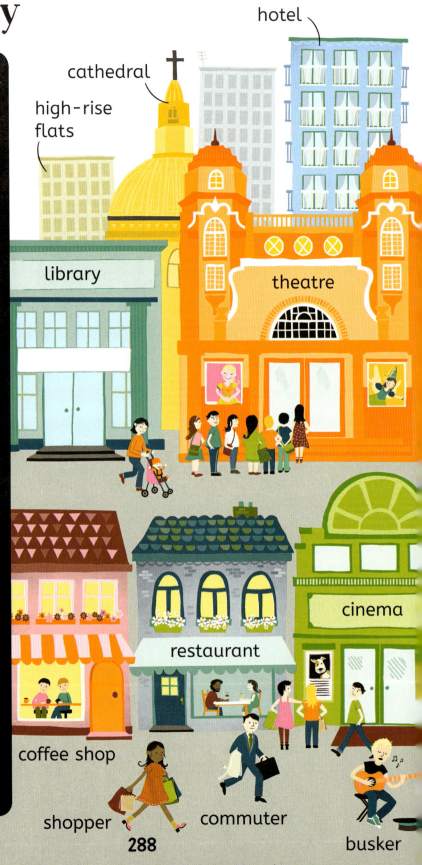

Cities can be ...

busy
bustling
buzzing
crowded
exciting
lively
noisy
packed

dirty
grimy
polluted
smoggy
smoky

empty
deserted
echoing
eerie

shabby
run-down
scruffy

shiny
gleaming
glittering
sparkling

Going shopping

greengrocer · barber · bookshop · pet shop · florist

toyshop · clothes shop · butcher · newsagent

cash machine · bank · hairdresser · post office · shoe shop · bakery

store	**cheap**	**money**		
department store	inexpensive	cash	card	coins
megastore	reasonable	change		
superstore	reduced	payment		note

At a supermarket

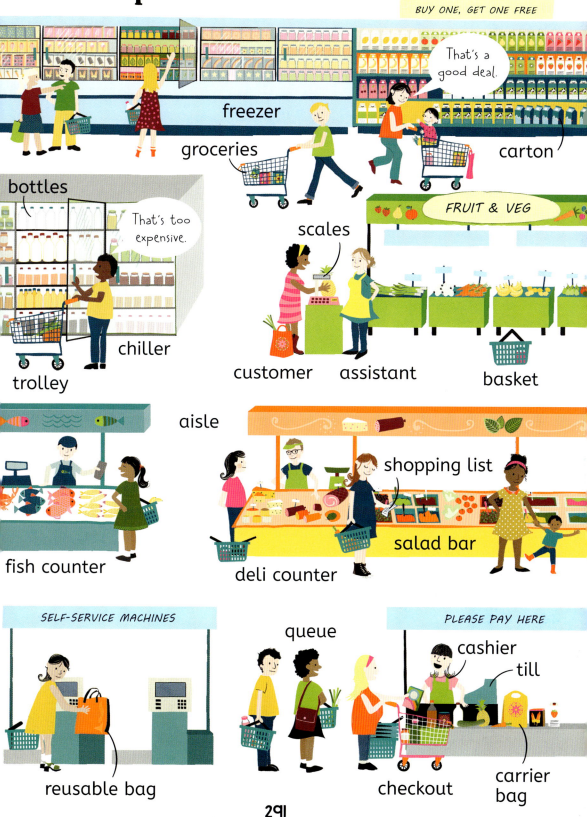

On the road

Vehicles may ...
accelerate
brake
break down
collide
crash
crawl
cruise
race
skid
slow down
speed up
squeal to a halt
swerve
veer

bus
bus stop
sports car
motorhome

pedestrian crossing

camper van

fire engine

roundabout
road sign

Cars can be ...
dented
gleaming
rusty
streamlined

steering wheel
windscreen
bonnet
boot
headlight
tyre

292

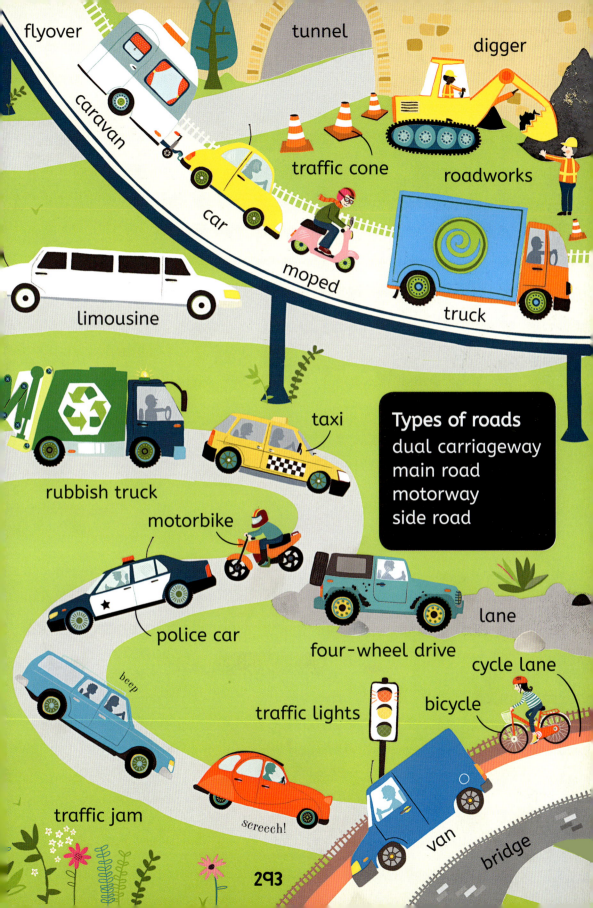

Ships and boats

Ships and boats may ...
bob up and down
capsize
cruise
dock
drift
float
moor
plough through the waves
put to sea
roll
set sail
sink
steam ahead

On board a ship
captain
cooks
crew
engineers
officers
passengers
sailors
stewards

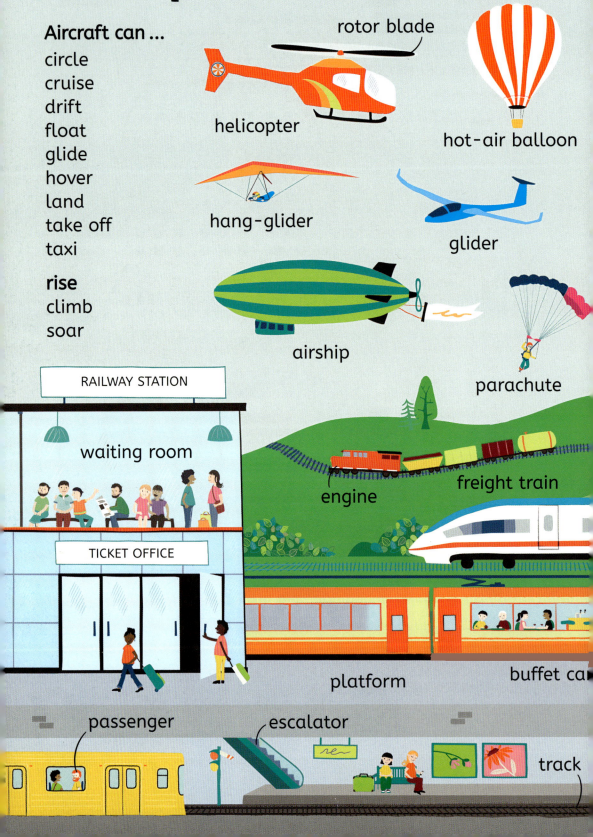

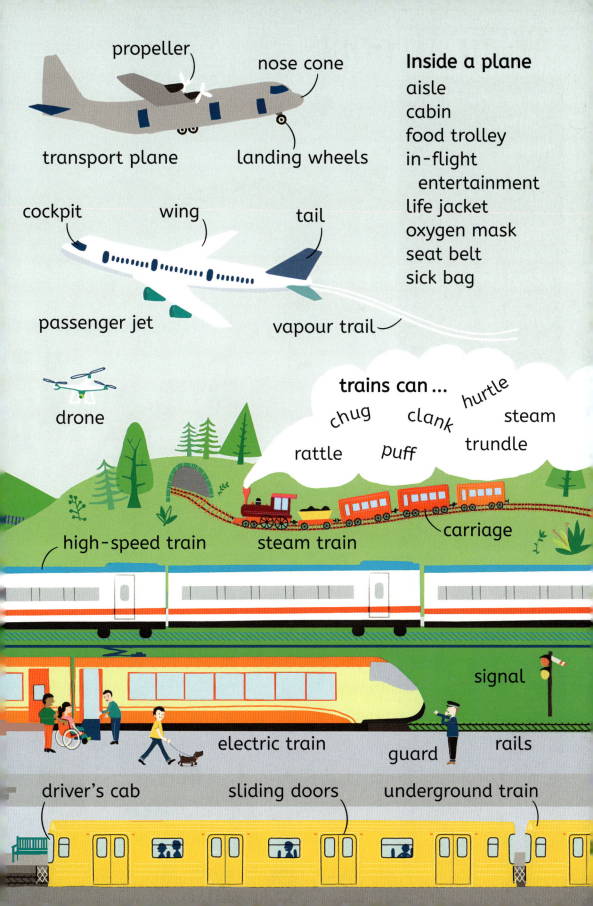

At an airport

We're going on a ...
flight
journey
trip

holiday
break
vacation

We may feel ...
excited
fidgety
tired
travel-sick

Flights can be ...
cancelled
delayed
on time
rescheduled

When do we ...
leave?
depart
set off
take off

arrive?
land
reach our
   destination
touch down

aeroplane
hangar
shuttle bus
baggage cart
laptop bag
wheelie case
backpack
hand luggage
SECURITY
X-ray machine
security guard

Jobs people do

job
career
work

boss
director
manager
supervisor

Jobs can be ...
difficult
easy
enjoyable
exciting
fun
hard
interesting
rewarding
satisfying
tiring

All sorts of jobs
accountant
architect
builder
designer
doctor
electrician
engineer
farmer
journalist
lawyer
librarian
musician
nurse
painter
pharmacist
social worker
teacher

dentist

decorator

chef

police officer

carpenter   hairdresser

plumber

gardener

vet

zookeeper

waiter

receptionist

mechanic

scientist

artist

firefighter

Fun and hobbies

We like to have fun
enjoy ourselves
have a good time

fun
enjoyment
entertainment
pleasure

Hobbies and interests
ballet
chess
computer games
cooking
dancing
drawing
fishing
judo
karate
painting
photography
reading
rollerblading
skateboarding
swimming

Art equipment
acrylic paints
canvas
chalk
crayons
easel
felt-tip pens
paintbrush
paints
pastels
pencil
rubber
watercolours

Things to read
atlas
comic
graphic novel
magazine
novel
picture book
reference book
storybook

Types of stories
adventure story
detective story
fairy tale
ghost story
mystery
science fiction story

Types of computer
games console
laptop
tablet
PC

Computer games can be…
amazing
educational
exciting
frustrating
fun
gripping
realistic
superrealistic
time-consuming
violent

easy
basic
simple
straightforward

hard
advanced
challenging
complex
complicated
difficult
testing

Dance and theatre

Some types of dance
disco dancing
folk dancing
jazz dancing
salsa
tango

Dancers may be ...
dainty
elegant
flexible
graceful
sprightly

Dancers ...
glide
leap
pirouette
spin
stomp
strut
sway
twirl
whirl

line dancing

ballerina
tutu
ballet

street dancing

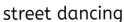
tap-dancing

ballroom dancing

At a theatre you can see a ...
ballet
comedy show
concert
dance performance
musical
pantomime
play
puppet show
talent show

Theatre words
actor
cast
chorus
costume
director
interval
make-up
rehearsal
scene
script
stage manager

On a set
lighting
props
scenery

In a theatre
aisle
balcony
box
curtain
stage
stalls

Film and TV

Films can be ...

exciting
action-packed
fast-moving
gripping
nail-biting

boring
dull
uninteresting
slow-moving
tedious

funny
comical
hilarious
ridiculous
side-splitting
whacky

sad
depressing
moving
tear-jerking
tragic

frightening
creepy
hair-raising
scary
spine-chilling
spooky
terrifying

WOW! SHHHH! AARGH! HA HA HA!

Films and TV programmes
cartoon
chat show
comedy
detective series
documentary
drama
game show
horror film
news
science fiction

Films may include ...
animation
close-up shots
computer graphics
flashbacks
slow-motion shots
sound effects
special effects
surround sound

In a cinema, you may hear ...
coughing
crunching
gasping
giggling
laughing
munching
rustling
slurping
sobbing
whispering

At a funfair

helter-skelter · big wheel · big dipper · carousel · ghost train

funfair
amusement park
fair
theme park

Fairground amusements
big dipper
bouncy castle
bumper cars
hall of mirrors
merry-go-round
simulator
swingboats
teacup ride

Rides can be…
exciting
fast
gentle
nail-biting
scary
thrilling

On a ride you may…
bounce
lurch
plunge
spin
whirl

Funfair lights can be…
blazing
colourful
dazzling
flashing
magical

Funfair music can be…
blaring
booming
deafening
pounding
thumping

At a circus

tightrope walker
trapeze artists

audience
clown
strongman
ringmaster
acrobats
eek!

Circus performers may …
balance on a tightrope
bounce on a trampoline
fly through the air
juggle
ride a unicycle
spin plates
swallow fire
take a bow
walk on stilts
walk on their hands

Acrobats do …
backflips
backward rolls
forward rolls
handstands
leaps
somersaults
tumbles
twists

Clowns may …
do slapstick routines
mime
throw custard pies

The audience may …
cover their eyes
gape
gasp

applaud
cheer
clap

laugh
cackle
chortle
chuckle
giggle
roar with laughter

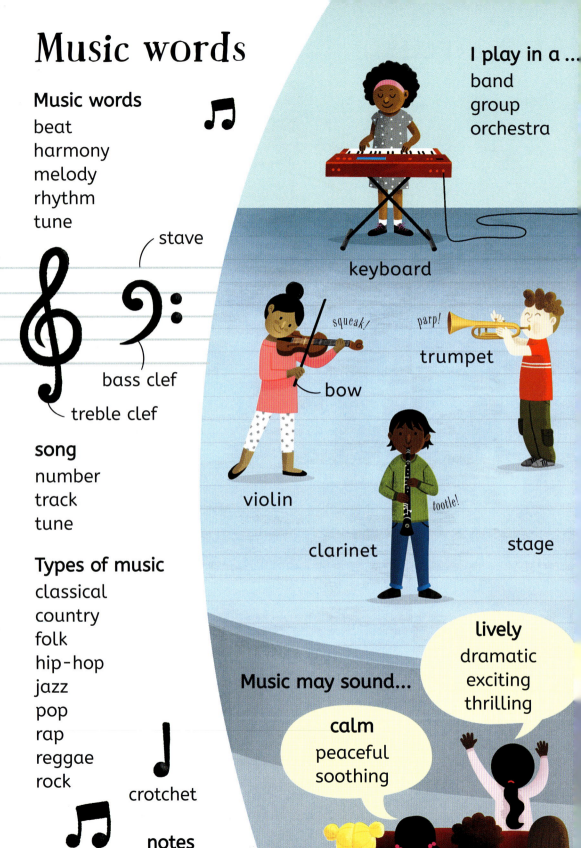

All sorts of sports

Types of sports
athletics
badminton
boxing
fencing
golf
gymnastics
hockey
ice hockey
judo
netball
rounders
rowing
rugby
show jumping
skating
snooker
squash
table tennis
wrestling

skateboarding baseball surfing
archery cricket karate
volleyball

Athletics events
decathlon
discus
high jump
hurdles
javelin
long jump
pentathlon
pole vault
sprint

Sports places
arena
court
field
pitch
ring
rink
sports hall
stadium
track

Athletes must be ..
athletic
determined
energetic
fit
in great shape
muscular
skilful
speedy
strong

Types of sporting event
challenge
competition
contest
cross-country run
final
game
heat
marathon
match
Olympics
Paralympics
qualifying round
quarterfinal
race
replay
semifinal
time trial
tournament

Sports moves

kick	hit	throw	dodge
dribble	drive	bowl	duck
pass	knock	chuck	sidestep
	putt	fling	swerve
catch	slam	hurl	
grab	strike	pass	
grasp	swipe at	pitch	
snatch	volley	toss	
seize	whack		

medal

trophy

Cats and dogs

Cats can be...
curious
independent
sleek
snuggly
timid

meow
cry
mew

kitten

purr!

Cats may...
yowl
hiss
scratch
slink

collar
lead
dalmatian
yelp!
woof!
labrador
greyhound
poodle
dachshund
puppy

Dogs can be...
affectionate
gentle
loyal

lively
bouncy
playful

obedient
well trained

disobedient
mischievous
naughty
wild

Dogs may...
bark
growl
wag their tails
whine

More pets

Pets may...
creep
flutter
slither

bite
chew
gnaw
munch
nibble
nip

jump
leap
pounce
spring

run
scamper
scurry
scuttle
trot

hamster
wheel
snake
budgerigar

chameleon

mouse
rabbit
gerbil
tank
tropical fish
guinea pig

Pets can look...
scaly
furry
fluffy
wiry

Horses and riding

Horses may ...
bolt
buck
canter
gallop
graze
jump
kick
nuzzle
plod
prance
rear
shy
stride
trot
walk

Horse noises
clip-clop
neigh
snicker
snort
whinny

Stable jobs
changing bedding
cleaning tack
feeding
grooming
mucking out

Horses may be ...
calm
gentle
good-natured
obedient
surefooted
well trained

or they may be ...
frisky
highly strung
nervous
skittish
stubborn
wild

horse
colt (young male)
filly (young female)
foal (baby horse)
mare (female)
pony (small horse)
stallion (male)

Horses eat ...
apples
carrots
hay
linseed cake
mash
oats
pony nuts

Riding equipment
crop
harness
leading rein
stable rug

Riding events
cross-country
dressage
flat racing
gymkhana
hacking
hurdling
point-to-point
pony trekking
showjumping

Types of horse
carthorse
hunter
polo pony
racehorse
show-jumper
thoroughbred

Horses can look ...
dainty
elegant
glossy
shaggy
sleek
stocky

Horse colours
bay
chestnut
dapple-grey
grey
palomino
piebald

Animal words

Some types of animals

mammal

bird

amphibian

insect

reptile

fish

animal
creature
beast

Animal habitats
desert
grassland
mountain
swamp
woodland

Animal sounds
bark
hiss
howl
quack
roar
screech
squawk
squeal

Animal groups
a flock of sheep
a herd of cows
a litter of puppies
a pack of wolves
a pod of whales
a pride of lions
a shoal of fish
a swarm of bees

Males, females and babies

animal	male	female	baby
chicken	→ cockerel	→ hen	→ chick
cow	→ bull	→ cow	→ calf
horse	→ stallion	→ mare	→ foal
pig	→ boar	→ sow	→ piglet
sheep	→ ram	→ ewe	→ lamb

Bird words

fly
circle
dart
flap
flit
flutter
glide
hover
sail
soar
swoop

hawk
bluejay
European robin
pheasant
peacock
crow
caw!
beak
egg
chick
wing
feathers
claw
nest
canary
puffin

More types of birds

bullfinch
cuckoo
dove
emu
falcon
goose
heron
jackdaw
kingfisher
kookaburra

lark
magpie
nightingale
ostrich
raven
sparrow
stork
swallow
thrush
woodpecker

Bird noises

cackle
call
chatter
cheep
chirp
chirrup
cluck
coo
gobble
hiss

honk
hoot
pipe
quack
screech
sing
squawk
trill
tweet
twitter

316

coo coo! pigeon
blackbird
hummingbird
seagull
HOOT!
owl
pelican
flamingo
quack!
duck
eagle
bird of paradise

Birds may...
dive
hop
paddle
peck
perch
plummet
pounce
roost
strut
waddle

A bird's feathers can look...
bedraggled
fluffy
ruffled
shiny
smooth

downy
glossy
colourful
speckled

Trees

acorn

conker

Trees can be ...
magnificent
spindly
spreading
sturdy

Tree bark can be ...
gnarled
papery
ridged
rough
smooth

Types of trees
ash
beech
birch
elm
hawthorn
hazel
horse chestnut
larch
magnolia
mahogany
maple
monkey puzzle
oak
olive
palm
plane
poplar
rowan
rubber
sweet chestnut
sycamore
walnut
weeping willow
yew

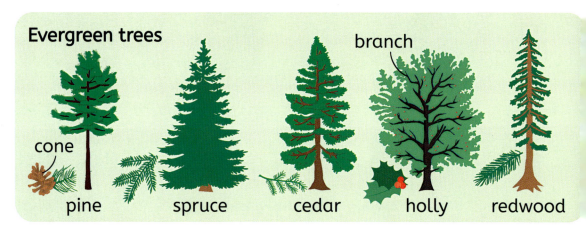

Evergreen trees

cone — pine — spruce — cedar (branch) — holly — redwood

Fruit trees

apple — lemon — cherry (blossom, trunk) — peach

Bushes and flowers

Types of flowers
carnation
cowslip
daffodil
daisy
dandelion
forget-me-not
hollyhock
hyacinth
marigold
orchid
primrose
snowdrop
violet
wallflower
waterlily

Types of bushes
bramble
currant
gorse
laurel
lavender
lilac
privet
rosemary
thyme

Bushes can be…
bushy
clipped
overgrown
prickly

Flowers can be …
beautiful
colourful
delicate
spectacular
straggly
sweet-smelling

buttercup
pansy 
iris 
rose  
seeds
petal
bud
sweet pea
leaf
lily 
poppy
stalk
foxglove
bluebell
crocus
tulip 
sunflower

319

In the country

field
meadow
pasture

path
lane
track
trail

hill
hillside
mound

wood
forest
woodland

Countryside words
barn
bog
cottage
fence
gate
grass
hedgerow
lake
pond
pool
scarecrow
village

In the country you may spot a...
badger
hare
hedgehog
mole
rabbit
squirrel

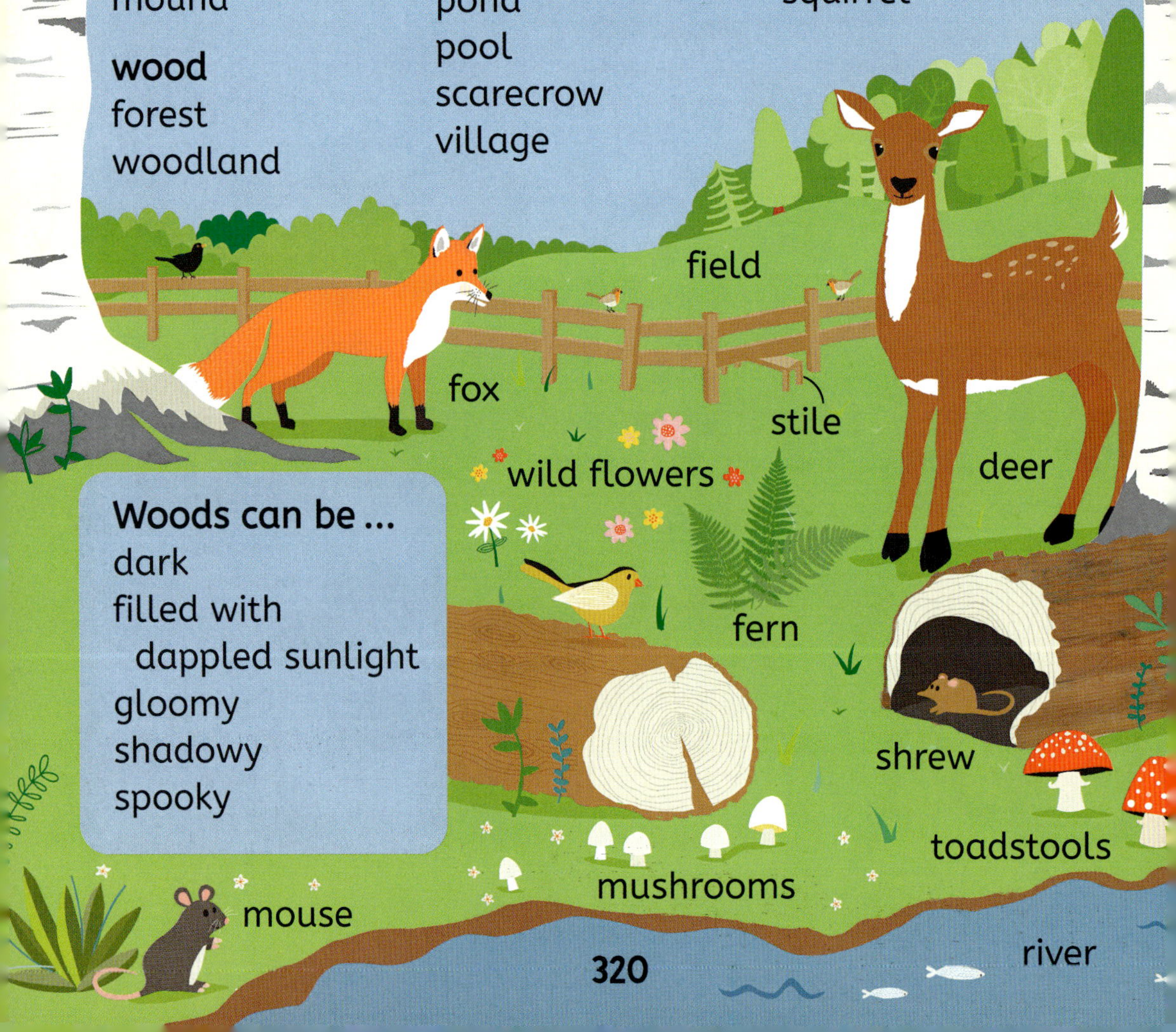

Woods can be...
dark
filled with dappled sunlight
gloomy
shadowy
spooky

fox
field
stile
deer
wild flowers
fern
shrew
toadstools
mushrooms
mouse
river

On a farm

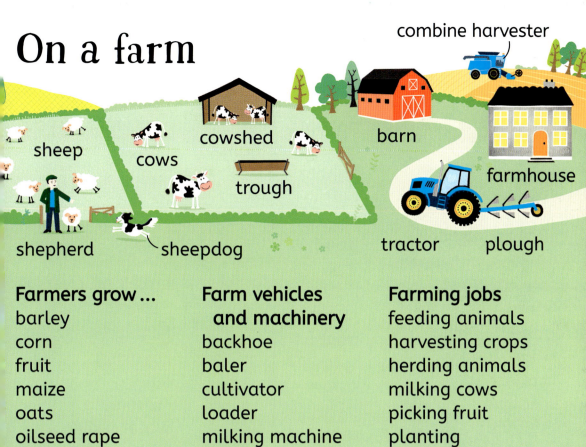

Farmers grow...
barley
corn
fruit
maize
oats
oilseed rape
sugar beet
vegetables
wheat

Some farm animals
donkey
goat
goose
pig

Farm vehicles and machinery
backhoe
baler
cultivator
loader
milking machine
mower
muck-spreader
seed drill
roller
trailer

Farming words
hay
manure
straw

Farming jobs
feeding animals
harvesting crops
herding animals
milking cows
picking fruit
planting vegetables
ploughing
rounding up sheep
shearing sheep
sowing seeds
spraying
weeding

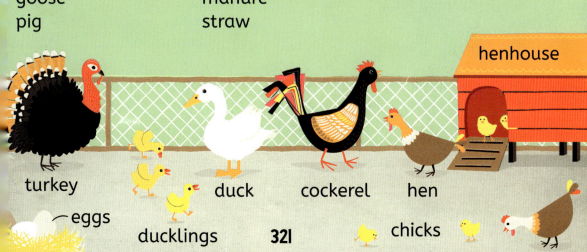

Rivers, lakes and ponds

river
brook
creek
stream
torrent

Rivers may be ...
choked with weeds
crystal clear
deep
fast-flowing
murky
polluted
shallow
sluggish
sparkling
stagnant

Rivers may ...
babble
break their banks
bubble
burble
cascade
flood
flow
froth
murmur
pour
splash
surge
swirl
trickle
twist
wind

Along a river you might see ...
gorge (deep valley)
island
lock
towpath
weir

Lake and river sports
fishing
kayaking
sailing
swimming
water-skiing
whitewater rafting

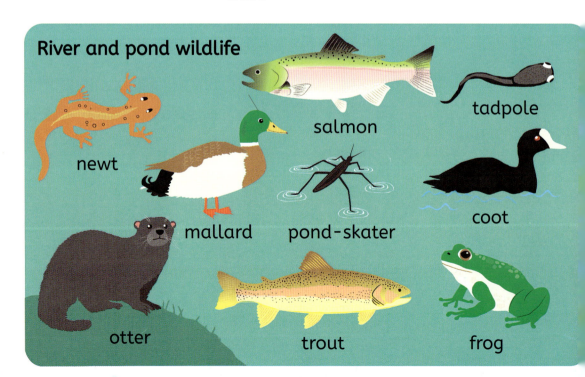

River and pond wildlife: newt, salmon, tadpole, mallard, pond-skater, coot, otter, trout, frog

In the mountains

Mountains can be...
high
lofty
snow-capped
soaring
towering

Their slopes can be...
craggy
forested
icy
rocky
steep

More mountain words
avalanche
black ice
glacier
snowstorm

top
peak
summit

chairlift

whoosh!

ski run

snowboarder

bottom
base
foot

snowmobile

toboggan
sled
sledge

Wheee!

husky sledge

fir trees

frozen lake

cable cars
climbing rope
ice axe
slope
slalom course
drag lift
button lift
T-bar
ledge
chalet
nursery slope
SKATE HIRE
skating rink
cross-country skiers

Mountain sports can be ...
challenging
dangerous
exciting
risky

Climbers ...
clamber
cling onto the rock face
lose their footing
reach the summit
scramble
tumble

Skiers and snowboarders ...
jump
perform tricks
race
speed
swerve

Skaters ...
balance
fall
glide
twirl
wobble

In a desert

Deserts are often...
dry
sandy
scorching

but some are...
freezing
rocky
stony

The sun is...
blazing
blinding
dazzling

You may be...
parched
sunburned/ sunburnt
sweaty

Some desert animals
desert fox
desert rat
lizard
locust
rattlesnake
tarantula

In a jungle

Jungles can be...	Jungle trees and plants...	Some jungle animals
dark	coil	armadillo
gloomy	dangle	chimpanzee
humid	loop	gorilla
lush	scratch	orangutan
noisy	snake	python
steamy	sting	tapir
swampy	tower	tiger

Grassland animals

Animals roam the grasslands ...
plains
savanna

Some grassland animals
antelope
buffalo
cheetah
crocodile
hyena
leopard
rhinoceros
warthog

The animals may ...
attack
charge
hide in the undergrowth
hunt
lie in wait
lurk in the bushes
pounce
prowl
snap their jaws
stalk their prey
thunder over the plain

You may hear a ...
bellow
crash
crunch
growl
grunt
hiss
howl
roar
rustle
screech
snap
snarl
splash
squeal

Under the sea

Fish and sea creatures
dolphin
eel
lobster
porpoise
pufferfish
seahorse
sea lion
sea snake
seal
squid
swordfish
whale

Fish may ...
crest the waves
dart
dive
drift
float
glide
leap out of the water
lurk
plunge
splash
surface
swim

Under the sea it can be ...
beautiful
cold
colourful
dark
mysterious
scary
silent

sea
ocean

sea bed
ocean floor

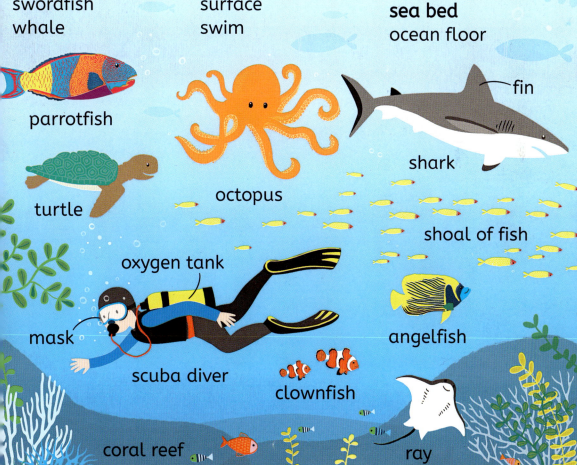

At the seaside

At the seaside you may see…
caves
cliffs
pier
rock pools
sand dunes

A seaside resort may be…
crowded
deserted
empty
packed
peaceful
picturesque
quiet
sleepy
touristy

Beaches may be…
pebbly
sandy
stony

Things to take to the beach
beach ball
bucket and spade
flippers
folding chair
picnic
snorkel
suncream
sunglasses
sunhat
swimsuit
towel
wetsuit

Seaside activities
building sandcastles
collecting shells
paddling
playing mini-golf
sailing
scuba diving
snorkelling
sunbathing
surfing
swimming
water-skiing

Sea words
high tide
low tide
spray
surf
white horses

Sea and shore

sea
ocean

beach
coast
sands
shingle
shore

The sea may be ...
calm
choppy
crystal clear
glassy
green
grey
raging
rough
shimmering
sparkling

The waves may ...
billow
break
churn
crash
foam
lap
pound
race
roar
roll
surge
swell

In a rock pool
anemone
barnacle
sea urchin
shrimp

Nature at the beach

driftwood
gull

jellyfish

crab

starfish
shells
cormorant
seaweed

promenade
beach café
campsite
lifeguard
parasol
pedalo
windsurfer
rubber dinghy
fishing net

331

Words for weather

Weather words
climate
temperature
weather forecast

Today, the weather is …

hot
baking
blistering
boiling
roasting
scorching
sizzling
sweltering
tropical

cold
bitter
bracing
chilly
cool
freezing
nippy
perishing
wintry

cloudy
gloomy
grey
miserable
overcast
dreary
dull

fine
dry
mild
sunny
warm

rainy
damp
drizzly
showery
spitting
wet

windy
blowy
blustery
breezy
gusty
stormy

weather vane

foggy
hazy
misty
murky
smoggy

steamy
clammy
close
humid
muggy

thermometer

Types of windy weather

breeze   gale   tornado/whirlwind

Types of wet weather

hail   shower
sleet   downpour

Ice, frost and snow

icicle

Snow may ...
drift
fall
float
melt
settle
thaw
swirl

Ice can be ...
brittle
cracked
glassy
hard
slippery
smooth

Snow can be ...
crisp
crunchy
dazzling
deep
powdery
slushy

Frost may ...
glisten
glitter
sparkle

The ground may be ...
as hard as iron
blanketed with snow
carpeted with snow
dusted with snow
frozen solid
sprinkled with snow

The trees may be ...
bare
covered with frost
laden with snow
weighed down by snow

In the snow you ...
plod
plough through
sink in
struggle
stumble

On the ice you ...
glide
skate
skid
slide
slip

snowflake

More ice, frost and snow words
avalanche
Jack Frost
snowball
snowdrift

snowman · sledge · snow angel

Storm words

storm
blizzard
hurricane
monsoon
snowstorm
thunderstorm
typhoon

Thunder ...
booms
cracks
echoes
growls
roars
rolls
rumbles

Lightning ...
flares
flashes
lights up the sky
strikes
zigzags

Rain ...
beats down
buckets down
lashes down
pelts down
pours down
teems down
tips down

Storms can be ...
awesome
deafening
destructive
devastating
dramatic
ear-splitting
frightening
powerful
raging
savage
terrifying
violent
wild

hailstones

forked lightning

Storms may ...
block roads
bring down power lines
cut off villages
damage crops
destroy buildings
flood homes
swell rivers
uproot trees

More storm words
billowing clouds
inky sky
thunderbolt
thunderclap
thundercloud

The wind ... howls gusts shrieks blasts rages blows

Night words

crescent moon

The night may be...
clear
moonlit
shadowy
starlit

The sky may be...
inky
pitch-black
starry
velvety

Night-time sounds
bats sqeaking
cats yowling
clocks chiming
doors slamming
floorboards creaking
owls hooting
people snoring
sirens wailing
windows banging

At night, it can feel...
ghostly
gloomy
hushed
peaceful
scary
silent
spooky
still

Times of night
dawn
daybreak
dusk
midnight
nightfall
the small hours

Some night-time animals
badger
glow-worm
hedgehog
nightingale

The moon may be...
bright
hazy
hidden behind a cloud
pale
silvery
waning (growing smaller)
waxing (growing larger)

The stars may...
flicker
glimmer
glitter
shimmer
shine
sparkle
twinkle

shooting star

bat
fireflies

owl

moths

Fire and fireworks

Fireworks...
blaze
dazzle
explode
fizzle out
flare
shoot
shower
sink
soar
sparkle
spin
spiral
whizz
whoosh
zoom

Fireworks can be...
dazzling
deafening
magical
spectacular
stunning

Firework sounds
boom
splutter
whine
whistle

Types of firework
banger
Catherine wheel
firecracker
fountain
rocket
Roman candle
sparkler

pop!
crash!
fizz!
hiss!
squeal!
bang!
crackle!
screech!

Fires...
blaze
burn
glow
rage
roar
scorch
smoulder

Smoke...
billows
chokes
curls
drifts
envelops
swirls

Flames...
dance
flare
flicker
glow

Noisy words

Stop that noise!
din
hullabaloo
racket
rumpus

Bells ring
chime
clang
jingle
peal

ding-dong!

Doors bang
crash
slam
thud

People shout
bellow
call out
roar
yell

Children scream
screech
shriek
squeal

Dancers stamp
clatter
clomp
stomp

Fountains splash
babble
glug
gurgle

splosh!

Drums boom
roll
thunder
rumble

squeak!

loud	quiet	deep	high
deafening	hushed	booming	high-pitched
ear-splitting	muffled	low	piercing
noisy	soft	low-pitched	shrill

Fairy-tale words

magic
enchantment
sorcery
witchcraft
wizardry

fairy
witch
dragon
pixie
gnome
toadstool
unicorn
prince
king
queen
princess
leprechaun
fairy godmother
goblin
giant
elf
horse and carriage

Fairy-tale characters may...
cast spells
change shape
come to the rescue
fight battles
grant wishes
solve riddles
vanish into thin air

The good characters are...
beautiful
brave
generous
gentle
handsome
kind
pretty

The bad characters are...
creepy
cunning
evil
menacing
sinister
ugly
wicked

giant
hulk
ogre

wizard
magician
sorcerer

cast a spell
bewitch
enchant
transform

Wizards and witches use a...
cloak of invisibility
crystal ball
flying broomstick
magic potion
magic wand

Wizards say...
Abracadabra!
Hocus pocus!
Shazam!

Fairy-tale places
castle
cave
cavern
cottage
dungeon
forest
lake
maze
palace
tower
tunnel
wood

Hey presto!

spell
charm
curse

book of spells

zap!

cauldron

bat

wizard

Magic potions...
boil
bubble
simmer
fizz
froth

Potion ingredients
bat's wing
dragon's blood
snake's tongue
unicorn's horn

Pirates and treasure

Pirates can be...
bloodthirsty
bold
brutal
cruel
daring
fearless
fierce
greedy
menacing
reckless
swashbuckling

Pirates may...
board ships
bury treasure
explore desert
  islands
fire cannons
force prisoners to
  walk the plank
go ashore
keep a lookout
scrub the deck
sing sea shanties
take prisoners

steal
loot
plunder
raid
rob

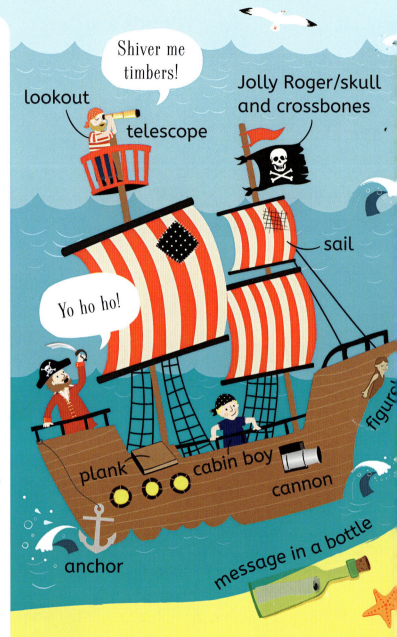

Pirate ships may...
brave the storm
cross the ocean
ride the waves
run aground

In a storm, a ship may...
groan
shudder
sink/capsize

treasure
booty
bounty
loot
riches

jewels
gems
precious stones

coins
ducats
doubloons
pieces of eight

Types of jewellery
bangles
beads
bracelets
brooches
earrings
necklaces
rings

Precious stones
amber
amethyst
diamond
emerald
pearl
ruby
sapphire
turquoise

Treasure can be...
dazzling
gleaming
glittering
inlaid with gems
sparkling

Or it can be...
dusty
grimy
rusty
tarnished
worthless

In space

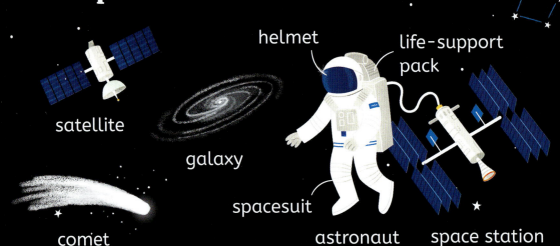

constellation
helmet
life-support pack
satellite
galaxy
spacesuit
astronaut
space station
comet

spaceship
rocket
spacecraft

Other spacecraft
moon buggy
spacelab
space shuttle

Other space words
Milky Way
universe

Spaceships may…
blast off
crash land
cruise
lift off
orbit the Earth
re-enter the Earth's atmosphere
zoom through space

Astronauts may…
contact mission control
conduct experiments
experience zero gravity
float
hover
moonwalk
spacewalk

Solar system

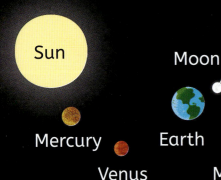

Sun
Mercury
Venus
Moon
Earth
Mars
asteroid belt
Jupiter
Saturn
Uranus
Neptune

planets

342

On a space adventure

You might travel by…
starship
teleporter

You might meet…
androids
extraterrestrial beings
Martians
shape shifters
space pirates

You might be…
caught in an intergalactic war
lost in deep space
stranded on a distant planet
stuck in a parallel universe
sucked into a black hole
trapped in a force field

Planets may be…
airless
baking
barren
dusty
frozen
glowing
icy
rocky
teeming with life
uninhabited
windy

Ghosts and haunted houses

Ghostly sounds
bang
bump
clank
clatter
clink
crash
creak
groan
hammer
knock
moan
mutter
rattle
screech
sigh
sob
thud

Ghostly sounds can be...
bloodcurdling
chilling
creepy
eerie
hair-raising
heart-stopping
spine-chilling
weird

Ghosts may...
appear
beckon
drift
float
glide
haunt
hover
vanish
waft

You may...
be rooted to the spot
be scared out of your wits
cover your eyes
hide
run for your life
scream
shudder

ghost
ghoul
gremlin
poltergeist
spirit

Haunted houses can be...
creepy
crumbling
dark
deserted
gloomy
menacing
moonlit
mysterious
neglected
rambling
shadowy
spooky

wail!
creak!
yowl! black cat
mist
howl! werewolf

In a haunted house
attic
cellar
dungeon
family portraits
four-poster bed
grandfather clock
library
locked door
looking glass

oak chest
panelled room
secret passageway
spiral staircase
stone steps
suit of armour
tower
trap door
turret

You may see or hear...
banging windows
clanking chains
creaking floorboards
fluttering curtains
guttering candles
hidden laughter
muffled screams

Monsters

Monsters may be...
curious
fire-breathing
friendly
greedy
one-eyed
slimy
smelly
spiteful

fierce
bloodthirsty
ferocious
rough
savage
violent

ugly
hideous
monstrous

Monster homes
bog
castle
cave
dungeon
forest
lake
swamp
well

Monsters may have...
tangled hair
wrinkles
warts
spikes
scales
hairy toes
shaggy fur
fiery breath
webbed feet
slime
tentacles

Monsters may...
belch
bellow
grumble
roar

Dinosaurs

Types of dinosaurs
brachiosaurus
diplodocus
iguanodon
stegosaurus
velociraptor

Dinosaurs may have...
bony plates
leathery wings
pointed fangs
scaly skin

Dinosaurs may...
attack
charge
chase
chomp
fight
hunt
kick
munch
pounce
rear up
snarl
snatch

Large dinosaurs may...
lumber
plod
thunder

Small dinosaurs may...
gallop
scamper
scuttle
trot

Volcanoes...
erupt
rumble
send out
 clouds of ash
smoke
smoulder

pterosaur
beak
lava
roar!
club tail
ankylosaurus
claws
horn
ferns
tyrannosaurus
triceratops

Adventure words

Some places for adventures: haunted mansion, pyramid, cave, desert island, hidden chamber, lost city, tunnel, castle, temple

Castles may be...
awe-inspiring
crumbling
gloomy
magnificent
ruined

Lost cities may be...
abandoned
deserted
empty
forgotten

Caves may be...
damp
echoing
freezing
icy cold
pitch-black

Cave walls may be...
dripping
gleaming
glistening
slimy
slippery

Hidden chambers may be...
airless
cramped
dark
musty
shadowy
stuffy

Tunnels may be...
narrow
twisting
winding

sliding panel
pillar
secret passage
urn
tomb
coffin
grave
mummy
statue
scarab beetle
hieroglyphics
picture writing

Adventures may be...
action-packed
amazing
dangerous
exciting
frightening
incredible
spine-chilling
terrifying
thrilling

Some adventure clues
chart
coded message
diary
inscription
manuscript
map
photograph
sealed letter
secret code

You will need to be...
adventurous
brave
curious
daring
determined
inquisitive

treasure chest

You may need...
camera
survival kit
compass
rope ladder
codebook
binoculars
notebook
torch
penknife

Knights and castles

Knights lived ...
in medieval times
in the Middle Ages

joust
tournament

Places in a castle
bedchamber
chapel
courtyard
dungeon
gatehouse
great hall
keep (central fortress)
kitchen
watchtower

Knights wore ...
chainmail
a suit of armour

Knights' weapons
battle-axe
broadsword
dagger
morning star (spiked ball on a chain)

Battle weapons and equipment
arrows
battering ram
boiling oil
catapult
crossbow
longbow
pikestaff
siege tower
slingshot

At a feast

Food at a feast	Guests at a feast	Lords and ladies wore...
boar's head	bishop	cloak/mantle
boiled custard	king	coronet
jellied eels	knight	fur-lined gown
marzipan swan	noble	headdress
pastry castle	priest	hood
pigeon pie	prince	robe/dress
roast heron	princess	tights/hose
roast peacock	queen	tunic
salted fish	sheriff	veil
venison	squire	

Word finder

Do you want to find an alternative for a particular word? This word finder will show you where to find other interesting words to use in its place.

a

afraid
see **scared**, 273

amazed
see **surprised**, 272

amazing
see **nice**, 262

angry, 272

announce, 270

annoyed
see **grumpy**, 273

answer, 270

anxious
see **worried**, 272

applaud, 305

arrive, 298

ask, 270

astonished
see **surprised**, 272

attractive
see **good-looking**, 266

b

bad, 262

bad-tempered
see **grumpy**, 273

bang (door), 337

beach, 331

beautiful
see **good-looking**, 266
see **nice**, 262

beg see **ask**, 270

big, 263

bite, 311

blue, 264

boastful
see **proud**, 275

boiling
see **hot**, 332

bored, 272

boring, 303

bottom (mountain), 324

c

bouncy
see **lively**, 275

brainy
see **clever**, 275

brave, 275

bright (colour), 264

brilliant
see **bright**, 264
see **good**, 262

build, 286

busy (city), 288

calm
(person), 274
(music), 306

car
(types), 292, 293

carry, 271

catch, 309

chat
see **talk**, 270

cheap, 290

cheeky
   see **naughty**, 275
   see **rude**, 274
cheer
   see **applaud**, 305
cheerful, 274
chest
   (treasure), 341
chew
   see **bite**, 311
   see **eat**, 282
chop
   (food), 283
clap
   see **applaud**, 305
clean (house), 285
clear
   (see-through), 287
clever, 275
climb, 271
cloudy, 332
clumsy, 275
cold
   (food and drink), 281
   (weather), 332

comment
   see **mention**, 270
conceited
   see **proud**, 275
concentrate on
   see **think about**, 270
confident, 275
confused, 272
cook, 283
cool
   see **cold**, 332
crash
   see **bang**, 337
crazy, 274
creepy
   see **frightening**, 303
cross
   see **angry**, 272
   see **grumpy**, 273
crowded
   see **busy**, 288
crown, 341
cruel
   see **unkind**, 274
cry, 273
curious
   see **nosy**, 275

d

daring
   see **brave**, 275
dark
   (colour), 264
deceitful
   see **dishonest**, 274
decide
   see **think about**, 270
deep
   (sound), 337
delicious, 282
deliver
   see **give**, 271
depressed
   see **sad**, 272
depressing
   see **sad**, 303
deserted
   see **empty**, 288
difficult
   see **hard**, 301
dirty
   (city), 288
   (clothes), 269
disgusting, 282

dishonest, 274
disobedient (dog), 310
dodge, 309
drag see pull, 271
dream see think, 270
drink, 282
dull see boring, 303

e

easy, 301
eat, 282
elderly see old, 274
empty (city), 288
enormous see big, 263
evil see bad, 262
excellent see good, 262
excited, 272
exciting, 303
exhausted see tired, 273

f

fantastic see nice, 262
fast see quickly, 282
fat see big, 263
fed-up see bored, 272
feel, 277
field, 320
fierce, 346
fine
  (healthy), 279
  (weather), 332
firm see hard, 287
fish (types), 280
fit see healthy, 274
fizzy, 281
flat (surface), 265
fly (bird), 316
foggy, 332
force see push, 271
forest see wood, 320
freezing see cold, 332
frightened see scared, 273
frightening, 303
fruit (types), 280
funny
  (person), 275
  (film), 303
furious see angry, 272
fussy, 275

g

generous see kind, 274
get better, 279
ghost, 345
giant, 339
giggle see laugh, 305
give, 271
good, 262

good-looking, 266

grab
see **catch**, 309
see **hold**, 271
see **take**, 271

grave
see **tomb**, 349

great
see **nice**, 262

green, 264

grey, 264

grin
see **smile**, 273

grumpy, 273

guess
see **think**, 270

gurgle
see **splash**, 337

h

hand over
see **give**, 271

handsome
see **good-looking**, 266

happy, 272

hard
(material), 287
(game), 301

hate, 273

healthy, 274

hear, 277

heavy
see **big**, 263

help yourself
see **take**, 271

helpful
see **nice**, 262

high
(sound), 337

hilarious
see **funny**, 275, 303

hill, 320

hit, 309

hold, 271

holiday, 298

honest, 274

horrible
see **bad**, 262

hot
(food and drink), 281
(weather), 332

huge
see **big**, 263

hurt
see **upset**, 273

i

imagine
see **think**, 270

important
(decision)
see **big**, 263

inquisitive
see **nosy**, 275

intelligent
see **clever**, 275

invent
see **think up**, 270

irritable
see **grumpy**, 273

j

jewels, 341

jingle
see **ring**, 337

jolly
see **cheerful**, 274

jump, 271

k

keen
　see **excited**, 272

kick, 309

kind, 274

knock
　see **hit**, 309

l

large
　see **big**, 263

laugh, 305

leap
　see **jump**, 271

leave
　(journey), 298
　see **put**, 271

level
　see **flat**, 265

lift
　see **carry**, 271

light (colour), 264

listen, 277

little
　see **small**, 263

lively
　(dog), 310
　(music), 306
　(person), 275

look, 277

look after, 279

loose
　(clothes), 269

loud, 337

love, 273

lovely
　see **nice**, 262

low (sound)
　see **deep**, 337

m

mad
　see **crazy**, 274

magic, 338

magician
　see **wizard**, 339

march
　see **walk**, 271

marvellous
　see **good**, 262

mean
　see **unkind**, 274

meat (types), 280

mention, 270

messy, 285

metal (types), 287

minute
　see **small**, 263

mischievous
　see **naughty**, 275

miserable
　see **sad**, 272

misty
　see **foggy**, 332

money, 290

move
　see **carry**, 271

muddled
　see **confused**, 272

munch
　see **eat**, 282

mutter, 270

n

narrow
　see **small**, 263

nasty
　see **bad**, 262
　see **unkind**, 274

naughty, 275

neat
  see **smart**, 269

nervous, 274

nice, 262

noise, 337

noisy
  see **loud**, 337

nosy, 275

notice
  see **feel**, 277
  see **hear**, 277
  see **see**, 277
  see **taste**, 277

o

obedient (dog), 310

old, 274

orange, 264

p

pale
  see **light**, 264

path, 320

pattern (types), 265

peaceful
  see **calm**, 274, 306

peak
  see **top**, 324

pick
  see **take**, 271

place
  see **put**, 271

pink, 264

point out
  see **mention**, 270

pointed, 265

polite, 274

press
  see **push**, 271

pretty
  see **good-looking**, 266

proud, 275

pull, 271

purple, 264

push, 271

put, 271

puzzled
  see **confused**, 272

q

quickly, 282

quiet, 337

r

rainy, 332

recover
  see **get better**, 279

red, 264

refreshing, 281

relaxed
  see **calm**, 274

reply
  see **answer**, 270

revolting
  see **bad**, 262

ridiculous
  see **funny**, 275, 303

ring (bell), 337

roar
  see **shout**, 337

rob
  see **steal**, 340

rough
  see **fierce**, 346

round (shape), 265
rude, 274
run, 271

S

sad
(feeling), 272
(film), 303
say, 270
scared, 273
scary
see **frightening**, 303
scream, 337
scruffy, 269
see, 277
see-through
see **clear**, 287
sensible, 275
serious (decision)
see **big**, 263
shabby
(building), 288
(clothes)
see **scruffy**, 269
sharp
see **pointed**, 265

shiny, 288
shocked
see **surprised**, 272
shop (types), 290
short, 263
shout, 337
shy, 275
silly
see **crazy**, 274
simple
see **easy**, 301
sit, 271
skinny
see **thin**, 263
slam
see **bang**, 337
sled
see **toboggan**, 324
sleepy
see **tired**, 273
slice
see **chop**, 283
slim
see **thin**, 263
slowly, 282

small, 263
smart
(clothes), 269
see **clever**, 275
smell, 277
smile, 273
smooth
(material), 287
snatch
see **take**, 271
snobbish
see **proud**, 275
snooty
see **proud**, 275
soft
(material), 287
(sound)
see **quiet**, 337
solid
see **hard**, 287
song, 306
sparkling
see **shiny**, 288
spell (magic), 339
spiteful
see **unkind**, 274
splash, 337

squash, 271

squeal
see scream, 337

squeeze
see squash, 271

stamp, 337

stand
see put, 271

steal, 340

steamy, 332

storm, 334

story (types), 301

strong
(person), 274
(material), 287

stuck-up
see proud, 275

stunning
see nice, 262

sunny
see fine, 332

suppose
see think, 270

surprised, 272

swerve
see dodge, 309

t

talk, 270

talk loudly, 270

talk quietly, 270

take, 271

take care of
see look after, 279

tall, 263

taste, 277

tense
see nervous, 274
see worried, 272

terrified
see scared, 273

terrifying
see frightening, 303

thick
(hair), 267

thin
(hair), 267
(person), 263

think, 270

think about, 270

think up, 270

thrilled
see excited, 272

throw, 309

tidy, 285

tight (clothes), 269

tiny, 263

tired, 273

toboggan, 324

tomb, 349

top
(mountain), 324

touch
see feel, 277

tough
see strong, 287

treasure, 341

truthful
see honest, 274

try
see taste, 277

tug
see pull, 271

u

ugly, 346

unhappy
see sad, 272

unimportant (mistake) see **small**, 263

unkind, 274

untidy see **messy**, 285

upset, 273

V

vain see **proud**, 275

vast see **big**, 263

vegetable (types), 281

violent see **fierce**, 346

violet, 264

W

walk, 271

wander see **walk**, 271

warm (food and drink), 281 (weather) see **fine**, 332

watch see **look**, 277

weak (person), 274 (material), 287

well see **healthy**, 274

weep see **cry**, 273

whisper see **talk quietly**, 270

wicked see **bad**, 262

wide see **big**, 263

wild see **naughty**, 275

windy, 332

wizard, 339

wonder see **think**, 270

wonderful see **nice**, 262

wood (forest), 320

work see **job**, 300

work out see **think about**, 270

worn out see **tired**, 273

worried, 272

Y

yell see **shout**, 337

yellow, 264

young, 274